A Decade with Dave

Dancing with the Devil

by

Ann J Graham

First published in Great Britain in 2022

Copyright © exclusive licence to Ann J Graham.

The rights of Ann J Graham have been asserted in accordance with the Copyright, Designs and Patents Act 1998.

No part of this book may be reprinted or reproduced or utilised in any form or by any electronic, mechanical, or other means, now known or hereafter invented, including photocopying and recording, or in any information storage or retrieval system, without permission in writing from Ann J Graham.

ISBN: 978-1-913822-22-4

This is a story inspired by true events. All the major events happened. Some of the people have been invented for anonymity while others are seeded from real people and then fictionalised. Dialogue has been created from memory.

To the wonderful memories of Moira and Iona - now long gone.

You both saved my life.

The bully, now known as a narcissist

Some traits of a narcissist—a person with a sense of self-importance and entitlement who frequently demeans, intimidates, bullies, or belittles others.

Foreword

Josie's story has been written in the passive third person (eg Josie headed out into the bright sunshine) while her abuser, Dave, is told in the active first person (eg I threw my keys on the table). In doing so, the author successfully unveils his dominance as the unreliable narrator.

It is with much trepidation that our writer steps onto a platform, not afforded to many, to make sense of what influenced her character for ten years. She appreciates that the cycle of abuse is now a well-known phenomenon, but that, even today, survivors cannot always speak about their experiences.

She, and only she, knows that there is much more to her story, but her hope is that with this limited revelation she can encourage those who have suffered a similar fate to speak out and walk away, physically and mentally, from their tormentor.

An encouragement to all who have spent any time in a destructive relationship, from a day to a year to a decade.

Prologue

Dave

I unfolded myself from the old couch that was never comfortable for my six-foot frame and rubbed the small of my back. I stared at Josie.

Her shoulder-length hair sprung back into soft waves with each brush stroke. She tied it into a loose ponytail, then put on some pink lipstick. Her casual trousers and a striped t-shirt flattered her slender figure. Humming along to a tune on the radio, she slipped into her new shoes.

I put my right hand to my forehead, but it was too late; rage was about to overtake me, no matter how hard I tried to control it. The frenzy built to a crescendo and there was no telling which form its vent would take. It all depended on what or who was in front of me.

It meant nothing to me that it was her twenty-first birthday. She had said she was going to spend time with a few friends; that meant something. She had no right to be going anywhere while I had to work. Living it up with her pals, having her celebration drink… and men would look at her, even talk to her. She would be out of my control. I glanced around the dull room, then focused on the worktop and the few unwashed breakfast dishes.

'So, you're going out and leaving the place like this?' I pointed in the sink's direction.

'It's only a couple of mugs and your plate.' She had the cheek to avoid looking at me. 'It's no problem. I'll wash them now.'

As I paced the threadbare rug; the left-hand side of my mouth twitched involuntarily. I felt my shoulders hunch and my fists clench.

The corroded tap resisted her grip for a second until warm water from the ancient boiler spluttered into the basin and forced the washing up liquid into bubbles. She watched as they rose, cloud-like.

In an instant, I moved behind her, grabbed her hair and forced the top of her head into the soapy water. Holding her there for a few seconds, I smirked as her wet hands slipped around the sides of the sink, searching for something to hold on to.

'No!' her yell was muffled. 'Please, stop!'

She unsuccessfully pushed against my last thrust, which momentarily submerged her face. Part of my anger subsided. After releasing my grip, I stood back and scoffed at her efforts to dry herself. Gasping and choking, she rubbed the nearest towel on her dripping hair. She chucked her soaked t-shirt towards the wash basket and missed. I burst out laughing.

'Why did you do that?' She didn't sound angry, more hurt and disappointed.

I'd won that round. Her confused face was priceless.

'I'll be calling you here at three o'clock.' I picked up the telephone receiver and pointed it at the wall clock.

She got my meaning.

I grabbed my car keys from the table. I didn't mean to knock the vase of flowers over, but it was a timely message and served its purpose. Cleaning up the water mixed with broken stems and petals would take up her precious time. Pity the vase didn't break. I never liked it anyway.

Josie

The slam of the door coincided with Josie sinking into the worn armchair. Her doe eyes laid bare her bewilderment at Dave's outburst. The one o'clock chimes from the nearby church bells echoed through her head.

Fighting back tears, she found another t-shirt and tidied up what remained of the flowers her friend had given her. The silver necklace from her sister had snapped and one of her favourite earrings was missing, probably down the drain. Too bad, no jewellery today.

With her jacket over her arm and a last glance in the mirror, Josie headed out into the sunshine. Running late, she kept her spirits up, knowing the afternoon chat would soon overtake the disillusionment of her relationship with Dave.

Once her eyes adjusted to the darkness in the small bar, she caught sight of her three friends at a corner table. The place wasn't busy, but the cheerful atmosphere allowed her to enter the spirit of the day and lift her broken heart. She had little more than an hour to share a bottle of birthday bubbly.

'We've not seen you out for ages, Josie. What've you been up to?' Sheila asked.

'You know what it's like. Between the job and the wee one, I don't know whether I'm coming or going. I'm just glad my mum could take Ginny. She went there last night for a sleepover, so I get her back tomorrow. It's been great to have a bit of time to myself but, yes, I'll need to make the effort and meet up with you all more often.'

The conversation went between work, kids, and nights out. Eventually, Josie glanced at her watch and made a sucking noise.

'Loved catching up. Look, I must dash in the next ten minutes because the landlord is popping round.'

Lying wasn't her strong point, but it worked and she arrived home with minutes to spare.

Unsure of how he might react to her birthday gifts, she had hidden the box of chocolates and the bracelet at the back of a drawer. There would be enough questions without bringing presents into the fray.

During Dave's grilling on the phone, he told her he'd be home earlier than usual but refused to give her a time. Her afternoon was spent sorting through washing and trying to concentrate on the dog-eared paperback she had found in a charity shop.

By seven in the evening, her stomach was in knots. She wished she'd been able to collect three-year-old Ginny from her mum rather than waiting until the morning, but she had no way of picking her up so late in the day. Anyway, if Dave arrived, and she wasn't in, life wouldn't be worth living. Better to bide her time and see what kind of mood he was in.

Even in his absence, his influence was tangible, and the tension prevented her from eating her sandwich. With hands gripping the arms of the chair, her thoughts returned to the times when Dave reminded her he was in control;

that she wouldn't go far on broken knees if she disappointed him. The invisible chain tightened as his key turned in the lock at seven-thirty; the interrogation was about to begin. Happy birthday, Josie.

Dave

I threw my keys on the table to let her know my temper hadn't subsided. Tossing my work jacket on the back of the couch, I glared at her.

'So, the make-up is still on? Did you go out like that? Who was that for?'

'It wasn't for anyone. It's my birthday, and I wanted to feel special. And I didn't know if you and I were still going out to eat.' Her voice sounded pathetic to me.

But that remark gave me another opportunity to disappoint her.

'Well, when it was *my* twenty-first, I was working on a ship, looking at New Zealand in the distance. I didn't get to go out for *my* birthday.'

She stood up and moved towards the kettle I jumped closer and, grabbing her by one shoulder, landed an expert punch on the side of her head, one that knocked her over the back of the couch. Her glasses flew somewhere under the table and I saw she had wet herself. Dazed, she got to her knees. I yanked her up by her ponytail. She yelped in pain. Apart from tousled hair and wet trousers, there were no other visible signs that I had been a bit rough with her; I always aimed for her head where bruises were hidden. Then, as I gripped her upper arm, she stumbled, and I pressed her face against the mirror.

'Look at you! Look at the state of you! That's what I've got to look at every day.'

Through her tears, she must have been aware of me turning on my heel and walking out. It's true I had thought about going out to eat with her, but there was no point in me spending good money on food when there was probably enough in the fridge. Plus, she wouldn't have been decent company with that miserable look on her face. I much preferred a drink with the boys. Anyway, I could stop at my mother's house to see what she had to eat and borrow a few pounds.

Around eight-thirty that evening, I greeted Steve and the other two guys who were already halfway down their pints. With my new leather jacket hanging over the back of a chair, I made for the bar.

'Ah well, another day, another dollar!' I joked with the lads as I laid my drink down and pulled my chair over.

The cool amber nectar hit the spot. In between talk of work, sport and money, we mentioned wives and girlfriends. The others made fleeting remarks.

'She knows her place.'

'I needed away from the constant nagging.'

'She'd better have my supper ready if she knows what's good for her.'

I was sure they weren't so macho in front of their other halves. I took them as weaklings, unable to stand up to a woman or put their physical strength behind their words. Not me. I was a proper man.

On the way home, I stopped at a garage to buy a bunch of half-price flowers. It was her birthday, after all.

Chapter 1

Josie

Four years earlier, seventeen-year-old Josie met her first serious boyfriend, Mark, at work. He was a year older and an apprentice baker; she was a typist in the factory office. Neither had experience with romance, but they laughed at each other's pathetic jokes, which made them think they were in love. The line manager accepted Josie's feeble excuses that allowed her to wander from the office to the factory.

'I need to take this form to payroll.' Or even better, 'There's no milk for our coffee. There's some in the bakery fridge. I'll go.'

Anything to walk past Mark as he prepared bread mix for the industrial ovens. If he was on confectionary and hidden in a corner, she was deflated. She couldn't stop thinking about his dark, collar-length hair, sultry brown eyes and playful sense of humour.

Fortunately, they got the chance to strengthen their relationship on a Christmas night out.

There had been very few laughs throughout Josie's childhood. A strict upbringing had restricted her and her younger sister, Iona. Despite attending mission halls for years, they had witnessed a complicated, violent, and unhappy home life that didn't tie in with the love and compassion preached from the pulpits. With parents who struggled in a doomed marriage, Josie had made a pact with herself; she planned to marry, never argue with her spouse, have four children and live happily ever after. Such naïve thoughts fed her dream of a wonderful future.

Mark told Josie his domineering father had had long-term contracts on whaling boats for years and every time he returned home, his mother was about to have, or had just given birth to, another baby. The fourteen siblings bonded but, as soon as they turned eighteen, each wanted away from the chaos.

As teenagers, Josie and Mark had very little in common except a dream to leave home; Josie was the first to make the move. She ventured to the city four months after they met, and eighteen-year-old Mark visited at weekends. Six months later, he proposed, and she accepted.

Josie got her pink two-piece costume dry cleaned and Mark borrowed a suit from his best friend. Their marriage ceremony was a simple one in the local registry office and, a few months later, it delighted them to discover they were to become parents. Their plan was to stop the cycle of unhappiness they had lived through as children and bring up their baby in an environment where there were two loving and understanding parents.

Sadly, even before the baby was born, there was a problem. Josie found it difficult to forgive her young husband when she caught him kissing another woman; she saw the ardent desire in what was supposed to be a simple, new-year greeting. At four months pregnant, Josie recoiled both mentally and physically from him. The marriage was over. So much for having four children and not arguing. After Ginny was born, Mark left and eventually settled down to start another family. It was two years before Josie felt confident enough to find a babysitter and a part-time job as a waitress in the Avonpark hotel on the outskirts of Falkirk.

She didn't see the harm when Dave, a regular customer, asked her and a colleague to join him for a drink after their shift ended one Friday. She tagged along as the support act to the serene Spanish Esme, who accepted his offer with a toss of her long, dark locks. The three amigos teased and joked with each other about clothes, looks and ages over a bottle of Rioja: a conversation that revealed Dave was in his mid-twenties, six years older than Josie.

With a broken marriage behind her and two-year-old Ginny to support, dating was the furthest thing from Josie's mind, but as the weeks went by, Dave became more attentive. He made sure he left her a generous tip at the hotel and complimented her when no one else could hear.

'Nice shoes!'

'You suit that colour.'

Often, he gave her a sultry look and sometimes a cheeky wink coupled with a raised eyebrow; there was no doubt in Josie's mind that he was interested in her.

When the after-work drinks continued without Esme, things turned serious; a coffee out here and a little gift there, all normal courting behaviour. Josie offered to pay her share, which he sometimes accepted, but more often than not he didn't, and settled the bill without batting an eyelid. He charmed her with a necklace and bracelet on her twentieth birthday. The next present, a few weeks later, surprised her. The bright red gift wrapping disguised a pair of deep red velvet trousers and a multi-coloured blouse. Both suited and fitted her perfectly. He smiled and nodded approval the following Sunday when he drew up in his Ford Escort and saw her waiting for him at the corner. Josie was grinning from ear to ear.

Dave

Josie caught my eye in the hotel. She smiled and responded politely when I passed a casual comment. It wasn't as if she could ignore me. I was a semi-regular customer and a bit of a looker. Seems that the few pounds she earned waitressing gave her and her little girl a treat.

I only appeared now and again, maybe early in the evenings to drink a beer in the bar then, with a smile and a nod, I was off. Sometimes I came back before closing time, but if I didn't, it was because I'd met an old acquaintance in another bar who was prepared to buy me a beer or two. I was out of the picture for a couple of weeks if I got a job repairing machinery on a site out of town. I didn't stay away for long because nine times out of ten, the boss became awkward, and I packed the job in. Every time I came back early, I told folk I had been working in some far-flung place but that the job had finished. It was none of their business anyway, so if they believed my work apparently entailed being called away at the drop of a hat and ending just as quickly, that was fine by me. My lifestyle created an element of mystery for Josie. After all, she had a boring routine existence as a single mum.

I asked her out on a few dates, then one night when I'd had a few drinks, I asked her out for a meal. I picked her up as arranged a couple of nights later; she was looking good and wearing the outfit I'd bought her. After the maître d' in the exclusive Indian restaurant showed us to our reserved bay window seat, we ordered from the *a la carte* menu. The little waiter was all over Josie, fixing her napkin and such like. He could do what he liked. She only had eyes for me.

He allowed me, as the man, to taste the wine, then filled our glasses. After a toast to the future, I asked Josie what she thought of my wine choice. I picked up the bottle and read from the label.

'Cabernet Sauvignon.'

'Hmm! Very nice,' she said.

She took another tentative sip. I could see she wasn't used to this.

'This is the same one I ordered for my ex, Evelyn, when it was her twenty-first birthday.'

I wanted Josie to know I was a bit of a connoisseur when it came to the finer things in life.

'Oh, I see.' She sat back and appeared to shrink into her seat. But I went on.

'I gave her Pagan perfume that day too; it was a real turn-on.'

I twirled the stem of the Bordeaux glass between my thumb and forefinger then gazed at the dark red elixir. I could see she was impressed so I swilled the ruby liquid and held it to the light. I placed it to my lips and breathed in the fruity undertones. The buzz of voices faded into the background and the aroma of the spices disappeared as I mentally relived some special moments with my ex.

Momentarily, I wondered if I should tell Josie how special Evelyn had been to me. Her raven hair, green eyes and cute hint of a lisp. We had been good together, but we had to split because of the physical distance between us. Evelyn had complained about having to spend two hours on a long bus trip each weekend when she visited me and tried to talk me into driving fifty minutes to her now and again. I did, but it was a boring journey and after two months of this arrangement, I told her she had a choice. If she wanted to see me, she'd have to do the travelling. After all, it was much cheaper for her to come by bus.

My thoughts were interrupted in the restaurant when Josie shook her head slightly.

'What's wrong with you?' I knew I was frowning.

'I'm OK. I was just thinking how lucky we are to be in such beautiful surroundings.' She blinked a few times, as if fighting back tears... of happiness.

'Nothing but the best for you,' I whispered as I reached for her hand.

The moment for questions from her about my ex had passed. More intense talk about families and plans followed our pleasant conversation.

A tall, dark-skinned waiter removed our empty plates, and I was surprised when Josie returned his smile and spoke to him as he lifted the unused cutlery. I wondered if she knew him. Although I felt rejected by her familiarity with him, I paid the bill then threw a few coins onto a small silver plate. I couldn't believe it when she hung back and exchanged some words with the male cloakroom attendant who helped her with her jacket. It was at that point I decided this wasn't her first time at that place. She had lied to me about not knowing the restaurant. They had all seen her before, definitely. I didn't respond to the young man's farewell, but walked as quickly as I could to the car park. When I looked back, I was about ten paces in front of Josie.

'So, you like the young foreigners then?' I mocked her as I left her to open the passenger door by herself.

I wasn't ready for her to see my expression, so I looked towards a nearby house just in case. The left side of my top lip was twitching when I got behind the wheel, but she wouldn't have seen that under my moustache. She leaned forward in her seat, turning her head to catch my eye, but I didn't want to look at her.

'That kid was about twelve! I think a two-year-old is enough for me.' She tried to make a joke of it while fastening her seat belt.

The fresh air had helped steady my breathing, so I held my breath a second or two before closing my door. She had clearly decided not to tell me any more about the Indian guys and I didn't question her lies. In fact, I didn't say another word all the way home. She had a one-sided conversation about food and wine and other rubbish until we drew up at the corner of her street.

'OK, I'll be in touch,' I dismissed her with a quick peck on the cheek. She didn't deserve any more.

I was suspicious, for sure. She sauntered towards the entrance to her flat, full of herself. My head was spinning with thoughts of her betrayal in the restaurant and what I could do about it.

It was difficult to pay attention to my driving as I made my way home and thankfully, there weren't too many cars on the road. The traffic lights had turned red before I knew what had happened. I slammed on the brakes and narrowly missed the taxi coming from the left. He honked his horn, but I growled and lifted my fist. Just as well he kept driving because it could have ended in a serious bit of road rage, all because Josie had angered me. It would have been her fault if things had turned out worse.

Josie

Josie pondered over the change in Dave she had detected throughout the evening. She had been near to tears on several occasions.

That was a feeble goodbye, she thought as her heart sank.

Curling up in her favourite armchair, she considered how her first meal out with him had gone. She frowned as she cupped her hands around her hot chocolate. Something didn't sit well with her. But thinking about the excellent wine and fantastic food, she smiled and stroked the red velvet of her trousers, then tapped her sparkling bracelet. Life was good.

The next day, she visited Moira. Roughly the same age, the two were bosom buddies.

'Look, I've known you for years. I can tell that something's up with you.' Moira squinted at Josie over her cup of tea. 'Are you going to tell me?'

Josie sighed.

'It's to do with Dave. I don't know how to begin, but I think I'm turning into an unreasonable female.'

Josie gave her account of Dave mentioning the wine with his ex, the comment about the perfume and the uncalled-for dig after she had spoken to the staff in the restaurant.

'Get away with you. You're not unreasonable. You want to please him because you're in love!' Moira waved her hand in the air. 'It sounds like he might be too. And about time. Get out there, girl, and do your stuff! If it makes you feel any better, get yourself some, what was it... Pagan if that's your only competition? He knows how good you look in those red trousers, probably didn't want to think anyone else might fancy you.'

That seemed a logical explanation. Josie decided she would save up for the perfume, a little treat for a future date.

When Moira insisted on meeting Dave, Josie engineered it to bump into him in a local café one day after a bit of shopping. He was sitting alone at a window table and nodded politely when Josie introduced her best friend.

Moira observed the new man in Josie's life while enjoying a coffee. He wasn't particularly handsome, but she could see the attraction. He was tall, medium build, with dark brown eyes, and held himself proudly. But his sense of humour bordered on being rude, especially when he directed his comments at others. The mention of a mutual friend gave him the chance to say she looked 'mumsy' with an oversized belly now that she'd had twins. That surprised Moira. The sneer on his face supported his view; the young woman was no longer attractive.

How else should the woman look two months after giving birth? Moira thought.

As they chatted, she saw him glance at Josie when she wasn't looking; he was paying attention. When they produced their purses to pay their share of the bill, he passed a remark about them treating him. They did and left him to finish his third cup of coffee.

'So, what do you think?' Josie asked as they turned the corner.

'Oh, he's certainly got the hots for you! Look, who can tell? Enjoy the moment and if it goes somewhere, that's fine. If not, you'll have enjoyed a few dates exploring fresh places.' Moira reassured her.

But Moira wondered about this kind of guy. She might have described him as overconfident and arrogant, but she also detected vulnerability. More importantly, she had seen a change in Josie. Moira remembered when she had first met her own husband, Ed. She had been tense, eager to please, and conscious of making sure she said the right thing. So, it wasn't a surprise that Josie wasn't her usual self with her new beau.

But Moira's confident, fun-loving friend appeared to have something else on her mind other than making sure she impressed Dave. Normally, she and Josie would have some harmless banter with the staff in a bar or a café, male or female, old or young. They were a bit of a double act, but Josie hadn't followed through when the waiter brought their coffees and Moira had passed a jokey, friendly remark.

She also reflected on Josie's silence after a comment Dave had made about a family they knew. He'd talked about the pros and cons of working away from home and ridiculed the husband.

'Well, he showed his true colours when he turned down the job on the rigs. His wife told him being together as a family was more important than big money. Now he's stuck in a nine-to-five job and driving a car that's like a sewing machine. No backbone. It's not him who wears the trousers in the house. That's for sure.'

Another incident from the café bothered Moira. She'd had a look at the ice cream selection and ordered a tub of vanilla. Josie had decided on a doughnut from the bakery counter. Once their orders were delivered, Dave had surveyed both and nodded a couple of times in the direction of the ice cream.

'Now there's somebody who knows what's good for them.'

He glanced briefly at Josie's doughnut, looked her up and down, his gaze lingering a second too long on her waistline, then he looked out the window. His comment and action were insensitive and unnecessary. Moira squirmed on Josie's behalf. The message was obvious; Josie hadn't made the right choice. She had lowered her head in shame.

Weeks after meeting in the café, Josie tapped her foot incessantly while she related another scene to Moira, affirming her friend's suspicions. She was delighted when Dave had offered to take her to a nearby craft shop. They met at the road end and headed to a garage to fill up. It was her outing, so she had offered to pay for the petrol, but he told her not to worry. He came out folding the receipt and carrying a bottle of lemonade, then drove away from the petrol pumps, stopping on a bit of waste ground inside the garage's confines. He unscrewed the top of the bottle and took a swig. Biting her bottom lip, Josie continued her story.

'Thirsty? Want some?' he had asked.

'OK.' Josie had reached out for the bottle.

She automatically wiped the top of the bottle. As she lifted it to her mouth, Dave grabbed the practically full bottle and threw it out of the driver's window onto the grass.

'Is there something wrong with me that you've got to wipe the bottle?' He had almost spat at her.

'Of course not. It's just a habit, I suppose. I meant nothing by it,' Josie assured him.

'Well, you won't be getting a drink now, will you?' Dave had said in a quiet voice before they drove off.

This was a red flag, one that Josie ignored.

Chapter 2

Dave

Little did Josie know that I sat in The Royal on the Friday after our Indian meal. She would never have guessed my plan was to stay away from her for a while. I smirked to myself as the thought ran through my mind that my absence should keep her on her toes, absence making her heart grow fonder and all that.

Into the bargain, I'd be able to catch up with the lads I hadn't seen for a while, find out what the gossip was and leave just before closing time. Someone was bound to question me about leaving before last call. I was prepared to listen to their jibes about me skipping out when it was my round; I had an excuse ready and it would deter anyone who thought about asking for a lift home. Picking up my mother and two of her pals from a ladies' night out was a good one; I'd never used that before.

They wouldn't have a clue that I was intending to park far enough away from the main entrance of the Avonpark to watch Josie and Esme leaving once the cocktail bar closed. If they had company, I would catch them.

Esme had been flirting with big Joe for weeks. I had seen them sneaking off together one Saturday night, and it was only a matter of time before they got together again; tonight might be that night.

Joe already had a wife, Maria, and Esme was his bit on the side. He admitted to me he had told Maria he was meeting a couple of mates in the Avonpark; a plan to make his presence look innocent. But I knew he was just the fellow to set Josie up with someone so they could all head off somewhere together. I didn't trust him one bit.

He wanted to stop the rumours about him and Esme before they spread. Joe's wife wasn't convinced of his innocence because *someone* had told a tale out of school. He reckoned he had enough on his plate, trying to convince Maria he was the most faithful guy on the planet. Joe never guessed I was behind the mysterious phone call. I wanted to create some excitement, not for any specific motive, but simply because I noticed an opportunity.

'She questioned me about an unfamiliar smell in the car,' Joe had told me in confidence. 'She has an inkling of what's going on. Seems my daughter asked if my wife was wearing a different perfume. I've told Esme she's not getting in my car if she's wearing hair spray or anything that smells.'

'Solution, Joe. Make sure you buy your wife the same perfume.' My answer made sense.

'She asked me who'd been in the car. Eventually, she let it go, but this, on top of the strange phone call, is worrying her. She's getting suspicious.'

Listening to the details he gave me, I smirked. I wanted to see if they tied up with what actually happened when I had called Maria.

'At ten o'clock three nights ago, she answered after a few rings. A muffled male voice had whispered, "Your husband. Do you know where he is? I can tell you. He's with the Spanish chica." Then he hung up.' Joe shook his head.

Apparently, it had worked. Maria stayed up for hours. The brandy helped steady her nerves until she heard Joe's car pull up.

It amazed me how controlled Joe was. Even when he encountered Esme, he was a master at disguising any feelings he had for her. He didn't spy on her or dread betrayal; neither did he fear rejection.

Esme was flirty. Behind the bar, she leaned forward to wash the tumblers, then sneaked a look at the men staring down the front of her blouse. A kind of, 'Anybody interested?' type of message. While every man in the cocktail bar drooled over her, Joe made sure he sat facing the opposite direction, pretending he didn't care. He left fifteen minutes before she finished her shift because they had planned their rendezvous in advance with the proviso that he might not turn up if things got difficult.

The Friday night I had sat waiting in the car was a prime opportunity to clock who left with whom, something I could use as a weapon in the future, if necessary, against Joe, Esme or Josie. I was prepared to follow them.

I fixed my mind on Joe's other friends. I suspected the older guy, Bert Toby, was interested in Josie. I called him Foxy Toby. There was something about the way he had looked at her after Esme turned him down. Old Freddy as well. He had got into the habit of leaving Josie a substantial tip and he'd done it secretly with great ease. Give her credit. When I'd asked her what Freddy was up to, she was honest about the generous tip.

But even if she was trustworthy then, that's not to say it would last. Look at the other night. What was she thinking about flirting with those Indian guys?

The cocktail bar had its regulars. They might offer her something she found difficult to refuse. After all, I knew some women liked that soft, caring treatment. That was alright at first, but men had to act like men. I knew I was a good catch, a much sought-after man. No shortage of offers for me in the past, but no, I would not let my guard down. Josie had to learn I was worth keeping. I would teach her.

Esme and Josie left the bar alone and I had mixed feelings. I could have driven past and offered them a lift, but I wondered if they might have arranged to meet someone further up the road, so I kept following them. It was disappointing when they got on the same bus. I went home.

When I went into the bar the following Friday, I asked Josie if she wanted to meet the next day. I felt obliged to go with her to a craft shop to show loyalty. My plan for later was to see Ricky about his garage. I didn't really want to rent it, but I hoped to talk him into letting me use it for a few weeks without charge. It was important to get my car off the road while I fixed a few bits and pieces.

Heading home from the craft shop, I stopped by a park and told Josie that I had to leave her there since Ricky was waiting.

She reached forward to open the passenger door and I had this overwhelming urge to hurt her the way she had hurt me at the Indian restaurant. I also felt like a leper when she had wiped the top of the lemonade bottle. I grabbed the back of her trousers and pulled her up and back. Before she could steady herself, I manipulated her and her jeans so that I could see skin. She yelped as I bit her as hard as I could on the fleshy part of her backside. She gasped as she stumbled out of the car. I drove away and couldn't help laughing at the rear end of her bending over. She seemed on the verge of vomiting.

It took me half an hour to wear Ricky down to the point that he agreed to give me the garage for two weeks. Outside, I saw a row of potted plants on the garage wall. The nearest one to my car had pink flowers. Just right. Without breaking stride, I picked it up as I passed and hid it from view in front of me until I opened the car door. It fitted nicely into the passenger footwell.

Later that day, I left the plant at the hotel for Josie. Not a peace offering as such, just a reminder of my spontaneous generosity.

Josie

Josie didn't immediately tell Moira about her day out. She was embarrassed to admit Dave wasn't as kind as she'd initially thought. After biting her nails, twiddling her thumbs and letting her cup of tea go cold, she spilled the beans.

'That's not on. No. That's practically assault,' Moira said.

They agreed this was manipulative behaviour. It was on the tip of Moira's tongue to advise Josie to get shot of Dave as quickly as she could. But she only suggested that she might bring up the biting incident next time they met and let him know how he made her feel. If he had any heart, he would take heed of Josie's feelings, but Moira wasn't convinced the outcome would be favourable for her friend. Her concern was building.

Josie confided in Moira that she felt she could be the butt of his jokes, ones which she didn't find funny. On a day out to Edinburgh, she and Dave had stopped off for a coffee then made their way back to the car park. He unlocked the driver's door, and she stood, waiting. But the passenger door had a fault and wouldn't open from the outside. Dave didn't do his normal leaning over the passenger seat to open her door. This time, he waved to her and drove a few yards. He paused, she went towards the car, reached out to open the door but he drove another few yards. This happened five times and it was all childish and stupid. It was raining and Josie thought it'd be best to let him drive off. Enough was enough. Anger rising, she made her way to the café, but he caught up with her and accused her of being too sensitive, saying it had only been a silly joke.

Things like that confused Moira. No one was laughing at his 'joke' but Josie had decided there seemed no point in creating a fuss over wiping the lip of a bottle, marking her with a bite or leaving her chasing his car in a car park. She wanted a boyfriend and Dave could be kind sometimes.

Aware of how new Josie's relationship was with Dave, Moira didn't want to put a spanner in the works by speaking out of turn, but there was something amiss. She wondered if Josie was digging a hole for herself because she continually excused his inappropriate actions.

Despite some initial second thoughts, the romance blossomed. Sometimes Dave's absence from the Avonpark made things more intense when he finally walked through the door after weeks of silence.

Josie's take on it was that he must have been called away for work and would tell her all about it later. Her hopes soared some weekends when he appeared minutes before closing time.

'Hah! Surprise, surprise!' she greeted him.

'See you outside once you're finished here?' Dave asked.

She nodded. Her heart skipped a beat, and she felt a warmth flood through her body.

After a few months, things were upside down since Dave had integrated himself into her life. He would leave, then reappear days later.

He would ask her out mid-week when it was too late to arrange a babysitter. But that didn't matter, she stayed home with Ginny. The good thing was she had a pool of babysitters for her work shifts, so there was no reason to get home immediately after the bar closed.

Esme and Joe occasionally joined them for after-work drinks, and sometimes they would meet at lunchtime. One outing Dave suggested was to Wiseman Farm on the outskirts of town.

'I've taken Josie there a few times now.' Dave lifted his chin proudly. 'It's an amazing place. The food is great. It's her favourite place.'

This was true. As they drove out of town, Josie felt her body relax while she took in the views of fields and rivers. She sighed as the aroma of trees and flowers filled the air. Away from the hustle and bustle of everyday life, this was a chance to lose herself.

Dave

In the farm restaurant, the four of us sat chatting and laughing over lunch. I could tell Josie was euphoric, she was babbling on. After tasting each other's dishes and then praising me for my choice of restaurant, we ordered coffees and Joe asked for the bill. When it arrived in a small box, the waiter laid it between Joe and me. I was frustrated because it was such an old-fashioned assumption that the men would pay. I couldn't help scoffing. I made it clear as I pushed the box in front of Josie.

'OK, I've paid a few times and I'm always filling the car with petrol, so it's your turn.'

I looked over at Esme and Joe.

'You sort her out with your half. I'm going to see a man about a dog,' I said as I got up.

I suppose that surprised Josie; I knew she didn't mind paying because she had offered several times in the past. Of course, I wasn't sure if she had money but if that was the case, this would teach her to come prepared and not expect other folk to pay. As it was, she had enough in her purse to cover it but I was glad to see her flush with embarrassment.

With the bill paid, we headed off, but her face was tripping her on the way home and she really pushed herself to have a conversation. Her mood almost spoiled what had been a delightful afternoon. I guessed she was thinking about having to pay the bill. She didn't realise I wanted to keep what was in my wallet. I'd planned to meet some folk for a drink the following afternoon and I wasn't sure how much I'd need. But there was honestly no room for complaint because I financed most of our outings. If I was between jobs, my mother always made sure I had enough money but even that supply wasn't limitless.

The truth was Mum had started asking me to pay her back. It was uncomfortable, but I reminded her of everything I did for her. I sold her items at a discount when they were no longer of use to me and got her chocolates on her birthday. She ended up slinking into the kitchen with her head down after my retort. No mother should ask her son for repayment. Parents are supposed to support their children.

Josie was difficult when it came to men acting naturally and taking control, but despite that, I liked her. One night, she organised and paid for a babysitter so that she and I could visit some of my friends. Within minutes of arriving at their house, I suggested the men headed out to the bar, leaving the women in the living room with a bottle of wine.

Her face told a story on my return three hours later, and we had to leave immediately. According to Josie, she felt abandoned, bored, and needed to be with Ginny again. Before I turned the engine on, I had to put her right.

'We only wanted to go for a pint,' I snarled at her, but she didn't say a word. 'Look at me when I'm talking to you!' I felt my neck stiffen. 'That's what people do; they go out with their friends.'

'Listen, I paid for a babysitter tonight so that I could go out with you. Not so that I could sit in someone else's house. That's all I'm saying about it.'

She'd said her piece, but I sat silently with the left side of my mouth twitching.

Wondering if I'd gone too far, I quickly absolved myself. I left a box of her favourite chocolate gingers at the Avonpark and the next time I saw her; I invited her on a day trip to the east coast. That's all it took; I could tell she was easy meat.

I could hardly believe it when the same thing about leaving the women happened the following week, but the outcome was different.

On Saturday, I bumped into Craig, an old friend who recently came back to town. With his wife Susan and their two children, they intended to settle nearby. I dropped into the Avonpark to tell Josie she needed to find a babysitter so that the four of us could meet up the following night, her Sunday off. Live music was scheduled for eight-thirty in a local club. Craig interested me because he owned a garage. I could have access to every conceivable tool I might need if we got to know the couple better.

The plan was to go to Craig and Susan's house at seven o'clock. Josie was ready and her babysitter was in place, so we set off. After a beer and a wine at their highly polished dining room table, Susan took Josie to see her new kitchen. While they were out of the room, I suggested to Craig that we both head to the club and the women could catch up later. When they came back through, Josie was raving about cupboards and worktops while Craig explained to his wife the plan of us men leaving first.

'What on earth are you talking about? Are you saying you're going out without me?' Ignoring everyone else in the room, Craig averted her stare. 'When did we ever go out without each other? We don't live like that and we're not starting now!'

Looking around, Craig hesitantly proposed that we all wait and leave together in approximately 30 minutes.

I didn't need Josie to speak about this. If the women we encountered were used to being compliant, I'd have an easier life. I hadn't liked her outburst the week before when I'd gone out for three hours. However, following the Craig and Susan incident, I found a way to manage her attitude and showed her an example of my disapproval of yet another couple.

'Look at Jimmy and Angie. Can you believe she's such a domineering cow? The poor man wants to relax with a bottle of beer after a week's work and all she can do is hand him a tea towel and tell him to dry the dishes. Not an appealing trait in a woman. She seems to forget he's working for her and the five kids. He needs to set her straight on that one.'

And so, I passed another message on. Not only were we men entitled to a break, we weren't to be asked to have anything to do with the household chores. I didn't think asking a man to clean up was normal. That wasn't the way to create a functional, happy family. Everyone should know their place.

Chapter 3

Josie

Dave left Josie in an awkward predicament at Wiseman Farm by assuming she could handle the bill. Yet, she felt unable to speak up in front of others. There had been an element of control and humiliation to his action. She rationalised it by thinking he might have lacked cash or even social skills in front of Esme and Joe. He did love her after all.

A few weeks later, Dave suggested Josie meet him on a Saturday afternoon. A problem arose as she had no babysitter for her little one. Although they had spoken about Dave meeting Ginny, a get-together had never materialised. He proposed they made it a family day out and visit the funfair with her?

They had a fantastic time because Ginny was the centre of attention. She jumped on and off the little cars and, with candy floss still hanging like a little pink beard from her chin, she chomped on popcorn and ran excitedly between each stall. Dave encouraged her to pick a numbered plastic duck with a hook and throw balls to hit a target. At three years old, she was captivated by the intriguing man who gave her the male attention she lacked.

Josie paid for everything, and rightly so. It was her daughter who was being treated. The situation became tricky for Josie when she saw the meagre contents of her purse. Her waitressing job didn't bring in much and, although Ginny's father, Mark, contributed a small amount, her weekly income didn't extend to costly days out at funfairs. This put her in a difficult position regarding money again.

Once home, Josie trembled as she broached the subject of income and spending after Ginny had fallen asleep. Dave lounged back on her couch, drinking a cup of tea with his feet up on the coffee table.

'So, what are you telling me? You're saying you don't have enough to spend on meals out or treating Ginny, yet you're happy to enjoy it all if I pay?'

He dragged his eyes up and down her body with scorn rather than approval.

He had missed her point. She didn't mean he should pay for everything. His reaction made her feel stupid, as if she was incapable of explaining herself. All that Josie had said was she couldn't continue living beyond her means and she would have to tighten her purse strings, otherwise there wouldn't be any food that week for her and Ginny. He glared at her and walked out without finishing his cup of tea.

Normal gossip consumed Josie and Moira every time they met. They believed they knew how the world and relationships worked and nobody could tell them any different. Ed sometimes tried to control what Moira did and who she met, so it didn't seem unusual when Josie admitted similar goings on in her liaison with Dave. Moira's savvy surpassed Josie's, often persuading Ed to consider different perspectives. The friends shared experiences like spending and saving, and the stock reply to a whine from one to the other was usually the same.

'My goodness, Dave and Ed are almost alike.'

If Josie and Moira had been wiser, they might have anticipated what was coming.

When they talked about uncomfortable things in their relationships, the other would occasionally suggest that such behaviour is normal. Josie was reminded of the turbulent relationship between her parents and the violence that ensued if her mother contradicted her father. Moira remembered the drunken battles between her parents. So, like their mothers before them, they assumed they had to grin and bear most situations. But Moira didn't like what she was hearing about Dave's unusual behaviour.

Once Dave met Moira's husband and discovered Ed wanted to rule the roost, he was more than happy for Josie to share some time with the couple. It delighted Dave because the friendship appeased at least one part of his character; it reinforced the need for the female to be subservient to the male.

While their little ones were in playgroup one morning, Josie and Moira passed by a café. Dave was inside and beckoned them to pop in and join him for a coffee. Just as they entered, Moira spotted Dave was with a male friend. She turned around and stood at the door, looking outside. Josie asked what the problem was.

'I can't go in there. If Ed ever found out I was sitting in a café with a couple of guys, I can't tell you what would happen. OK if Dave was there on his own, but...' She put her hands up in horror.

It was then that Josie realised Moira was facing her own dramas at home.

Later in the week, when Dave asked why they had left so quickly, Josie repeated Moira's reason.

'Hah!' he sneered. 'Why can't you be like her? See, that's what normal relationships are like. That's what loyal people do.'

Josie couldn't see what harm there would be in having a coffee in a public place with someone. She couldn't remember ever being with anyone else, especially a man, but Dave's statement held a cautionary message. In time, his remarks relating to other couples and families carried warnings.

Josie and Moira soon questioned the intentions of Dave and Ed but lacked the courage to confront them. All they could do was put the world to rights when the men weren't there.

Dave went from job to job, labouring or repairing broken machinery, and sometimes doing shift work. It wasn't uncommon for him to start a job in another city and turn up at her door a few days later, saying the boss didn't like him or the job had finished.

If Dave found the boss OK, he stayed, but after a couple of weeks or months, he started taking days off. His feeble excuses didn't always hold up, so either he had to face up to being disciplined or come up with better stories for his absences.

Josie didn't know that this was what he had been doing all his working life, skipping out when he was asked to pick up a tool and, consequently, losing wages.

Dave

After I'd been two weeks on a mechanical type job, I was told I'd have to travel seventy miles to Aberdeen where a new site was opening. The choice was either daily travel or staying in an on-site caravan with fellow workers. I didn't like either option, so the day before I was due to leave, I called in to say my father had died and I wouldn't be able to fulfil my obligations. I happily took a week off, allowing the others to find their way around the new site.

I had to join them eventually because I was running out of money. On my return, a colleague said he was sorry to hear about my father.

'Oh, I know. It was a difficult time, but he's pulled through.' The other man was astonished by what I said.

'I thought he passed away?'

My jaw dropped when I realised I had made a blunder. Within seconds, I came up with an answer.

'Well, technically, he passed away. He died on the operating table, but they resuscitated him,' I said with a straight face.

None of it was true. My father had never been in hospital; he was alive and well and cutting the grass in his back garden, but my story had given me a week at home where good old Mum looked after me.

I confessed to Josie that I had falsified certificates and manipulated my CV to appear as if a well-known petroleum company had employed me. In future interviews, I was hired without being asked for evidence of my qualifications. I'd wondered if she would ever use that knowledge against me. I kept her straight on that one.

Thanks to a friend's recommendation, I secured a job in an oil refinery after a phone interview. I'd be away for a couple of months in Holland. Josie was excited for me but disappointed that she couldn't come along because she had Ginny and other responsibilities. She even suggested giving up everything and following me to Holland where we could start a new life. But I told her these kinds of jobs didn't work like that. Nothing was permanent unless you had a long-term contract. She was jealous because I had an exciting life, on and off aeroplanes, in and out of different hotels and the freedom and the money to choose what I did and didn't do.

It was great when I was in a job like the one in Holland, everything was done for me the three weeks I was away and I didn't have to pay for much. I tried to spend as little as possible even when I was home for my two-week break. One of my better ideas was to flit between my parent's house and Josie's flat. Only after many months, I let it slip that I never paid my mother board money because I wasn't there every day. Neither did I contribute to Josie's housekeeping for the same reason but I felt quite comfortable putting the kettle on, opening the fridge and helping myself. Buying or bringing food for Josie was as good as paying rent in my mind. With that kind of arrangement, I could afford a decent car and spend on whatever I liked.

Josie's cupboards never had what I wanted. I had to complain if there was no brown bread. That was the only way she would pay attention,

'Why do you insist on buying this white rubbish? All I'm saying is, buy a brown loaf now and again. That way, I can at least have a sandwich when I'm here.'

She was so selfish.

Josie

As well as Dave not paying his share, he was light fingered when it came to other people's money. A friend of Josie's, Linda, had paid outright for a pair of boots she had ordered from Josie's catalogue. She wanted to pay them in full rather than weekly. They cost £30 and Linda had given Josie two £20 notes and got £10 change. The two notes were still lying on the sideboard when Dave arrived. Picking up the money, he asked whose it was. Josie told him but, before she could say any more, he handed her £20 and kept the other for himself.

'I'm sure this is what folk do if someone gives them the full amount in cash. They spend it then pay by instalments. Everybody wins,' he announced as he pocketed twenty.

It took Josie a few minutes to work out what had happened. She had given £10 to Linda as change and now Dave was taking £20. She found herself in debt for the boots. Looking at the £20 now in front of her, she knew he had tricked her, but was afraid to challenge him.

Their circle of friends widened, and he constantly compared her to the other women. She made mistakes every day, according to him.

'Why don't you show Josie how to get her hair like yours?' or 'Why don't you buy a dress like Sharon's? You look dumpy in that one.'

It wasn't so much that it was difficult to please him; it was more that the goalposts of what made him happy changed rapidly and without warning. Her knotted stomach and tense shoulders were in preparation for his unexpected blows to her self-esteem.

Moira and Ed joined them for coffee one day and it transpired that Moira had forgotten to pay an electricity bill. Ed was livid, and it seemed obvious to Josie that he would have vented his anger more forcefully had he been at home rather than in a café. After scowling at Moira and asking her if she was stupid, he lifted his hand to bang the table but thought better of it. Dave guffawed at the scene that was playing out in front of him. Ed shook his head.

'Can you believe that? I told her it had to be paid by today and here we are, three in the afternoon and she's sitting drinking coffee!'

'That's women for you.' Dave sat back, shaking his head.

The young women shrank under his gaze.

At Josie's a few days later, Dave picked up his jacket to leave and asked her if she was going into town.

'I hadn't planned to, but I might.' She had learned to give answers that covered all eventualities.

'Pay this then.' He threw a bill and a £20 note on the table and walked out without saying goodbye. If she'd had her wits about her, she would have pocketed the money because it had been hers from the catalogue payment fiasco. But she didn't. She had learned, most likely from her parents' battles, it was better to leave well alone and not antagonise a fragile situation.

Once he left, Moira popped in to ask if Josie would like to take the little ones to the park, so she left his repair bill and decided not to go into town after all.

Later, with his eyes darkened and his mouth set, the veins on his neck stood out as he picked up the bill and the money.

'Completely incompetent, aren't you? That bill was supposed to be paid today. I promised the guy in the garage I wouldn't let him down and it's still here. What do you do? Sit on your arse all day no doubt. You can't even follow a simple instruction.'

'Isn't it funny that when Moira didn't pay a bill, you laughed? Is it because it's me that it's no longer funny?' Josie had become daring, her chin jutting out in a challenge.

She expected a response and backed away but Dave said nothing. He picked up the bill and the money, then left. Now it was all her fault.

He was cunning in getting money from others, too. His sister was selling a nearly new pram. Dave said he was sure he had a buyer for her. Telling the buyer the pram was £20 when his sister only wanted £10 meant he pocketed the profit. He picked up other people's change in a bar or café, sometimes even the tips for waiters, and would borrow small amounts from friends but never pay them back. Josie soon realised his lifting the catalogue money was typical behaviour. Cash wasn't safe in her house. She began to hide it because she had to put food in the little one's mouth.

One evening, they stopped in at a local hotel lounge and a group of six came in. Dave knew a couple of them. They had dressed more formally than normal.

'Huh! So, what's the occasion? Have you won on the horses or something?' he asked Charlie.

'It's Jane's twenty-first, so we're going out to celebrate. We've booked The Atholl, but we're going to have a drink here first.' He stood proudly in his new suit with matching waistcoat.

'So, who's paying for all this then?' Dave asked.

'It's my treat. I'm taking them all out.'

Dave moved closer and ran his hands and fingers swiftly over Charlie's suit jacket. Josie looked on as he touched the collar and down the front; he mentioned the quality of the material before he sat back on the barstool. And then the group ordered their drinks. Just as the barmaid was tallying up the bill, Charlie felt his inside jacket pocket and then his side pockets before his face went pale. He turned to one of the group in a panic and said something.

'Anything wrong?' Dave called over.

'I've lost my wallet! There's a lot of money in it; I put it in my inside pocket. I can't believe it. It's gone. My jacket's been on my back since I left the house and I paid the taxi driver five minutes ago, then made sure I tucked it back in my pocket. I mentioned it to Jane.' He was almost in tears as he looked pleadingly at his wife.

'I saw you,' Jane announced as she patted his inside pocket. 'I was keeping an eye on it because I know there's £200 there.'

Another member of the group paid for the drinks, but between them, they agreed they wouldn't be able to go for their celebratory meal. Then Dave called Charlie over.

'Is this what you're looking for?' he held out a black leather wallet.

'How the hell did you get that?'

'Well, you weren't paying attention when I was looking at your suit jacket. All it took was for me to feel where your wallet was and pick it out,' Dave replied smugly.

Of course, Charlie was grateful and Dave made out he was teaching him a lesson about being careless when he was carrying so much cash.

Josie thought, *I don't believe for a minute that's the reason he took it.*

She had been watching everything and never saw his sleight of hand. Something puzzled her; she wondered why someone would do something like that? Dave hadn't kept the wallet given that he was adept at stealing.

Maybe it wasn't worth the risk of being discovered.

Dave had dark, hidden talents that Josie was finding out about. She felt a knot in the pit of her stomach.

Chapter 4

Dave

There came a point when Josie couldn't do anything right as far as I was concerned. Sometimes I arrived thinking I'd be able to find something decent in her fridge or cupboards but often all I saw was the meagre lunch she had made for her and Ginny. It was laughable. I told her she was anything but an exemplary mother and housewife if she couldn't keep decent stuff for eating. But, now that her daughter was of an age to sit at a table for at least half an hour, I was happy to drive to seaside towns where we sometimes had lunch out. When it came to paying, I was fed up hearing that she was trying to do the best she could with the money she had.

She seemed proud that she never borrowed money from anyone. That was something I did constantly; it never bothered me. I didn't owe *her* anything and all I had to do was buy a treat, take her out for a drink or a meal now and again if I ever thought she was becoming distant. I knew how to reel her back in with promises. It didn't matter if I *forgot* about them. By then she was dangling on my hook once more. and had forgotten the petty things that bothered her.

Not even twenty-one, Josie told me she was unsettled in life, but she didn't know what she wanted. To me she just wasn't content. Ungrateful I would call it. But she always accepted my gifts and kind gestures, so I learned how to create little dramas that displeased her so that I would have an excuse to make it up to her and show her how kind I was. It was easy to take her spirit down then boost it back up again, toying with her emotions like a yoyo. The idea was to keep her confused, slightly out of touch with reality and focused on the pleasant things I did for her.

Sometimes I challenged myself. How far could I push her? Initially, I was careful not to lose my temper completely. I had to take it step by step until I had her where I wanted her. There was such satisfaction in watching her deflate, her crestfallen face blinking back tears.

One day, I waited outside a department store while Josie ran in to get thread or something. When she came out, she was all smiles and held up her wrist to me.

'So, what do you think? Smell that,' she said.

'Why? What is it?'

'It's a free sample of Pagan. Do you like it?'

I did, but I wasn't intending to tell her that.

'Smells like cat's piss.'

She was trying to bring up my ex Evelyn, but I wasn't giving her the satisfaction of a compliment. She could wait for that.

Meeting up with our friends became increasingly difficult. Now and again she refused to come out because she was feeling down, but I didn't let that stop me from getting a few pints and mixing with folk. I needed time out. I was convinced she was worried that I would do or say something to make her feel bad in front of others. But, if she asked to come out and I didn't want her there, I had ways to create uncertainty about what she was wearing, her figure or her make up and put her down before we even left the house. It was most satisfying.

Many times, I would either comment on how she was losing her locks, or I said nothing but simply stared at her in a way I knew was unsettling. She said I was scowling when I looked at her shoes, then she scurried away to change them. I tested my methods by saying now and again that she looked great. Giving her compliments never failed. Then she was relaxed and keen to go out with me. I could store the negative comments for later if she started talking to other men during the evening. Then I could throw in the odd remark. Now and again, it was good to keep her on her toes. If new friends invited her out without me, I had no choice but to point out they were making a fool of her or that she couldn't trust them.

'You're getting above your station trying to mix with them. Don't forget where you come from. Why on earth would they want *you* in their company? Look at them, successful with decent clothes and houses. What do you think you'll look like beside them? They just feel sorry for you. They'll be laughing at you!'

Initially, I approved of her friends. But my instinct told me she was talking about me, so I often put her right about people she encountered, including her friends. Eventually, she complied and read my suggestions as best to stay away from people and certain places like the local cafés. For a while, she only went out if I was with her. I rewarded her with compliments and little gifts.

Out shopping or in town, she often averted her eyes when she caught sight of a friend.

'There's Sandra,' I said one day at an open-air market.

'Oh right. I can't talk to her just now.'

She didn't seem to have energy left to even hold a conversation, like a timid little rabbit.

If we went out together to a café or a bar and she sat down first, I joined her but passed a few remarks to keep her on the ball. She said I had a dour look on my face when I pointed out her mistake.

'You shouldn't have picked this seat. Never sit close to the door; too many people coming and going,' or 'Never sit next to the kitchen; the staff are always passing by and bumping your chair.'

I even tried this. 'Why did you choose a table near the young men? Do you want to sit and stare at them?'

I think Josie was avoiding taking the wrong seat when she let me go into places first, but I made a point of holding the door open for her; others saw me as the proper gentleman that I am. She stood inside, looking awkward and not knowing where to sit while I stood shaking my head as if trying to understand her dilemma.

'Well, sit down!' I would say loud enough for other customers to hear and nod towards the empty tables.

Even our nights out in company were excellent opportunities to remind her I was in charge. If there was a special night in the local social club, she wasn't always keen to make the effort, but I insisted she get a babysitter and I let her join me. We often sat with folk at their table, even if we weren't part of their group. That wasn't a problem because most of them were familiar and it was a way to meet new people. Sometimes they even paid our bill.

One evening, we pulled our chairs into a group of eight where two young men were bouncing jokes and comments off each other. She said she didn't know them but I didn't believe her. I was surprised to see Josie relaxed and in stitches, chipping in now and again with a smart remark. The young men encouraged her, so she had leant forward, far too engrossed in the chitchat. Others were laughing and eventually, the entire table focused on the two men and Josie. I was excluded and I'd had enough. I leaned closer to Josie and hissed in her right ear.

'I'm glad you find their jokes funny.'

Not for the first time, Josie's shoulders tensed, her face froze, and she slumped in her chair. That had stopped her. Seconds later, she got up and made her way towards the toilets. The men were trying hard to take her away from me but I had managed to get her away from them first. She looked like a burst balloon as she walked out with her head down. Pathetic. I hadn't lost my touch. I could still change her mood with the right words.

Josie

Josie was still wiping her tears as she came out of the toilet cubicle to find one of the older females from the company sitting on a stool in front of the mirrors.

'Are you OK, love?' she asked.

Josie nodded then shook her head. Her actions were as confused as her thoughts.

'We all knew he had said something to you, but we didn't know what. He completely spoiled your fun. I don't want to interfere, but I'm a lot older than you and I can tell you now, I've got a gut feeling he's a bad one.'

'I'm not sure what I was doing wrong. I was only laughing at the funny stories,' Josie offered through sniffles.

'Wrong? You're not doing anything wrong, pet. Can I ask you how old he is? Are you married?'

'He's twenty-six and no, I'm only going out with him.'

The woman thought for a minute.

'I don't know how he treats you in private, but if he's doing that kind of thing in public, I think you deserve to be warned. If he's as jealous as that because you're laughing at a joke, I would put money on him getting angry at practically everything you do because he'll have trust issues about who you're mixing with.' She stopped for a moment, but Josie was choked with tears and could only nod her head. 'He'll come across as the big, bold boy, the important know it all, but he's really masking a lot of anxiety and insecurity. You're a lovely lass, but I'm sure he never tells you that, probably tells you he doesn't like this or that about you. He's no oil painting, but I'm sure every day you do your best to make him feel good about himself and ignore what you need for yourself.'

Josie had calmed.

'A lot of what you're saying is true, but I want to make him happy. I want this to work for us. Maybe soon he'll realise that and see I'm not interested in anyone else, whether they make me laugh or not.' Josie tried to defend Dave as the woman took both of Josie's hands in hers.

'You'll never change him. I think you're going to stay with him though. I hope I'm wrong. Maybe someday you'll sit back and wonder why you wasted so many years on such a bully. I can spot one a mile away. You deserve a lot better, pet.'

She smiled, then let go of Josie's hands. While they had been talking and there had been that brief physical contact, Josie felt strong and was glad to have someone else's opinion, even if she didn't feel she could act on the advice at that precise moment.

It was as though someone cared about how she felt. But when the woman had let go and Josie's hands had fallen to her sides, she was on her own, isolated, with no support. The world was going on without her and she was left to fight her own battles.

She felt a tide of anxiety wash over her and rubbed at the front of her neck as if to stop herself from choking.

Leaving the ladies' room, they spotted Dave on a chair in the hallway. He didn't get up. It was Josie's moment. She could have gone back into the lounge with the woman and carried on the fun, but she didn't. After thanking the woman, she walked over to Dave and said she needed to go home. Fun over; he'd won.

They headed off towards the car park. She said nothing much on the journey, even when she got out of his car. There was no way she was waiting to discuss any of what had happened, because something told her he would turn it around and make it her responsibility.

Once she closed her front door, she leaned her back against it and shook her head in despair. Her shaking hands steadied as she filled the kettle.

Sitting down with a cup of tea, she surveyed the pile of college prospectuses on the table. One stray leaflet about evening classes had fallen from the top and looking at it, forlorn and lying apart from the others, a lump formed in Josie's throat.

She so badly wanted to go to college, but she doubted she was even good enough for that. There was significance to the fallen leaflet. Abandoned and of no importance. Josie cradled her head in her hands and broke her heart.

Dave

Josie needed to learn there wasn't anything wrong with me showing my disapproval at her laughing with the group of guys. After all, I was the one she was out with. She was being over friendly and the men were getting the wrong idea. I had to stop her and protect her from these scoundrels. I couldn't physically pull her away, but I've always been good at a sharp comment. No matter who she spoke to, I had a choice; belittle her or attack the infiltrator. Other folk tended to back away immediately, not wanting to get involved, so the perfect solution was to focus on Josie. I was protecting her. The only problem with shielding her was that if she misunderstood my intentions, she went into a huff. After that I usually stayed out of her way until she had cooled down. It wasn't difficult to persuade her that she had caused the problems. I forgave her and presented her with a few flowers or some chocolates. Good girl.

I explained the problem about her laughing at other guys jokes; I wanted us to live together. I knew I would feel secure if we were a proper couple and shared more than dates. I reminded Josie I saw Ginny more than her biological father, and if I had more confidence in our relationship, I could provide a pleasant life for all. The choice was hers. Josie didn't immediately jump at my offer, but she had passed the point of questioning or accusing me about my actions in the club. I gave her time to realise what she had done wrong,

I made noises about us finding a place together. Although I knew she wasn't entirely happy with life, she and Ginny were secure and sheltered in their rented flat but I had to let her know I wasn't being unreasonable about asking her to move. I needed her to rely on me and treat me like the man of the house, well, except for the financial side of things. I had no argument against her bringing in her own money.

Things between us would work if she did what pleased me. The answer was for me to feel needed and proud to have a place of my own.

Time and time again, I told her she was mad to stay in the area she lived in. I wanted to choose where we went even if it cost more. But that had to be with her contributing financially. Of course, it was crucial to keep the supply of cash coming in from my mum when I was out of work. Good old Mum wouldn't see me stuck for rent and there was no need to think any further than that.

Before any suitable flats came up for us, an agency offered me a job in a rig supply business in Dundee. I suggested that Josie and Ginny join me to test the waters of us living together. We'd have to stay in a paid for caravan like the other workers, but it would be a start and give us time to speak about a permanent place. To see the lay of the land, I took them up to the area before I was due to start and organised a family room at a bed-and-breakfast in Dundee for three nights.

The friendly owner showed us around. He pointed out the shared toilet and bathroom and handed me a key to the room. Everything was clean and Ginny would have her own junior bed.

It didn't take long for me to unpack. I was keen to locate places of interest nearby and got fed up waiting for Josie.

'I'm heading out for a pint, so I'll meet her you at the corner in half an hour.' I left her to it.

It was easy to chat with some guys in the bar who were working on a similar site, so I lost track of time. I was surprised that Josie was annoyed having to stand at the corner for almost an hour with Ginny. She said she didn't know where I was and was worried. But there were only three bars nearby. She could have popped her head round the doors to see if I was there. By the time I arrived at the corner, I needed to eat and the moment for sightseeing had passed. All I wanted was some food and a rest after all the driving. I made sure she paid her share of a quick lunch nearby, then we headed back to the bed-and-breakfast.

'I'm going for a bath,' I told her.

'I'll take Ginny over to the park and I might buy some snacks at the shop.' Josie unfolded a pair of dungarees for her daughter.

I stopped in my tracks as I picked up the soap, a towel and three magazines. I bared my teeth.

'You're not going anywhere. You'll stay in here until I'm finished.' I thrust my head forward to show I was deadly serious. The dungarees fell from her hands.

My way of relaxing was to spend no less than an hour in a bath and, as I had warned her before, without interruption.

'There's nothing for Ginny to do in here. We need to go out, even for a breath of fresh air. You'll be ages in there,' she pleaded.

I picked up the key, walked out and locked the bedroom door behind me. They wouldn't be going anywhere. For the next hour and a bit, I relaxed and topped up the deep, warm water every so often, browsing through my Exchange and Mart magazines. I finished by washing my hair and took my time drying myself with the thick, pure white towels. I didn't have my comb so I had to use my fingers to slick my hair back. That took a few minutes. Then I leisurely picked up my things and made my way back to the room.

Josie was angry at me when I unlocked the bedroom door. I stood there with a towel secured round my waist, but I didn't get a minute to draw breath before she started moaning. Apparently, Ginny had announced she needed to go to the toilet five minutes after I had locked them in. I hadn't thought about that, but it wasn't my problem. How was I supposed to know when other people, especially children, needed to answer the call of nature? Josie should have been forward-thinking enough to take her daughter to the toilet before I went for my bath. Seems there had been no option but to let Ginny do her business in her underwear. Josie held it up to me the moment I came back. That was all I needed to see. Disgusting little animal

'I'm speechless!' Josie knew if she said much more, I might do something she regretted. But she went on, ranting as if I had done wrong. 'Do you know how selfish you are? You locked us in a room with no way out and this little girl had nothing to do. Her needing the toilet is one thing. What if there had been a fire? She's a child, Dave.'

If it hadn't been for me feeling calm after my bath, I would have told her it should have been her saying sorry to me for not reminding me to bring a comb. I glanced across at Ginny huddled on a chair, her gaze averting mine.

Chapter 5

Josie

Things were not looking good for Dave and Josie in Dundee, and they hadn't even moved in together properly.

Josie wanted to pack and go home, but she didn't have the train fare. Her family allowance could only be cashed away from home twice unless she informed the benefits office so she would have to wait until the following Tuesday for money. Dave was in control financially and that frustrated her. She was a prisoner who had to stay silent to appease her captor.

But she felt the fire in her after the locked door incident. Ginny was being treated inappropriately because of Dave's selfishness. Here she was again, at a crossroads. Thoughts of changing her mind about moving in with him dissipated over the next few days when he showed more affection and consideration towards her and Ginny. They went to visit the caravan and the surrounding area. It didn't surprise Josie that the seaside town of Arbroath consisted of beaches and parks, fish and chip shops and tourist attractions. Perhaps this could be a good life.

With their brief stay at the bed-and-breakfast over, Dave packed his things to take up his new contract. There were almost ten days before Josie was to join him. She had enough time to collect her belongings and catch up with friends before leaving Falkirk. She confided in another friend, Sheila, that she wasn't sure if she was doing the right thing and explained about his temper and selfishness.

'Look, I don't want to get involved. I've known Dave for years, and he's never changed. I only put up with him because of you. Why do you let him treat you like that? Why are you giving up everything and moving away?'

'I honestly don't know. When I talk about it, it's as though it's all happening to a different person. I want to be strong and tell him to get lost. I want a peaceful life. Something keeps pulling me back to him. It's like he's always there, round every corner, coming in and out of my life. Hiding in the background, waiting with some offer of a better life. I'm so confused.'

'He's making sure you'll never meet anyone else.'

Initially, Josie tried to make sense of what Sheila was implying, that he was controlling her. With Dave never far away, he monitored and dominated each aspect of her life. But Josie let events roll along, silently hoping she could prove Sheila wrong. Friends said he was rude and inappropriate but, although Josie agreed, now and again she saw him differently. Somehow, she felt sorry for him.

But Josie also had ideas for her own security that she didn't share with Dave. Sheila's friend, Doris, lived in Oban, miles away on the west coast of Scotland, but was looking for a property in the Falkirk area to be nearer her mother. With a six-year-old boy, she had enough to buy a small place, but she wanted to rent for a few months to get a feel for the district.

After speaking on the phone, Josie came to an arrangement with Doris. If it worked, she would sub-let her flat and, because she didn't need three bedrooms, Doris agreed Josie could use one as a store. Josie only needed to take a few personal things to Arbroath, so most of her furniture would remain. The only uncertainty was if Doris found a place to buy sooner than a few months, Josie decided to cross that bridge when she came to it. By then, she would know if Dave was a man of his word. She invited Sheila and Doris for morning coffee to iron out the details.

Josie tried to convince Sheila, Moira and her other friends that if she and Dave were living together, he might understand how important it was to have a secure family without jealousy. He would have to keep a job to survive and life might become normal. She was prepared to try given that she was not burning all her bridges in her hometown.

Once set, she and Ginny made their way up north. Dave collected them at Arbroath train station. On the outskirts of Dundee, caravans faced the sea, with a nearby children's park and trampolines. They were a couple of miles from the centre of town, but a small shop on the site provided essentials. Ginny was so excited about her new life.

But, within the first week, Josie was bored. She needed something to do rather than hang around a caravan all day. She took Ginny to the play area and beach, but they wanted a more vibrant location with other children to interact with. The man in the next caravan, Lou, worked with Dave and told Josie his wife, Liz, was coming up for a couple of weeks, so she would soon have some company.

Liz was a lovely lady who had just started her annual two weeks summer holiday. Although she slept late then enjoyed many cups of tea in the mornings while reading the paper, she always had time for Josie and Ginny. Sometimes they walked along the beach to a café, and other times they sat and chatted outside of the caravans as Ginny played in the sandpit nearby with a newfound chum.

After a week, Liz popped into town on the Friday to meet Lou after work. They were going for a drink then to enjoy some fish and chips in a seaside café. There was nothing much to eat in the caravan cupboards because this was pay day for Dave and he'd said he would bring something back with him. He was later than usual coming home and it didn't surprise Josie he'd been for a drink with the boys.

Dave stumbled into the caravan and threw a paper bag next to the stove. He rattled through the pots to find a frying pan. From the bag, he produced an onion and some other vegetables. Finally, he unfolded a piece of greaseproof paper to reveal an oversized steak.

'What's that for?' Josie asked.

'It's my dinner,' he slurred.

'Only one?'

'Yes. One is enough for me.'

Josie stood back. She and Ginny had been waiting to see what plans he had for eating because he was the one with the money.

He rummaged for cooking oil and turned on the burner.

With the steak falling over the edges of the pan, he cut up the onion and tried to find space next to the meat to fry it. He roughly chopped a couple of carrots, throwing them into a pan of water. The gas was too high for the steak and it burned without cooking through. The onions were a mix of over-fried and still white. He had to take the steak off the burner; it was cooling quickly, so he removed the half-cooked carrots. Finding a suitable plate, he sat and ate.

Josie waited for a few seconds; she was stunned at his selfishness. Not for her, but for her little girl, who sat staring at the plate. Josie's thoughts were unsuitable for a child's ears. She had to summon all her strength to control the raging fury. After the force of her teeth caused the inside of her bottom lip to bleed, she walked silently over to the tiny worktop and made toast. With some margarine and the last bit of cheese on the top, she put it down in front of Ginny and helped her to cut it up. She fought back the tears, knowing she would find it difficult to sleep while hungry.

As he cut through the undercooked steak, the blood slowly found its way onto the vegetables. After eating two thirds of the meat, he laid his fork down and scraped the other third and what remained of the vegetables into the bin. His attitude, mixed with his belly full of alcohol, prevented Josie from confronting him. She was frightened of the consequences. Her stomach groaned that night as she lay awake wondering what she'd done to deserve such a life.

The following day, Dave drove to town and returned with a huge bag of groceries. It was as though the steak incident hadn't even happened. The entire weekend was tense. Josie feared a repeat around food but lacked the courage to address it. Her life was becoming a constant roller coaster of emotion.

On the Monday, she and Liz took a stroll into town. As they walked, Liz sensed Josie was much quieter than normal. Her speech was calm but she was repeating some stories. She appeared to be on another planet.

'Josie, probably none of my business, but if there's anything you want to talk to me about, you can. I feel something is desperately wrong.' Liz put her arm around her new friend.

Then Josie let it all go. Her words came tumbling out when she told Liz she and Dave weren't married and that Ginny wasn't his. Her explanation about coming to a caravan to stay with him sounded pathetic. It shocked Liz that Josie had left her old life behind without any concrete plans. When she told the story about the single steak he'd bought and allowed her and Ginny to sit and watch him eat. Liz was horrified. She knew how much the men were making, but Josie said she didn't have a clue about Dave's finances.

'Seems like you need to take some action,' Liz announced.

They got back half an hour before the men arrived, so Josie boiled some water that might do for pasta then waited to see what Dave's plans were for eating.

Dave

'Right,' was my first word as I stepped into the caravan on the Monday evening. 'There's been a change of plan. You'll never guess. The job is finishing on Friday, so that's the end of the caravan.'

'What does that mean?' The wooden spoon slipped from Josie's hand.

'That's it, the job's over. Four weeks is all we got. That's what happens with this type of work.'

Before Josie could ask anything more, I announced that I'd be going back to my mother's house and would look for another job. Josie didn't have to tell me she had nowhere to go or remind me she had a child. But she did.

'You can ask someone, one of your pals, if you can stay with them.' I always had a solution for her. I was good at that.

I only had my mother, and she kept my bedroom ready for me. Josie had Moira, Sheila and a group of others she could ask. Knowing I had a place to rest and a free meal, even in my toughest times, was incredibly convenient.

The next day, I came back to a much more relaxed Josie. She was reading a magazine while Ginny was having her ten-minute nap.

'Glad to see you've calmed down. Your face looks much nicer when you smile you know.' I hadn't given her a compliment for a while. She was due one.

This time, I had brought back fish and chips from the shop in town. Being early, I was certain Josie hadn't even started making food. In fact, it wouldn't have surprised me if she'd started on about where she was supposed to go after Friday. All I would have said was that it wasn't my problem.

I admit that, by Thursday, I wondered why she hadn't broached the subject of what was to happen to her and Ginny. As I moved stuff out of the way so that I could put my feet up, I noticed two holdalls.

'What's all this?' I asked, sweeping my arm in the direction of the floor.

'Just our bits and pieces,' she replied.

'So, do you have something in mind?'

'Well, yes. You're going back to your mother's because they will lock the caravan up, so we're going somewhere as well,' Josie said in a strangely calm voice.

'OK, that's clear. Where?'

She turned to face me.

'What does it matter to you? You do your own thing, I'll do mine.'

This was her trying to be smart. All evening I tried to get more out of her but she wasn't opening up. Letting me go without a fight hadn't been in my plans. I'd get her back.

Josie

What Dave didn't know was at the beginning of the week, instead of enjoying her morning tea and reading the paper, Liz called Josie and Ginny right after the men left for work.

'Lou told me last night the job was finishing next Friday and that Dave is going back to his mother's. My first reaction was to ask myself what on earth you were going to do? Is he able to take you and Ginny with him?' she asked.

'No, that's not possible. I am completely up in the air. I can't even think straight.' Josie's voice cracked.

'Let's work something out. Do you realise every day in the paper there are ads asking for live-in childminders? Let's see if we can find something.'

Liz grabbed that day's paper and passed an older one to Josie. They looked at the vacancies section and finally, Liz found something of interest. It was an advert asking for someone to look after two children in Aberdeen. In exchange, there would be free accommodation, food and a bit of pocket money. There were other ads, but that was the one that jumped out at them. Aberdeen was about an hour away by train. Liz tore the advert out and handed it over. She told Josie not to worry about the train fare, to call the number and see what the outcome was. For the first time in a few months, Josie had hope.

After making sure she had enough money to make a call, Liz watched Ginny while Josie ran to the site telephone. She steadied her shaking fingers on the plastic dialling circles and prayed that if this was meant to be, it would all go smoothly. Her mouth was dry and she swallowed twice involuntarily.

The single father at the end of the line asked if Josie was available immediately. That wasn't a problem, but she told him about Ginny. Thankfully, a child would be welcomed in his home, the room was a double. Divorced and doing shift work at a local factory, he needed someone to make sure his two children were up, fed and out to school on time. He also wanted someone there when they came home. There would be a bit of child minding in the evening thrown in now and again. It seemed simple enough. She agreed to travel up on the Friday and he said he would meet her at the train station, holding a piece of cardboard with her first name on it.

Liz handed her some pound notes to help her with travel and said to post the money in the future when she could save from her family allowance and the small amount she hoped to earn.

Thanks to Liz, Josie could start again. The more she thought about a future and where she would live, the more she took in the simpleness of the caravan. The compactness of the cupboards, storage and beds were perfect for a short stay, but it wasn't the right environment to try to make a home. Things were limited, kept to a minimum; four of everything, even cutlery and crockery, which meant a constant stream of washing up. Pillows had to be used as cushions, blankets were folded and spread out constantly depending on Ginny's sleep pattern. There was no respite.

So that Thursday, when Dave had almost tripped over the holdalls, he had no idea Josie would stick to her plans.

On the Friday morning, Josie tidied the caravan for the last time after Dave left for work. The train was at two o'clock, so Liz made sure she ordered a taxi in plenty of time. Josie was shaking and her stomach was churning when she stuffed last-minute things into the holdalls and folded the pushchair.

She didn't bother to leave a note for Dave. There wasn't any point. He would head off in a completely different direction from her. She was going north; he was going south. Part of her was sad, but she also felt relieved. She was doing what was right for her and Ginny. It was unlikely she and Dave would ever meet again.

Chapter 6

Dave

We left work as soon as we got the relevant paperwork on the last day. Lou had wanted to stay until the end but I persuaded him that with our pay in our pockets, we weren't obliged to give the company any more of our time.

I was more shocked than surprised as I drew in at one-thirty to find a black cab in my parking space beside the caravan. Lou got out of the car and said hello to Josie who was making her way down the caravan steps with one of the holdalls I had seen the night before. I jumped out and asked what was happening. Clearly, my arrival hadn't been in her plans. Luckily, I had got back in time. Josie addressed me briefly.

'We're leaving now.'

The taxi driver helped to put the holdalls and Ginny's pram in the boot while I hovered, going from one foot to the other. Neither Josie nor the taxi driver paid attention when I raised my hand to a stop position. The driver closed the door after Josie and Ginny were in and they took off.

The nerve. That can't be the end. I thought. I wouldn't let it be.

I got back into my car and reversed to turn at Lou's caravan. I didn't care that I churned up the grass, but in my rear-view mirror, I saw Liz's expression. They'd have a fair bit of work to straighten that out before they left. I could bet that cow Liz had put Josie up to this. She would never have thought of it on her own. I followed the taxi to the train station and, once Josie was on the pavement and unfolding the pushchair, I tried my best to get her to reveal her destination.

'Where?'

I was back to my one-word questions. I guessed she was going back to Falkirk, although that didn't make sense. Why would she get a train south when she knew I'd be driving in that direction? If I'd known the time of her train, I could have figured out her destination by asking at the ticket office. She avoided my question.

'Do you have a watch?' I asked.

'You know I don't. You know I don't have anything.'

'Here, take this.' I took my wristwatch off and put it in her pocket. I wanted to help her more but she turned away and walked to the ticket office.

I couldn't follow her any further because my car was in a drop-off-only zone. I watched her trying to balance the two holdalls while pushing Ginny's pram.

Josie

Once Josie reached the waiting room at the bottom of the station stairs, the thumping in her chest caused her to stop and take a deep breath. For all she knew, Dave might find a way to follow her and emerge from the shadows of the dingy platform. The corners of the tickets in her hand were dampening from anxious sweat as she scoured the faces of the waiting passengers.

A wave of movement towards the edge of the platform let Josie know the train was pulling in so she folded the push chair and told Ginny to hold on to the strap hanging from a bag. The obedient child climbed up the enormous step on carriage B and headed to the first available seat. She pulled herself up on the faded imitation velvet and immediately asked Josie to open her packet of raisins. Josie looked at her little girl and felt more than a pang of guilt that their lives consisted only of a terminus. A woman opposite smiled at Ginny. The child's face was full of anticipation because all that mattered was a handful of dried fruit.

Must be great to trust in someone so much that you know they have your best interests at heart. The thought brought a lump to Josie's throat.

Once again, Josie looked around. Wringing her hands and bobbing up and down to see into the carriage behind, she was certain they were on their own. There was something comforting about physically getting away. She had heard of people who could mentally cut themselves off from their problems and get on with life, but Josie knew she was different. It was crucial to put a geographical distance between her and the devil.

The longer the bridges over rivers and estuaries, the better; the sensation of moving at speed calmed Josie's troubled soul. Ginny wanted to know about the animals in the fields and tiny boats on the water.

'Can we count the cows, Mummy?'

'Do the boats stay in the water when it's raining?'

'I don't like my shoes now. I want white ones.'

The chatter continued and Josie checked herself when she tried to unjumble her thoughts instead of answering questions about where squirrels lived.

When Ginny snuggled in and drifted off to the rocking of the carriage movement, Josie breathed a sigh of relief. She found compartments in her mind for her muddled thoughts. In life, survival was paramount; food, clothes and a place to live. The philosophical thinking that nothing else could be achieved until these needs were met was a reality facing her every day. She began to question herself.

What is it that I need?
Why can't I get what I need?
What is it that I want?
Why am I not achieving what I want?

The answers scared her. The basics for survival didn't grow on trees, someone had to provide. Every day, she counted each penny to see what she could spend. There were no real treats. It was all about food and the odd pair of socks for Ginny. This wasn't the dark ages where women had to depend on men to support them but it seemed to be that way for her. There was work to be had. But Josie didn't have a choice of jobs because for a start she had Ginny and she wasn't qualified to do much more than clean toilets or stack shelves in a supermarket. Time for a rethink.

Now she had an opportunity to take Ginny to work. She wasn't going to be earning a fortune but at least she would have a constant roof over her head for the first time in a while. Josie smiled at what might materialise over the next few months.

The train trundled along while Josie ate the sandwich she had prepared earlier. The guard's whistle disturbed Ginny but only for a second. She turned round and cosied in again. Josie went back to her thoughts.

Education. That was the real answer. It wasn't that she hadn't been bright at school but the 50s and 60s hadn't really been a time for women to shine. It's true that some did but in the environment Josie had grown up in, it was all about boyfriends, marriage and children, and not necessarily in that order. She made a promise to herself. Forget the idea she had when she met Mark and the plan of four children. She would get herself an education, not overnight, but slowly fitting in with her lifestyle and Ginny. When she had been looking for work, Josie remembered seeing an advert for free evening courses at local schools. That thought took her back to the collection of college prospectuses she used to treasure. Time to start. She had no idea what her final dream job would be but the first step of the ladder was beckoning her.

Ginny woke up and nibbled on her cake. When she asked to sit on Josie's knee, her big eyes stared out from her tiny face. Her hair was tousled so Josie smoothed it back into place.

'Do you know how much I love you?' she asked her daughter.

'Do you know how much I love chocolate cake, Mummy?' Ginny replied.

The woman opposite burst out laughing.

They arrived to meet their host and embark on their new adventure. Her well-behaved wards were at home to greet her. Josie understood all that needed to be done and got herself into a routine within a matter of days. The only people she wrote to were her mother, who didn't know much about Dave, and Moira. Both were under strict instructions to get rid of the letters after they'd read them. She gave them the house phone number but asked them not to share it.

Dave

I couldn't figure out where Josie had gone, but I was almost certain something would come up that would reveal all. Once I drove back from the train station, I went to see Lou and Liz to speak about handing in the keys for the caravan and to find out if they had anything to say about the churned-up patch of grass. They didn't, but it looked like a bulldozer had run over it. I sat inside with a cup of tea and looked around. Liz had washed the floor and put some old newspapers down to prevent foot marks before it dried. As I glanced down, I saw a page where something had been torn out. I instinctively knew that's where the key to Josie's whereabouts lay.

I made my way to the site shop to ask if they had a copy of the paper. My luck was in. They did, and I found out what the missing part contained, a name and a telephone number. I made sure the advert was safely stored in my wallet.

That night, the guys from work went out for a few beers to say goodbye. Most of them had picked up another contract but Lou and I were in limbo. To avoid making food, I got a Chinese takeaway. It saved making a mess of the cooker and sink after Josie had done a decent job of cleaning it. The next morning, I made sure Liz knew I had nothing to eat or drink, hoping she would offer me tea and toast. It worked.

I packed my bits and pieces, and Lou took the caravan keys to hand in. I wasn't sure what the procedure was, so I needed to pass the buck to Lou in case the manager came snooping around to check the inventory. My mother would like the miniature bedroom clock and I'd keep the unusual corkscrew. Nobody would miss these things or, if they did, I'd be well out of the way.

It was just after seven when I pulled up outside my parent's house in a small town next to Falkirk. Mum appeared at the window with a big grin. Before I got out of the car I waited to see if she turned to announce my arrival to my dad. She didn't so I knew he was still in the bar at the end of the road boring someone to death about what a wonderful husband and father he was while throwing in snide comments about the people he had fallen out with.

This was good news. There'd be time to get my mother to cook a decent meal for me, ask her for a sub after I'd given her the clock and get out for my first pint back home. The thought made me tingle. I'd be facing warm welcomes from the guys and no doubt a few free pints. I could tell them anything about why I was back and these losers would believe it. To have the attention focused on me was going to make up for the Josie situation. I'd deal with that later.

The following weekend, I called her. She was startled to hear my voice and asked how I had found the phone number. I mentioned the torn newspaper on Liz's floor and kept my voice slower and calmer when I told her I was concerned. Being careful not to overdo it, I put on a slightly shaky tone. I needed us to meet; I wanted her address. She wouldn't tell. She had nothing much to say to me at that moment, but it was only a matter of time until she cracked.

About three weeks later, I called her again. I'd had a fine time with the guys at the club most nights, but I needed to find out what Josie was up to. It surprised me when she needed a shoulder to cry on during the call. She had received a letter from her mother's friend, Madge. It explained that her extremely ill mother had passed on the address. I had only met her mother a few times, I got the feeling Josie didn't want to explain our on again off again lifestyle, even when we moved into the caravan. Maybe it was just as well because that hadn't lasted. Now her mother had been taken into hospital. It was all very sudden. Madge knew Josie was struggling and might not have the money to travel, so she had enclosed some notes that would allow her to take the train back home.

I could tell Josie was upset and it was good to hear she was coming back. My offer of collecting her from the train and dropping her off at the hospital was well received. She had little choice.

Moira had said Josie could use her spare room for a while, so she had to make alternative arrangements for the two children she should have been caring for in Aberdeen. That was the end of her adventure and she made her way home to see her dying mother. Sad as that was, things were working in my favour.

I explained I was trying to make amends by looking for somewhere we could live together. I wouldn't agree to anything like a caravan again and told her I had some job interviews lined up. When she was at her most vulnerable, I showed some concern and gave her support. That's just the kind of guy I was. I was patient. I would have my moment.

Chapter 7

Josie

It was sheer luck Dave found out about a two bedroomed flat to rent in Mary Street, Falkirk. He had been driving by and noticed a sign on the door. Ripping it off to make sure no one else saw it, he headed to the nearest phone box to call the number. Once Josie heard he had made an effort, she was impressed, but still felt unsure. She didn't want to tell him she was hedging her bets by keeping a tenant her flat in case things didn't work out. She couldn't risk being turned out again with nowhere to go, especially with little Ginny.

They viewed the Mary Street accommodation later that evening and Dave signed on the dotted line. They were to take over the following week. He seemed to have changed and was more caring towards her and Ginny. He listened to what Josie wanted and what she considered a successful future. College, work and a steady income but, more importantly, peace and trust in a relationship.

During the first week at the flat, Dave was away. He had landed a job in acquisitions on a site near London so Josie and Ginny moved into Mary Street on their own. Dave's car was there but not the keys; he said it wasn't safe to drive without explaining why. She let that go.

Josie worked like lightening to make the flat more homely. This move was to be permanent, a chance to be cherished and be a family. She sighed with relief that things were working out.

The place was looking cozy by the time he returned on the Friday. Josie had made dinner, and they happily sat around the wobbly table while enjoying spaghetti Bolognese. There was only an outside toilet. no bathroom or shower, but it hadn't bothered Dave and that surprised Josie. Although the toilet was only for their use, it was more than inconvenient when Ginny needed to get ready for bed. But it wasn't that much different from how people had lived a few years before. Many a family had spent their whole lives in such cramped conditions. Josie had to boil a kettle then wash in the kitchen sink, but this was his choice of flat and she was not going to complain.

Within a couple of weeks, she had enrolled Ginny at the local nursery and got a part-time job with a secretarial agency. It was a fair bit of work to get ready and catch buses to work, but she was delighted to have an income. She chose to work in offices where they only needed a short-term substitute for a few days.

Dave's job in London didn't last, the boss didn't like him. It wasn't long before Josie thought about his erratic work pattern and wondered if he was qualified to do the jobs he was applying for. There was always a period of instability when he had to work a week's lie time at the start or was waiting for payroll to sort out his money when he left. Sometimes he didn't give notice and lost the week's lie time or times when he made up absurd excuses and left his shift early, putting his job in jeopardy.

Into the bargain, whether he was working or not, he started going out at night without Josie, sometimes spending the housekeeping money on beer and petrol. He had kicked her out of the way more than once, leaving her shocked and trembling. Josie wanted to be fair and gave him time to settle, but she found that increasingly difficult, especially when he slapped the back of her head and told her if she wasn't happy, she could leave. More humiliating was when Josie gathered things together for the washing machine.

'Wait!' he shouted.

Josie's hand hovered over her underwear and Ginny's nursery apron.

'What?'

'Let me see that.'

He ripped the few items from her hand and held her underwear to his nose.

'What are you doing?'

'Just checking.' He smirked. 'Maybe you don't realise it, but I can tell if you've been with someone else by the smell of these.'

The idea of such an animalistic accusation left Josie speechless and repulsed.

He didn't appear to have a healthy work or home ethic. She began to realise he hadn't changed. He had got worse and she had fallen for his lies. With nowhere else to go, she was keeping quiet more often rather than stir up his anger; she was afraid of him and could only listen when he raved about a local job he'd been offered. She was sure it wouldn't last.

It was on his back shift one Sunday when Josie had been looking forward to celebrating her twenty-first birthday that he had kicked off. Unwashed dishes in the sink led him to grab her roughly, force her head into the water then with a strong backhand, knock her over the couch. The day following the assault and after he left for his next back shift, she got out of the house. She needed to think and breathe.

An hour before she was due to pick Ginny up from nursery, she walked into a café, head down and shoulders drooped. After looking into the froth on the top of her coffee, she asked herself how much more she could do to make Dave happy with her and their relationship. She shuddered at thoughts of how brutal he could be. And the accusations never ended. He always thought she was doing more than looking at or laughing with other men. Shortly after he had signed up for the flat, they had been about to get into the car when a couple walked by.

'Hello Josie.' the young man had called out.

'Oh hi. How are you, Mike?'

'Fine. Good to see you. Are you living here?' He lifted his hand in the direction of the front door.

'Yes. Are we neighbours?'

'We're just round the corner.'

The questions began even before the car door shut.

Who was he? How did she meet him? Is that why she was so quick to agree to live in this particular area?

At times like these, Josie was empty. Devoid of any emotion, she couldn't answer. There was no anger in her, only frustration because she didn't know how to answer for fear of his irritation increasing.

One solution was to avoid being in company, just as Moira had done in the café when Dave had sat with his friend. She hadn't even gone in for fear of Ed's reprisal. That's what Dave had said he wanted; her to be like Moira.

Although he purported to have much sought-after jobs, he didn't appear to have money. Josie couldn't tell what he was doing with his wages. When he was living with his parents, he had enough to change his car regularly and pay for meals out. Now and again, he had come in with a gift for her or Ginny, but that had stopped. Josie told herself she shouldn't be surprised because now he was paying rent for the flat. She bought most of the shopping, but sometimes he would come in with plastic bags full of food. It seemed he had gone to the supermarket without her. The strange mix was often things he never ate: porridge, chocolate biscuits or custard powder. It was as though he had gone into someone's cupboard, maybe his mother's, and helped himself.

Josie was transported out of her thoughts when a clock chimed time for collecting Ginny. She paid for the coffee and left. The little one fell asleep as soon as her head hit the pillow that afternoon; nursery had exhausted her, so a nap was the answer. Sitting down with her coat still on, Josie looked around. She took in the living room's bleakness. The pattern on the faded chairs no longer bore any resemblance to their matching couch. Over years, direct sunlight must have streamed through the cracked glass window to kill the former splendour of their red, velvet rose design. Not only did their glorified position disguise most of the threadbare rug, but it also reduced the risk of tenants treading the hessian backing into the woodworm-infested floorboards. The sadness of it added to her despair. But it was all she had until she could sort out her life.

Dave had a temper, but usually he could control it when he was in company. He acted differently in front of Josie. She was easy pickings, but he couldn't reveal himself in front of others. The only time Josie witnessed him flying off the handle outside the house was on a night out with Moira, Ed, and their two friends, Derek and June. After some joking around, Josie saw Dave's reaction when a couple of young men and Derek got into a trivial altercation in the bar. It passed and, when it was time to go home, the group left at the same time as the young men. Josie didn't see what happened except that, within seconds, Derek was on the ground and the men were laying into him. Rather than trying to stop them, in two strides Dave was beside Derek and kicking into his side as he lay curled up. They all knew Derek had been through major surgery for bowel cancer and had to use a colostomy bag.

Josie and Moira screamed at the same time, 'No! No! Leave him!'

June knelt on the ground beside Derek and wept as the young men ran away. The horror of what Dave had done began to sink in. It seemed like the others hadn't noticed because they didn't challenge Dave. Maybe they were afraid he would turn his unwanted attention to them. Josie asked herself what could have made Dave so angry, given that he could have helped to stop the argument rather than booting an ill man four times; a man who was their friend.

Dave

It was only after I had made numerous promises that Josie agreed she and Ginny would move in with me. When I found the flat on Mary Street, I put down a month's deposit kindly donated by my mother. Josie didn't need to know that. As luck would have it, the flat was in an established part of the town. Even though it was in an old building and the furniture seemed ancient, that wasn't important. Josie seemed to like the flat and I was ready to try a place of my own with a ready-made family.

Before we moved in, a company had offered me a temporary job in London. It was a great feeling to be offered something in the capital, I guess I was being head hunted. I was to leave each Sunday night and return the following Friday afternoon and likely this arrangement would be for a month until they gave me a permanent contract, something I could almost guarantee because of my experience.

Before I left, I handed Josie some money for groceries and any emergencies that might arise. Again, thanks to the generosity of my mother, this was a good start. She knew I might not be able to keep my promise to pay her back out of my first pay but at least Josie was grateful for my contribution. I suggested if she ran out of money, she should ask somebody for a loan, but she only stared at me without saying a word.

The first few weekends I was home, Josie was bustling around and smiling. I added to her happy mood by telling her I was uncharacteristically enamoured with my boss. At an informal meeting, he had glanced at my CV and said he didn't have to ask any questions, he knew what guys like me were capable of, he was sure we'd had amazing training from the biggest and best petroleum companies in the world. It had made sense to doctor most of the dates on my CV and hide the dates when I was unemployed. Everyone knows you can bank on these managers being too busy to check out the finer details. I only had to tide myself over for a short while until my permanent contract appeared and then I could settle into a routine and get time off with full pay.

Josie and Ginny were also settling. As usual, Josie was careful to plan her spending carefully, but I was disappointed at her reaction to a little joke I played on her. I couldn't see the logic in creating an atmosphere over something that was meant to make her laugh.

She and Ginny caught the bus at quarter to eight each morning and one Monday Josie opened the side pocket of her bag on the bus to find, not the usual fifty pence, but a note from me.

'I owe you fifty pence.'

When I came back on the Friday, she told me she had needed the money and not a promissory note.

I knew she only needed £1.50 for the weekly nursery fees but what I didn't know was each weekend she put a fifty pence piece in the side pocket of her bag. That way, she only had to make sure she had £1 on a Monday morning.

I had been going through her bag, found the money and took it. She was lucky I left her a note, or she'd never have known what happened to it.

That day, she had been short of money and had to make a choice; pay the nursery or pay the bus fare on the next leg of her journey to work. Later, I roared with laughter that her whole day had been a disaster, all because she didn't have fifty pence. She had to pay the nursery double the following week.

From what I understood, things were going well for me at work. I knew how important I was to the job and through the grapevine, I heard I was about to be promoted. The job was good, but I didn't understand everything. It was easy to take a back seat when I found things were too difficult. To get my job done and when the coast was clear, I called out to one of the young trainees.

'Listen, I've been called away to deal with another job. I'll be about half an hour. Here's a chance for you to try out your skills. The readings from here need to go there. Do you think you can manage that?' I handed him my clipboard.

'Yes, no problem. I learned some of this on my last job.'

The trainee beamed. This was the kind of job he wouldn't normally be asked to do without supervision. I didn't know exactly what figures I was supposed to record, so I reckoned there'd be at least two good outcomes from passing the work on. The boss would think I'd done a good job and, if I checked what the trainee had done, I'd know what I had to do the next time. After I asked him to cover a few jobs in quick succession, he was more than happy.

The stupid boy didn't keep our arrangement to himself because one of the twats in his group reminded him that what he was doing for me counted as nothing unless someone signed his work sheet. Of course, I had to refuse because I didn't have the authority. That created a problem. It came as a shock to me when he sneaked off and asked my immediate boss to sign off the tasks. Complete betrayal and disloyalty after me giving him the chance to show his worth. My boss reacted without thinking. Where I felt he should have been pleased that he now had two people to take the readings, he wasn't. He was more interested in what I was doing and where I had gone when I gave the trainee the job. He took to checking up on me, as if I was new to the site. I reminded him of my CV and my experience.

One day, the boss appeared from nowhere, steam coming out of his ears and waving what looked like a month's worth of sheets. He had misunderstood me when I told him I could do everyone's job standing on my head. He started to call me out, so I told him he hadn't listened or let me finish what I was saying. He muttered a few words then stormed away, still holding the sheets.

So, I walked off the site. I arrived home with the news that the boss didn't understand me. It wasn't a big deal because I was confident about the next interview I had lined up; it entailed doing shift work locally.

A matter of weeks after I started the local job, I realised shift work wasn't for me. Around the same time, I found faults in the flat. I had to call the landlord every few days to complain about this and that just to get him moving. I had rented it as seen, but it was only after living in it that I noticed problems the landlord had hidden from me. I saw how old and worn everything was.

I became frustrated and Josie just happened to be in the wrong place at the wrong time on her twenty-first birthday. It was a relief to vent my anger though, and I'm sure she understood that. She wasn't really hurt, just a bit shaken.

The landlord was making plenty money out of me or more to the point, out of my mother, so I had to make sure he was keeping his end of the bargain and providing a decent place to live. But I wanted out of the deal.

We were getting ready to go out with Ginny when I became bored waiting. I dialled the landlord's number, wondering if he would bother to answer this time. Josie knew who I was speaking to when I forcefully told him we'd already complained about the cracked window and nothing had been done.

'You've not fixed it, so we're moving out. You won't be getting any rent this month.' I threw the receiver on its cradle.

Josie's mouth fell open.

'What have you done?' she asked.

'I'm not putting up with this anymore. He never fixes things on time. I'm going back to my mother's so you can call Moira or Doris and say you and Ginny are going to kip there for a few nights until you fix things.'

Josie would know how to cope. It wasn't the first time she'd said she could survive on her own, and the dilemma of uncertainty for her and Ginny would be short-lived. She looked crushed, but she deserved what she got because she needed to find friends who had big houses and enough money to help her in a time of need. Although I knew the immediate issue for her would be finding a place to stay, I was surprised at her question.

'How is it this kind of thing keeps happening?'

'What are you talking about now?' I could feel my temper rising.

'All this jumping from job to job and house to house.'

'You need to realise this is life. This happens when you're looking for the right type of work or house. Move forward with your life and leave that kind of stuff behind. You keep bringing up the past. It's so annoying.'

Josie

Dave's comment made Josie wonder if she wasn't being realistic. People lost jobs and gave up houses all the time. Maybe he was right and she was being idealistic. Reminding herself of the disappointments with Dave from before was likely clouding her vision of the future. A worthless feeling swept through her as she began to believe their unstable relationship was all her doing and she had to live with the consequences.

But she also felt stuck. There was no way she could impose on her friends again; she had a job and relied on being a bus ride away from the nursery and her work. She couldn't afford the rent on her own and, even if she could, she didn't want to stay in such a dilapidated flat. Dave had chosen it. He had signed the contract and she had moved in, hoping that he would try to make family life work.

Their discussion ended with them agreeing that they should go back to their original arrangement of living separately. He needed independence and she and Ginny were out on a limb. He wasn't interested.

They left the flat and its outside toilet to the next tenant. Dave went to his mother's and Josie sat staring out the window of a temporary bed-and-breakfast accommodation. Despite the hustle and bustle in the street below, she felt marooned. The isolation and sorrow were second to the dread that washed over her. Ginny put her head on Josie's lap.

'Are you crying, Mummy?' the little one asked.

She was but, unlike Dave, Josie was determined she wouldn't be abandoning her work ethic no matter where she was living.

The timing of everything was almost perfect. Doris had found a place to buy and was planning to move out of Josie's flat within the month. Perhaps this was a sign of better things to come. Ginny needed stability.

Chapter 8

Dave

I remember another day I saw Josie's face fall further than usual. She hadn't understood when I tried to call my sister, Paula, in Canada and she hung up. Josie didn't know the background to our family. I told her to make a cup of tea and I'd fill her in with the details.

My mum had a spell of good luck when my sister moved away from Scotland around her twentieth birthday. Paula and Mark had moved abroad not long after they got married. A year later, six months after their first child was born, they had paid for my mum to travel over to Vancouver. She came back after a month, tanned and healthy. Seems Paula wouldn't let her lift a finger. It was all about relaxing by the pool and tucking into home-made food. And they wouldn't take a penny off her.

Paula wanted her to stay there for good, but no, my mum knew her place was looking after me and my dad. He was a grumpy, lazy old sod and years of running around after him had worn her down. I always stayed out of the way until she'd done the shopping and the housework but she never complained about me, only my dad. I couldn't bear to be in the same room as him. When she was making dinner, I waited in my room until she shouted on me while he spread himself out on his old armchair, dominating the living room.

Every year, Paula sent my mum the money or flight tickets to Canada as a treat and to give her a rest. At the end of each holiday, she tried to persuade my mum to stay but the answer was always the same.

After eleven years of visiting Canada, I could tell my mum didn't have the same energy as before but that didn't stop her from doing housework and cooking. It was such a shame that every time she decided to go shopping, I had to take my car to meet friends. But she managed with four shopping bags She always found a way to balance the groceries and walk home. I often arrived back minutes after she had unpacked the shopping to ask for a sub, she never refused me because I'd learned to ask quietly out of my dad's earshot or when he was at the pub. He was a pest when he had a drink in him and would have gone on about me asking for money to run a car when I wasn't working.

One night, in his drunken state, he sat down to watch TV around eleven o'clock. It was loud. My bedroom was next to the living room and the sound was booming. I knew Mum was sleeping in another room down the hall and she wouldn't have heard the crap he was apparently listening to. It was clear he had done his usual falling asleep in his chair because, in between conversations on the program, I could hear him snoring.

Mum wakened the minute I shook her and told her she'd need to get him to turn it down. The neighbours would complain and I couldn't sleep. She was really annoyed at having to get up and I'm not surprised. He was being his usual selfish self. Worse was to come because that night, instead of wakening him up and telling him to get to bed, she walked over and turned the TV off. That's when I heard him shouting.

'What are you doing? You idiot. I was watching that.' Seems he threw his slipper at her.

'You couldn't have been watching it. You were sleeping,' she fired at him.

I snuggled back under the blankets and tried to block out the sound of him screaming obscenities at her. It wasn't my problem. She had to sort it out. But I could hear him every now and again throughout the night, berating her.

'Get out of this bed. Get out of this room. Sleep on the couch because that's where you deserve to be.'

When I heard the squeak of the living room door, I knew later she'd be grumbling about her disturbed night.

The next morning, she tried hard to be polite to the postman who arrived with a couple of letters. One was her usual summer flight ticket to Canada from Paula. She was to leave in four weeks.

I was right of course. The poor woman looked so tired and worn out. Even reading the letter didn't cheer her up.

'Right now, I can't think about Canada. It's a long flight.' She sighed.

At that very moment, I had a brainwave.

'Well, you don't have to go. You can stay here and get the jobs done in the garden that you've been talking about. The ticket is transferable and I'd love to see Paula. You've been loads of times. I've never seen her house or anything.'

Mum put her head to the side. I could see she was thinking about it so I wouldn't let up until she agreed. My idea was to keep reminding her of how long each leg of the journey was. After half an hour of discussing it with the minimum amount of pressure, she saw sense and handed me the tickets. I was going to Canada.

'Don't tell Paula. I'd like to surprise her,' I said.

It was easy enough for the name to be changed and the date brought forward. The travel agent was very helpful.

The following week, I found myself in Canada and double checking I had the right address. Mum had given me money for a taxi from Vancouver airport because I told her I wasn't taking public transport. After all, I didn't know the area and it might not be safe.

Once I'd shown the taxi driver Paula's address, he remarked that I was going to a nice area so I sat back and took in the sights. It seemed ages later he pulled up in front of an impressive house and garden. I didn't give him a tip. I wasn't sure what the custom was in Canada but he was polite enough when I said goodbye.

I finally stood on the tree-lined pavement, but I was mixed up with days and times because of my travels and it took a minute to calculate that it was noon on a Sunday. All the driveways I could see sported more than one truck or car, clearly an affluent area.

I had hoped Paula or Mark would have heard the taxi draw up, looked out and had the decency to come and help with my cases. There was no sign of anyone being home, even when I rang the doorbell four times. How inconvenient it felt. OK, they didn't know I was coming but I couldn't help thinking someone must be inside. I lifted my hand to bang on the door when a voice interrupted me.

'Hello, can I help you?'

I looked behind me as a heavily built male leaned out of an upstairs window in the house next door.

'I was looking for Paula. Now I'm wondering if I've got the right address.'

'Paula, yes. And who are you? Clearly from Scotland, eh?'

'Aye, I've come a long way. I'm Paula's brother.'

'Wait a minute. I'll come down.'

The man, Jim, was good enough to explain that Paula, Mark and their two girls were away for a long weekend in their van. That's how they spent most holidays. In fact, they wouldn't be back until the Wednesday because Jim said Mark had taken an extra couple of days off.

His wife appeared and we started a decent conversation. I find it's good to do that, to tell people you like their house or car and make enquiries about what goes on in the area. They love it, they think you're interested. When I hang about long enough, folk sometimes help me out. Not everyone is that kind, but I can tell quickly if I've struck a chord with them. Jim was one of that kind.

'Hmm. Now I don't know what to do. My mum told me all about their van. Raved about it. You've probably met my mum because she's been here a few times. She's getting older and didn't feel up to the travel. So that we didn't disappoint Paula, I've come in Mum's place. But we kept it a surprise, otherwise Paula would have been here. She'll be so disappointed that no one was in when I arrived, knowing how much I like my cup of tea.'

That was the crunch. Jim's wife took the hint and invited me in so that they could give me directions to Paula's van. After two cups of tea and asking them if I could call for a taxi, I set off on my next adventure.

We drove through a couple of towns before hills and green fields spread out before us. The roads weren't busy on that particular holiday weekend. I was more than thankful that my mum had given me much more money than I asked for, especially as we overtook coaches full of people who clearly couldn't afford the luxury of a taxi.

'So, there's buses that come out here?'

'Oh yes. They're comfortable and reasonably priced here. The only drawback is they stop at random places between towns. Takes a bit longer but all in all, a very good service,' he drawled on in his Canadian accent.

That's when I wondered how people on the bus could live like that. I was sure they were looking down at the taxi, jealous that we were overtaking and getting to our destination long before them.

An hour later, we stopped at the entrance to an enormous van park. From the automatic gate and security guard, it was clear this was no measly camping ground with communal toilets that I would never visit. It was an attractive area for those who had bought a static van on an expensive and sought-after piece of land in a prime location.

From the gate, a tree-lined driveway disappeared into the distance and tiny boats bobbed on the water to the right. Delighted that I had arrived when it was almost time to eat, I let my driver put my suitcases next to the camp entrance.

'I can't take you in. Only private vehicles allowed.'

'No worries. I'll find out where I'm supposed to be.'

He had told me the fare before we set out, so I had it ready for him. Once again, I hadn't thought about a tip and wondered at his slow blink as he stared at the exact amount in his hand. I might have asked him to wait until I got some change, but I felt his facial expression was out of order. He did his job, he got paid, end of story.

All I could do was ask the security guard where I'd find B129 and eyed my cases a few times.

'How far away are we talking?'

He screwed up his eyes then signalled for me to wait.

'I'll help you.'

I let him wheel the biggest case because I had a small one and a holdall. He clearly wasn't as strong as he looked. I must have mistaken his fat for muscle. The exercise would be good for him; he struggled to get through the puffing and panting stage.

Next thing, I was standing outside B129 and really proud that our Paula had found such a beautiful spot. A beast of a truck sat at the side of the van. I did a double take. It was immaculate. What a life. No wonder she wanted my mum to share it. Well, now she and her family would pander to me, the baby of the family. This was going to be something to boast about once I was home.

I rattled on the door, and I mean rattled.

'What the—'

An irritated female voice filtered through the open window.

I yelled back.

'Aye well, get your arse out here and have a look.'

Paula opened the door. She looked radiant. I stared back at her. She was definitely my sister, but there was something different. Her dark hair was in an attractive bob style and the velvet leisure suit looked good on her. She'd put on a bit of weight. Not much, but enough to make me look her up and down a couple of times. I decided not to say anything about her size until later. Finally, I spoke because she suddenly looked lifeless.

'Surprised?' It seemed a daft question. 'Mum couldn't face the journey, so I came instead.'

Even though she wasn't smiling, I could tell by her glistening eyes she was over the moon to see me. Paula took a step back and muttered a few indecipherable words before turning towards whoever was inside.

'Dave's arrived, unannounced.'

I took that comment in the spirit it was meant. Surprise and delight. Mark and my two nieces, whom I'd never met, exchanged a few words of wonderment as I stepped past her.

'Hi Mark. How's you?'

'Dave, what a surprise.'

'Who is he?' One of the girls stood up. She must have been about ten.

'That's your mum's brother, Uncle Dave. From Scotland. Grandma's son.'

'So, where is Grandma?' A smaller girl joined the other one at the end of the table.

Strange to hear my mother being referred to as Grandma, but of course they'd had a relationship for years, one that I hadn't witnessed.

'Hope you've got the kettle on.' I started as I meant to go on.

Mark got up and did the necessary while I explained that Jim, their neighbour, had given me the address of their van.

For the next half hour, we spoke about Mum, Dad and some of our relatives. Who had children, who was ill and who was doing what with their lives.

I filled Paula in on my successes and how life working abroad could be difficult. There was no chance to ask how things were for her because time was marching on.

'So, what's the plan going to be for tonight? I'm getting tired now after all my travelling. Could do with a bite to eat then turning in.'

Paula sent Mark off to ask a friend if another van was free. There were keys somewhere and it was good of her to suggest I have my own space for the night.

After I'd eaten the ham and chicken salad she made me, I told her I hadn't expected such a paltry plate of food but that it had tasted good. The joke seemed lost on her, so it was important that I kept quiet for the time being.

'So, you've done OK here. Mark must be earning big bucks.'

'Mark works hard. Ever since we came here, he's taken every job he's been offered and stuck with the contract.'

I wondered at her remark. I wasn't sure if Mum had told her that, although I was successful in getting jobs, there was always someone who made life difficult and I often had to leave after a couple of weeks. Of course Mum had helped me out financially, but I had a feeling she would never have told Paula that.

Years before, I'd heard the story that Mark had started out as a bellboy, a sort of porter, in a hotel. He had to ferry racks of clothes and piles of suitcases around. At the beck and call of all and sundry, he earned very little and depended on tips. You would never have caught me doing a job like that. Give him his due though, in the early days he was doing three jobs at once to provide for Paula and the kids. At that time, I was surprised that *she* didn't get a job. All she was doing was staying at home and getting the kids fixed. Hanging around the house all day must have been boring for her. But eventually, he landed lucky and got an office job. Looked like they'd made it good.

Mark came back with the keys for a van in the next row and didn't sit down until he'd helped me out with my cases.

My accommodation for the next three nights was fine. I had a look around, checking in every cupboard, wardrobe and set of drawers. There were a few personal items, toiletries, towels and extra food in a small fridge so I was delighted that I could make myself at home. Such kind friends Paula had. I was tired and a bit put out that nobody had made up the bed, but it didn't take me long to figure out how to do it before I curled up for the night.

The following day, Paula, Mark and the girls had to go out because they'd planned to visit friends in the next town. I admit to being upset that they didn't cancel that arrangement. They left me behind in a place I didn't know, with no transport and no reference to meals. Thankfully, the on-site supermarket was open, so I bought some bread and milk. There were a few jars of sauce and some pasta in my temporary accommodation. I made my own dinner and opened a bottle of red wine that had been hidden at the back of a cupboard. I wondered if I should replace it but thought better of it. It was unlikely that the supermarket would sell such a good wine and if they did, it would probably cost an arm and a leg.

I told Paula when she came back that I'd bought food at the shop. If she jumped to the conclusion that I'd bought enough for a few meals, then that was her mistake.

A couple of days later, it was time to leave for the drive home, I made sure the whole family knew I needed leg room. They packed the truck and I packed my things back into my case. I saw the girls were helping to take bags out of the van and tidy up. I got my cases over to the truck, then Paula handed me a black plastic bag.

'Maybe you could drop that in the trash?'

'Trash? Trash? Oh my, we've become all foreign now.'

I was hacked off that she expected me to be a bin man. It wasn't as if it was my rubbish. But I didn't say another word. I turned on my heel and made my way to the bins. The stretch of water was close by and I enjoyed a good fifteen or so minutes sitting on a bench. I watched the holiday makers get their boats and vans spick and span before they left on their homeward journeys. By the time I walked back to Paula's, the truck was packed, and my suitcases were safely tucked away.

'Almost ready?' I asked as I eased myself into the front passenger seat.

There was plenty of room in the back for Paula and the two girls. They were able to hold bags and a small case on their knees while I stretched out for the two-hour journey.

Once home, Paula showed me the room Mum usually slept in. The cleanliness and extras like shower gel and shampoo were nice touches to go with the deep pile towels in the en-suite.

'Well, I can see why Mum likes it here. Kind of like a luxury hotel, isn't it?'

Paula didn't reply.

'I'll go down for my cases and unpack.'

The space in the wardrobe and the four empty drawers were just perfect. It was nearly an hour later when I went downstairs. I had lain on the bed to rest and almost fell asleep. I didn't want to help water the plants anyway.

I was glad I was in my sister's house because I would be able to do more than put the kettle on whenever I wanted. Basically, I could make myself at home and find what I wanted in the cupboards. We were family.

During the next ten days, I noticed Paula leaving the room at odd intervals. At one point, I asked Mark if Paula was going outside for a cigarette, although I didn't think she smoked.

'No, she gets a bit overwhelmed sometimes. She likes her own space.'

From that, I took it she wasn't used to having decent company.

To make sure I wasn't caught out having to pay for meals in restaurants, I had asked who was paying when Mark suggested we eat out. He only had to pay for one other person, whereas I'd have to pay for four extra people. He understood my reasoning.

When my brief holiday was ending, I asked Paula what her plans were for getting me back to the airport.

'Mark will take you. He can take advantage of going in that direction and drop in to see his friend.'

What a stroke of luck that was. Otherwise, I'd have been made to dig into the pile of notes I had in my wallet for a taxi fare. I was saving to buy another car, or at least a respray for the one I had, so I hadn't spent more than a few dollars of my own money. As it was, since Mum had given me a tidy sum, I was going home with only a little hole made in my pile of cash.

On the journey to the airport, Mark asked what I thought of their country of choice.

'Not bad at all. I've been to some smashing places earning mega bucks. But it's all about the cost of living. What's the point in earning good money if it's all gone by the end of the month? There's something to be said for getting paid from the UK but living where it costs practically nothing to feed and clothe yourself.'

Mark didn't have an answer for that. He didn't have a clue what life was like in poorer countries. So, I continued.

'Anyway, the main thing is that you're happy with your choice.'

We said our goodbyes. There was no need to offer him something towards the petrol. His trip was essentially to see his friend. I was just being dropped off on the way.

I heard from my mum that Paula hadn't been too pleased with my visit. She had really wanted Mum to go and might have wondered if she'd ever see her again. True, Mum was getting old and was unlikely to make it over to Canada, but the idea that I had stolen Mum's holiday was a ridiculous idea. It had just seemed daft to waste the ticket. It was difficult not to say anything to Mum, but I felt Paula was jealous that I would be going back to live with the very person she wanted to see.

Months later, my mum told me our Paula in Canada had cancer. By the time we heard about it, her breast had been removed. Scary stuff. I think Mum told her we were all sorry to hear her news. That was all. There was no need for an expensive international phone call or even to write a letter. But I had plans to visit Canada again and that went through my mind the year before I met Josie.

At one point, I had a few weeks' spare because the guys at work had badmouthed me to the boss. They were furious because now and again I arrived ten minutes or so late for my shift. Leaving the job meant I had time on my hands. That's when I had the idea of taking myself off to Canada again. Nice cheap holiday and I knew Paula had a place big enough to give me my own room. No bills to pay, no shopping to buy and no cleaning to do. Spending three weeks in and out of the swimming pool with a few beers by my side. Who wouldn't want that? All I had to do was give her a bit of warning this time.

I visited an old workmate, Rob, for a chat. I sat nursing my cup of tea and waited for Rob to leave the room. It was when he went to the toilet that I put in my request to his wife.

'Oh, I forgot. I need to pass on a message. Any chance I could make a quick phone call?'

I was up and heading to the phone in the hall before she replied. Mary was always obliging.

I dialled the code and the number for Canada, hoping she wouldn't hear the dialling going on forever.

Mark answered and I told him I was hoping to speak to my sister.

'Ah, she's not back until six o'clock your time tonight.'

'Tell her I'm coming over to see her. Two weeks' time, first week in September. I'll call back later.'

And that was all. He sounded happy enough, so I was made up when I said goodbye to Rob and Mary. I stopped by the bar and talked a couple of guys into buying me beers. Being well oiled by the time I got back to my mum's, the couch and the TV were beckoning me. I fell asleep and wakened just before seven. I reckoned Paula would be home. The only way I could call was to ask my neighbour. He didn't mind me using his phone, but he always made me pay for the call.

I was surprised at Paula's reaction. From the moment she answered, she was in a mood.

'Don't you dare call my home and say you're coming over. You think it's acceptable to announce your arrival without asking if it's convenient for *me*. I was so ill a while ago and there was never as much as a card or a phone call from you. Don't you dare turn up at my door like you did the last time. You had the cheek to take my mother's ticket and sat on your backside when you were here. Paid for nothing and used everybody. You are no brother of mine.'

Well, that was certainly a rehearsed speech. All evening, I thought about her slapping me down like that and wondered who was the one with the cheek? All I had wanted was to see my big sister. Eventually, I looked at things from her point of view. She'd had her breast removed, likely lost some weight and no doubt was embarrassed by the way she looked. She was a proud person and probably conscious of not being a complete woman. She wouldn't want me to see her like that. I'd have to sit it out until she came back down to earth.

When I finished my story, Josie must have understood why Paula hung up on me. She was still finding it hard to talk about her illness. Josie shook her head but was looking at me through saucer eyes. For a brief moment, I thought she was taking Paula's side. She knew better than to do that.

Chapter 9

Dave

It came as a complete surprise to me to find out that Josie hadn't given up her flat. At first, I was raging that she had kept Doris a secret from me and told her that was why things weren't working for us. But I kept her actions in mind for a time if and when she discovered I had a few secrets of my own. In the end, it was great for me because I didn't have to keep her or pay rent. It must have been something I said that gave her the idea of sub-letting. She would never have been able to think of such a notion on her own. Clearly, she had been listening to me but I passed it off as her being smarter than I ever imagined.

That was a difficult time for me. I was between disappointment and relief that our trial period together had ended. I went back to my parent's house and Josie settled into life in her old flat again.

I left her alone for a week or two until she got things in order. It would only be a matter of time until she needed help with jobs she couldn't do on her own. Her flat was nice but lacked a few mod cons.

There was no way of letting her know I was intending to visit, so I suppose to her it looked like I was appearing out of the blue. I felt at home in her flat and kept my thoughts about her boring friends to myself. They wallpapered or cut grass at their own houses on the weekends, but I helped around the house for Josie. I washed up, set the table, and even installed a shower which she bought after saving up for a few weeks. My mother didn't have a shower, so this was a chance for me to clean up quickly if I wanted. But I never forgot the luxury of a bath. I also offered to repair a broken worktop and fit shelves in Josie's bathroom. It was a chance to start pointing out my skills.

Josie joined an evening class, something she kept banging on about.

'What you've got to realise is you really don't have the intellectual capability to be part of a study group. I'm just worried that you'll overdo it and end up becoming ill with the pressure,' I told her when she went off to register.

But she stuck with it and went two nights a week for several months to achieve her goal of shorthand and typing certificates. Her day job with the agency was still on the cards but she only accepted office work near home. When her certificates finally arrived in the post, that's when I shook my head and threw the envelope across the table. I had already told her I was a well-qualified engineer but that I never bothered to keep or boast about any certificates.

'These folks who sit in a class for years, no need for that. I've tried it. I knew more than the guy who was trying to teach us. Waste of time.'

Josie turned up for her agency work but there were a couple of times she had to leave jobs and she had the cheek to pass the buck, saying it was all because of me.

If I was between jobs, I was bored so I arranged some things for us to do. When I told her we were going out one Friday at lunch time with my cousin and his wife, she asked me what I was playing at. She had to go to work. She didn't agree with me that most people take a 'sickie' now and again. I know I did. Taking two or three days off seemed much more authentic an excuse for the flu because one day off might be construed as having a hangover. On the Thursday evening, I told her to call in sick and leave a message on her boss's answering machine. She didn't. I think she couldn't be bothered going to the phone box. I stayed that night and got up before six in the morning. While she was still sleeping, I went to the phone box and left a message on her work's answering machine to say she had been up all night with an upset stomach and wouldn't make it into work. She finally got up and started her daily routine but, when she came out of the shower, I laughed and said there was no point in her going in, her boss thought she was ill. Who would she embarrass if she turned up? That forced her to stay off work and, despite her protesting about me calling her work and reminding me the agency didn't pay her for days off, we had a nice lunch.

'See, wasn't that a much better way to spend a Friday?'

Apparently, after the third time I did that, they questioned her about her last-minute absences. The agency let her go.

Once, on a long-term contract, she was the only secretary in a builder's merchants, she took her work seriously. I learned it delighted the men she worked for that her methods were meticulous, and it seems they praised her. She was happy to bring snippets of their compliments back to me. I knew the men had ulterior motives, that their praise wasn't for what she produced. They were making veiled suggestions. I turned up at her work several times unannounced, bearing take away coffees and doughnuts for us to enjoy so she had to stop working. She had an office to herself and I sat in there with her until her boss said she could go home early and see to me. She couldn't have been that good because they finally handed her a month's notice. She lied to me and said it was my fault for keeping her off her duties.

Josie told me she still had her vision of going to college but she wasn't sure if she was ready for full-time study. The odd evening class had been enough, but she implied I had distracted her dream when we moved to the caravan because of my job. But that was just how life went. I was right, she wasn't able to keep up.

When I successfully secured another job, this time with an offshore company, I was more than proud. I had been impressed when I heard of other men who had got jobs on the rigs. The general opinion was they were making big money, mixing in prosperous circles and being admired by those at the bottom of the ladder. I wasn't at the top yet, but people looking at me weren't to know that, so I wanted to dress accordingly for travelling to my extremely important first rig post in the oil and gas industry.

I persuaded my mother to open an account at a men's outfitters and bought clothes I felt gave me the much sought-after look of a successful man. Josie came with me to choose shirts, ties, and a belted brown corduroy coat. I caught her look as I checked myself out in the shop's mirror. I walked over to her, still wearing the coat.

'Is there a problem?' I asked.

'It's lovely. I just don't know why you need a coat.' She didn't refer to the price.

'Because I need to look the part!' I stared at her; she was so bloody stupid.

I was flying to Europe to get a connection and knew people would look at me, admiring the status that a good coat would bring. It was the height of summer, and I was unlikely to wear it on the flight, but at the airport, people would see me.

After my first trip, I asked Josie if there was any way she could cut the coat to make it into a jacket because it was uncomfortable sitting around in a full-length coat at airports.

'It won't work. A jacket needs a different shape. I can't do that.' She admitted her skills were limited.

'Just cut it and see.'

'Dave, if I cut it, you won't have a coat or a jacket. It'll be a useless piece of cloth.'

I could feel the side of my mouth twitching. She risked repercussions if she didn't agree with me.

'Why don't you just do what I ask? You want to make all the decisions, don't you? Everything about the house, everything that I ask you to do you've got an argument about. Do you know what your problem is? You want to stand up and pee.'

That was enough to get her back to earth. She asked me what length I wanted it and she cut the coat later that day. But, after spending ages at her sewing machine, I was disappointed in her. She didn't do it right and the bottom stuck out like a wee girl's party dress. My mother had paid a lot of money for it and Josie had ruined something that was now only fit for the bin.

When I was asked to work onshore for a week, I jumped at the chance. Meeting some of the big bosses was an opportunity to find out who was who. I was given a boiler suit and a hard hat. On the last day, I handed my gear back but not before I spied someone's hard hat with *Supervisor* taped to the front. It easily fitted into my holdall. On the way home and out of sight in a layby, I took it out and sat it on the back window ledge of my car. I was only two trips in and hadn't yet done the course to achieve the dizzy height of supervisor, but I could do the job anyway. It would be a good talking point when I gave folk a lift. Josie asked if I'd bought the stick-on label myself, but I told her she must have forgotten our previous conversations where I told her I was working onshore with managers and supervisors. She unsuccessfully tried to burst my bubble.

Josie

Ed had also secured work offshore, so without Dave knowing, Josie spoke to Moira about the coat and the hardhat. Moira laughed and told her in the world of offshore workers, some wanted to look the part because the powers that be bandied titles about to encourage the men. Ed had told her some guys felt they were in inflated positions even when they weren't responsible for anyone. Josie was sure Dave was pretending he had made it, nearly to the top, within a month. The supervisor hat was on display to the world, and he visibly swelled with pride every time he glanced at it. She had spent hours studying for a few paper certificates and was nowhere near ready to boast about her achievements, if ever.

'What's the final qualification for that then?' he had asked when she spoke about enrolling full time in college.

'It'll take me a year, but it's a Higher National Certificate. They call it an HNC.' She beamed.

'Do you know you can buy a leather-bound HNC for a few quid?' In a sentence, he had emotionally slapped her down again, almost convincing her that everything she did was pointless.

Within the month, two major things had happened. Dave packed in his job and Josie had stopped thinking about furthering her studies. With a sick feeling that she'd had each morning for a while and an uncomfortable fit of her trousers, she made an appointment with the doctor. Dave drove her round to the health centre where the nurse messed about with a glass container and confirmed Josie was pregnant.

Dave was livid that he had been waiting outside for over ten minutes in the car.

'What took you so long?' he snarled.

'I guess it was them telling me I'm having a baby.' Instead of being happy, she was almost in tears.

Speechless at his next remark, wide-eyed, she stared ahead.

'Well, I find it hard to believe it's mine!'

At that moment, she knew she had made a terrible mistake. She would never get support from him. Sadly, there seemed no way out. She realised it would have been better if they had walked away from each other when they had, not one, but two opportunities, the caravan and the rented flat in Mary Street. She knew she would never again bring up the subject of him being the father of her baby. He wasn't a family man.

A surge of courage and strength filled her body and from that moment on, she knew she was on her own. Soon to be with two children. In her mind, she took a step back from him. It was the only way she knew how to protect herself from falling apart.

She shelved the idea of college and couldn't think of anything other than family and home. Naïvely, at twenty-two years old, she hadn't considered what direction her life would take if she found herself with another mouth to feed. Ginny was nearly four years old and in many ways an independent girl. Now Josie would have to start again.

This was a blunder; this wasn't what she had planned for her life because she wasn't completely sure about Dave and the way he operated. He had kept her running back and forth, meeting him at the drop of a hat, helping to find bits for his car and making sure she had enough snacks when he appeared out of the blue. He exhausted her with his demands and was responsible for her unreliable work record. She had to face bringing a new life into her already complicated one.

Despite the confusion, good news arrived for Dave the following week. He had secured a job with a marine company and would head off soon for a three-month trip on a ship. Not only was it good money, but the company had already put a month's salary into his bank account. The new boss was sure they had an extremely experienced worker at their fingertips and arranged a pickup for him in London.

Josie tried to be happy for him but thought more about the results of her pregnancy test. Not that she didn't want another baby; the time just wasn't right. She wasn't even sure if the man was right. There was a question mark hanging over her future. Dave was good at making her feel as if she mattered, but he was also a master at making her feel nervous and rejected. And there was the violence that reared its ugly head now and again.

A few days later, as they drove to pick up Ginny from nursery, she quietly contemplated her situation. Dave broke the silence.

'So, what are you thinking?' he asked.

'I need some time to take all this in, another baby and all that. We can talk about it tomorrow, or at least before you leave for London. I can't think straight right now.'

'I've decided I'm not going to take the job.'

He took his eyes off the road for a couple of seconds. She stared ahead.

'But you need a job and they've already paid you!'

'Tough luck. That's their mistake. I'm staying here.' He finished the conversation.

This was the most ridiculous thing Josie had ever heard of. He was unemployed with the offer of a very well-paid job and here she was, pregnant. It wasn't as though she was asking for any monetary support, but it seemed morally wrong for a healthy man to turn down the offer of work. If he'd been staying to support her and the baby he found hard to believe was his, that would have been a different matter. But there was nothing for him to do, not for another six or seven months at least. He wouldn't be spending his time with her while waiting for the new arrival. He'd be off out to see his mates at the bar.

'And don't you go telling folk about this.' He glanced down at her stomach. 'It's got nothing to do with anyone else.'

So that was her, trapped again and now silenced, unable to share the good news of what should have been a glorious celebration. Naturally, she told Moira, who was supportive as usual and who, coincidentally, had just found out she was pregnant too. But, as the months went by, Josie could tell her other friends felt sad for her. They had financial stability and support from family. Josie's mum had passed away the year before, so there were no relatives to support her. She only had a roof over her head, her saving grace.

Dave never returned the salary the marine company had paid him by mistake. Neither did he put anything aside for the baby. And he could carry on living what Josie termed the high life without a regular job because his mother continued to support him. He always had a car. He didn't mind changing it when he became bored. His choices ranged from Minis to Daimlers. And when he saw a television or some other household item that took his fancy, he would impulse buy, put down a deposit and agree to a payment scheme. He led Josie to believe he was buying things for her: TV, video and such like. The payments were never kept up for more than a couple of months, after which time he would appeal to his mother saying the gadget wasn't suitable and she could have it if she took on the payments. She always agreed, and that gave him scope to go out again and buy the latest model of whatever he had talked her into paying for.

When it came to buying everyday items, an experience in a chemist one day almost sent Josie over the top. Dave's strategies for getting someone else, invariably her, to pay, usually happened when he took her by surprise in front of others, as had happened in the restaurant with Esme and Joe and many times since. She had seen a shampoo that was good for Ginny and had paid for it at the counter while Dave strolled around the chemist picking up various things. He chose the expensive toothpaste and bath soak he liked, plus he had picked out some special skin cream he used. Along with a few other items, he laid his bundle on the counter beside the shop assistant. She tallied it up and told him how much it came to. He looked at Josie, then tapped her on the arm.

'Go on then. Pay her,' he said in a cocky voice.

There were two things that happened. Josie saw the assistant was extremely attractive, so Dave was acting the bold boy in front of her, and it instantly became clear that he thought Josie would never refuse him when he had an audience. She was just about to shock him. At over four months pregnant, she knew she had to put her foot down, irrespective of the potential to allow his bad mood to develop further.

'I don't have enough money for that,' she answered in a semi-confident voice.

'Come on. The lassie's waiting.' He made it out to be Josie's responsibility.

'What part of that don't you understand? I only had enough for Ginny's shampoo.' She kept her head held high.

He tried a couple of times more then turned to the shop assistant.

'Huh! Give me a minute.'

Stomping off, he replaced most of his collection, then stormed back to pay for one remaining item. But Josie felt she was taking liberties when he dropped her off at home that day. She didn't like being beholden to him and his taxi service, but it was raining, and she hadn't brought a raincoat for Ginny. If she had been on top of things, she would have walked away and let him drive off in his rage. Once home, she felt satisfied that she had stood her ground. It was unfortunate that she had humiliated him in front of such a lovely lady, but Josie had to stand up for herself.

However, that wasn't the end for Dave. He was furious and didn't come to see her for days. When he arrived at half past ten one night, she was in bed. The sound of a constant rapping on the door told Josie she could forget about sleeping. The interrogation about how she had spent her weekend was about to start.

'Where have you been? Who did you meet? Who were you with? What time did you get in? What were you wearing?'

She hadn't been anywhere.

The questions came thick and fast, and she couldn't think straight. There wasn't even time to answer one when he was spouting out the next. Her head was in a spin. He talked and talked so much while Josie was trying to formulate answers. She didn't stop to ask where he had been and what he'd been doing. When she didn't have time to think, there was a different type of adrenaline that kicked in and her mind froze. Once he had vented, she was exhausted and wanted it all to end. Better that she kept quiet.

After a couple of minutes' peace, she read the scowl on his face as another barrage of insults waiting to come her way. But she was wrong. His body language was unfamiliar. He wasn't tense, although Josie wondered if it had been time at the bar that had relaxed him. He leaned back on the couch and crossed his legs.

'Think you are getting along OK then? Happy?' He half-slurred his questions.

'I'm fine.'

'I probably shouldn't have come over so late, but I have something to tell you.'

Josie furrowed her brows anticipating his version of an apology.

'I've got gonorrhoea.' He averted his eyes. Neither of them spoke for a moment. He smirked. 'Just thought you should know.'

He's lying! Josie thought.

It surprised her that he reckoned she was so gullible.

This new cool slant to something so horrific did not marry with his normal approach. It would have been more believable if he had done his usual, stormed in, taken her by the throat until she almost passed out and accused her of sleeping around. Then he would have thrown some medical paperwork at her and blamed his unfortunate situation on her. But, having said his bit, he walked out.

Instead of going back to bed, Josie lay down on the couch and burst out laughing.

What an idiot! He thinks I can't read him, she thought.

He had wanted a response. He wanted her to think he was living a double life while she was barefoot and pregnant. She didn't know if he was being unfaithful, but she also wondered if he wanted a reaction that would show she cared. She didn't.

There was no sign of Dave for a week. He came back with yet another strange aura about him. Unsure of where he would go, she jumped in.

'And, by the way, that disease you've got.' She stared straight into his eyes. 'I've not got it!'

'What? Do you mean to say you—'

A week away from him and now she was giving just about as good as she got but the tension involved in keeping up these mind games was draining. He had energy for it and was more than prepared to continue with his emotional abuse.

Dave

I dropped in from the bar later than usual one Saturday afternoon and told Josie about a group of ladies who had come into the lounge to promote cigarettes. I joked about how the men had said they'd be more than happy to start smoking if the lovely ladies were involved. Suddenly, I became aware of Josie's appearance. Pregnant and dressed in an oversized t-shirt, I looked her up and down.

'So, who were the ladies and what were they like?' she asked.

'Gorgeous.' I closed my eyes as though conjuring up the vision with a half-smile on my face.

Underneath her make-up-free face, she must have felt fat and unattractive.

'You look tired,' I said with a smirk.

That was my revenge for the incident in the chemist and her non-response to my so-called gonorrhoea confession.

Make her feel inadequate and unappealing, I thought.

It was evident I had touched a sore spot when she dropped onto the chair. I was right, she was tired.

That day, she had the same look on her face as the times when I called shop assistants and waitresses *sweetheart* or *honey*. It must have made her feel jealous because I never used these intimate terms for her.

Chapter 10

Josie

More stress came Josie's way. It didn't work out when they went into town together to look at something for the new arrival; something she would be expected to pay for. He walked at least six feet in front of her and she could never catch up. They would exit a shop at the same time and within two strides, Dave was off. It wasn't as if they had to walk separately to avoid crowds of people. It was as though he was ashamed to be walking next to her.

She spoke to her confidante. Moira suggested she disappear into a shop and see how long it took him to realise she was missing. It was a good idea, but Josie was too afraid to try it.

It was around this time that Dave mentioned how much he respected a couple who lived on the other side of town. He had known the man when he had his eye on a lovely young lady. She didn't respond to his advances initially, but the man didn't give up. He finally dragged the girl into a back garden and beat her to within an inch of her life. Dave thought it was wonderful that the woman finally agreed to marry his friend. As far as he was concerned, that was the way to win a woman's heart. Josie couldn't speak after he related the story. Her mouth fell open.

Surely that's not what he's intending to do to me? The thought made her sick to her stomach and she protectively clutched her belly.

It wasn't usual to believe someone could beat love into you, but Dave talked as though that was an option he might try. More popular was the belief that you could grow to love someone but Dave was demolishing her feelings one at a time by undermining her, mentally and physically.

She didn't want trauma in her life, but it was hitting her daily, like a ton of bricks. Little Ginny wasn't getting enough attention. Sometimes she and Josie could have gone out to the park or relaxed at a beach, but they had to make sure they were home when Dave appeared. He was never clear about his plans, so there was nothing Josie could do but wait to see if he came round. If she wasn't at home or in her usual haunts, he could make her life hell or at least threaten to.

Like most pregnant women, Josie created a nest for her growing family. The agency work dried up, but she was entitled to some benefits and had splashed out when she saw the local painter and decorator's shop had a sale. After days of cutting, pasting and hanging the pale green wallpaper herself, the kitchen had a fresh look.

Once Ginny's bedroom was tidied and her old toys disposed of, Josie bought two large tins of emulsion paint for the small bedroom and the bathroom. It would take her longer than usual to do the jobs, but she knew if she took it a step at a time, she could make an attractive nursery in time for the baby's arrival.

Moira and Josie had bumped into each other at the antenatal clinic. The next day, they took the children for a picnic. They took a walk to the park, and both apologised for not having caught up for weeks. Josie never told Moira but Dave had started bad-mouthing her and Ed and was almost successful at putting a wedge between them. But it was as though they had never been a day apart and they chatted while Ginny and Peter jumped on and off the swings then ran towards the picnic rug to pick up a sandwich or a piece of fruit.

It was the most wonderful afternoon Josie had spent in a long time. She confided in Moira that there was a strong possibility she would eventually look for a change of house and get away to another town. She'd been on her own for two years before Dave came on the scene; she felt she could manage alone again, but it couldn't be at that precise moment. She needed to keep appointments and wait until the baby was born before she could think about moving. Moira didn't say a word. She knew the time would come when she could help Josie. She didn't know how, so things would have to roll along for the moment.

Around four o'clock in the afternoon, Josie helped Ginny climb the two flights of stairs to their flat. She dumped the bag of empty juice bottles and sandwich containers and put Ginny down for a nap. Putting her feet up, Josie took a slow sip out of a welcome cup of tea. By now her bump made her uncomfortable. Thankfully, she no longer looked like she only had a fat stomach; the world could see she was pregnant.

The rattle of the door handle alerted her. Dave had arrived. She seldom locked the front door, so it didn't surprise her when he finally stood in front of her.

'Right,' he said with force in his voice.

'What is it?'

'Last Monday. Where were you?' He towered over her.

'What are you talking about?'

'Dundas shopping centre. Two o'clock. Who were you talking to?'

'I don't know. I don't think I was at the shopping centre. I can't remember.' Josie felt the fear grip her.

He moved his face closer to hers and his voice became menacing.

'I heard you were talking to a guy at two o'clock last Monday at Dundas shopping centre,' he repeated. 'I want to know who he was.'

The tension in the air was unmistakable. Josie was terrified and had to move. She stood up, slowly walked into the kitchen and laid her cup on the counter. He followed her, sat on a kitchen chair, reached into the centre of the kitchen table and picked up an eighteen-inch narrow blue glass vase that held a single stem. Josie looked on in horror as he lifted it high into the air and smashed it in two over his right knee. Splinters of blue glass spread around the floor.

'What are you doing?' She gulped, her hands shook uncontrollably.

'Well, all you have to do is tell me.' He cocked his head to one side, his grip tightening on the broken vase.

'I don't know. I don't think I was there. Where is all this coming from? I don't understand.'

'I have my spies. A good friend of mine saw you. Don't think people won't report back to me.'

Josie could only shake her head in disbelief as he tossed the broken glass at her feet. He stood up, opened the cutlery drawer and picked out a soup spoon. Using it as a lever, he flipped open one tin of paint. As the lid rattled against the worktop, she saw drops of paint splatter against the net curtains and the new wallpaper. She gaped at him then back at the paint tin.

'Look, look what you're doing!'

Leaving the lid where it had landed on the work surface, he picked up the tin, walked into the living room and stood at the door. Gripping the tin with outstretched arms, he swung around with such force that the paint flew from one end of the living room to the other. It was everywhere. On the couch, the walls, the curtains and anything else that had been lying around. Ginny's dolls were now magnolia and the paint slid down the mirror and around the picture frames, dripping slowly onto the carpet.

'Please!' Josie begged him even though she could see the damage was done. She feared he could do more.

Without a word, he walked back into the kitchen, chucked the now empty tin back on the worktop and opened the second tin. This time, he threw the contents around the newly decorated kitchen. He dropped the empty tin beside the other one and walked out.

Josie's flat was in chaos. Her body turned this way and that while her breath came in short pants. Looking at the floor, she saw it was impossible to walk anywhere without treading on paint or broken glass. Without a telephone, she couldn't call for help, but looking out of the kitchen window, she caught sight of a neighbour, Paula, in the street. Josie called out and signalled for her to come up. With a feeling of sparks flying round her head, causing a muddled sensation, Josie thought she might pass out. But her body was in automatic pilot and, gasping for air, she opened the door for her friend.

'Josie. What's going on?'

When Paula saw the devastation, she was horrified. She couldn't believe what Dave had done. Before Josie could stop her, she moved down the stairs as fast as she could and went back to her flat to call the police. Returning with her husband, Alex, they helped Josie sit down and tried to calm her crying. It was embarrassing and soul-destroying to think the police would be coming to the door but, after Paula had started the ball rolling, nothing could stop it.

The officers came within the hour. Once they had a description of events, they questioned Josie.

'So, how do we know you didn't do this yourself to get Dave into bother?' they asked her when they heard about her turbulent relationship. The police had to cover all eventualities but by now Josie was almost hysterical.

'Please, look at me.' She spread her arms. 'I've been trying to build up a home here.' Their reaction hurt her.

'Josie, let them look around. Come here.' Paula did her best to comfort her.

After checking out the flat, they told Josie that even if she decided not to take things any further, Dave would still be in trouble. They intended to charge him with malicious damage, and she was to be informed of a court date.

Initially, Josie was scared at what Dave's reaction would be now that the police were involved, but he did his usual and stayed away from her for a couple of weeks.

Despite her shock and utter disbelief at how Dave could be so violent and destructive, Josie got on with it. She made calls to specialist cleaning companies to see what could be done with the couch and the carpets. Friends came round to help, and she regained a bit of confidence.

She caught up with Moira, and they compared notes about their pregnancies and preparations for their new arrivals. Josie's intended move from the area came up in conversation and Moira encouraged her to put her name down on a council exchange list. Josie couldn't easily view properties because travelling long distances on buses at her stage of the pregnancy, and with Ginny, was practically impossible. She knew she could wait because she had a super flat that someone would jump at when the time was right.

One afternoon, while walking out of the supermarket with two heavy bags, she bumped into Dave.

'Can we talk?' he asked. She was sure he must have been following her because the supermarket was not his domain. 'How are you? I just wanted to speak to you on your own and see how things were going.'

He offered to take her home in the car, something that was a welcome relief. On the way, Josie spoke about what had happened, the paint and the police. But he wasn't saying anything.

'Where's the tape recorder?' he asked, as he mockingly looked around the floor of his car.

'I'm not into playing these silly games. You know what you did, and I know what you did. I got word that the court date is in a few weeks, so let's leave it at that. I'm tired of this. I'm moving on with my life.' She left him sitting.

The following weekend, Josie walked out to see him standing next to his car at the end of the street. Ginny saw him and pointed at the car. Dave got out and before Josie could stop him, he had lifted Ginny into the back seat.

'I'm going for a coffee, and I want to speak to you,' he said.

'No, look, I'm not coming with you. We've got somewhere to go, so please let her out.' She was as forceful as she could be without alarming Ginny.

But he stood blocking Josie. Not wanting to make a fuss, Josie stood back, thinking he would tire at the thought of having to cope with a child, let her out and go away. He didn't. He closed the passenger door, jumped into the driver's seat and began to drive away. Ginny's little face gazed out the back window at Josie. Not knowing what to do, Josie felt completely helpless but pretended to cry, screwing her face up. Ginny copied her. Josie watched the brake lights suddenly come on and Ginny was left on the pavement. Dave drove off alone.

But he didn't give up. Josie could never understand why he was interested in flogging away at a relationship if he didn't trust her, didn't want her and didn't think the baby she was carrying was his.

It wasn't true that she had spoken to someone at a shopping centre and she couldn't get her head around it. The incident had apparently taken place in the afternoon, in broad daylight and somebody said she had been talking to a man, nothing else. She had been six months pregnant, so it wasn't clear what was so inappropriate even if it had been true.

Dave

I tried again to bump into Josie, but she had changed her routine. Three weeks before the court case, I was confident Josie wouldn't turn me away if I went to her door. Rather than create animosity and risk another assault on the flat, I knew she would let me in. I was right.

Some light fragrance hung in the air; her new perfume I presumed. Very pleasant. I made noises of approval when I saw how much she'd changed the place.

'So, you've finally got a phone in.'

'I think it's important now that I'm about to have the baby. I might need to call for help.'

Two new coffee tables sat at each end of the couch and held little vases with a mix of flowers.

'Are these real?'

She tensed as I stared at her. I was waiting to find out who they were from.

'Yes, they're real. No, nobody bought them for me. Yes, I bought them myself and no, there's nothing more to tell you.'

Praise didn't come easy but I had been advised to temper my emotions if I wanted a favourable outcome at court.

'You suit that colour.' I nodded towards the green and white spotted top she was wearing.

She smiled cautiously.

We spoke about the interior design of the flat and how I could see a way to improve the nursery with a cartoon theme Josie agreed that a fireplace would liven up the living room and I told her of an unusual wooden design I had seen in a *Modern Homes* magazine. She was hesitant, so I did my best to encourage her.

'It's up to you, but you're missing a great chance. I can get you the wood at cost price. I'll be able to build it in a few hours.'

She told me she'd have to wait until the following week when she was getting double benefits. That happened if there was a holiday Monday coming up. It seemed strange to me that she didn't want to borrow from one of her friends. I pointed out that their husbands were working and likely loaded, but Josie always frustrated me with situations like that. No way was she prepared to *go begging*, as she called it.

For my part, I needed to do things to assuage her fears. Not everyday things, impressive things like changing doors, renewing work tops or renovating the whole flat if necessary. I reminded her she'd have to pay for any alterations.

The new frying pan and set of crystal wine glasses I brought for Josie were peace offerings. I had added them to my mother's store account once I found her card lying on the sideboard.

'What's the story with the Co-op card, Mum? Is it a buy now pay later sort of deal?'

'Kind of, son. You buy now, but the payments are split over the next twenty weeks.'

That was just what I needed and I was able to get the pan and the glasses. I said I'd give my mother a few shillings each week, but I knew she would take over the payments. Ideal. And Josie was full of thanks, thinking I had bought them. Result.

Josie

When Moira or Sheila visited, they agreed with Josie that Dave seemed to have turned a corner. Maybe he realised he'd almost blown it and had learned his lesson. They witnessed him acting like a responsible adult. He arrived with bags of groceries and slipped the odd pound note into Josie's pocket. Something major had changed him.

They saw the planks of wood and tins of varnish on the living room floor and were taken with the new fireplace design Josie described. Part of her wanted to be proud that her flat would be kicked into shape once more but lingering doubts crept in and threatened to destroy sporadic peaceful moments. There was no rest in her mind.

At the sheriff's court hearing about the malicious damage, Paula and Alex were called as witnesses, along with a heavily pregnant Josie. Dave didn't contest the charge even though he hired a criminal solicitor. When his counsel told the court that Dave was making amends by renovating Josie's flat and subsidising her, it all became clear. The fireplace and the decorating had been a ploy to make sure he did as his solicitor had advised, keep his nose clean and, if the opportunity arose, make peace with Josie by supporting her and his soon-to-be baby.

The sheriff fined him but he was bound over for a year. If he stepped out of line during that time, he would be answerable to the court. A stark warning, which he heeded.

The weeks passed, Josie expanded and Ginny looked forward to a new baby in the house. It was difficult to keep the flat looking tidy as it was impossible for Josie to bend over to clean the inside of the bath or get on her hands and knees to clean the kitchen floor. In the not-so-distant past, that would have been fodder for Dave to point out her shortcomings but he didn't comment. Neither did he offer to help with a few bits of housework, which would have made life so much easier for Josie. His foot was back in the door and he didn't see why he had to put in the effort.

Chapter 11

Dave

A month after the court case, Josie told me Moira had a baby girl. She and Ginny went to visit. I didn't bother, not really a man thing. One night three weeks later, I stayed overnight with Josie and slept on the couch. I told her I was giving her room to sleep peacefully, but I really wanted to watch the late film. It was impossible to see anything on television at my mother's because my dad would be in his drunken stupor, sleeping in the chair with some daft programme booming in the background. If I changed the TV channel, he would start his usual roaring that he had been watching a programme. My mother had said she had to listen to his rants if I made any demands on the TV.

'Well, if he wants the TV to himself, so be it, but you'll need to buy me a portable TV for my bedroom.'

My mother couldn't see the logic behind my argument, saying the disagreements only started when I arrived unexpectedly. She never really watched TV but said she was forced to go into another room or sit in the kitchen, reading a magazine or the paper if I put him in a bad mood.

'Leave him in peace. Don't give him anything to argue about.' She was almost begging me.

Seems I had no idea what she had to put up with when they were alone, but like most women, she was always prone to exaggeration.

I settled down to watch the latest James Bond film at Josie's, but I fell asleep on the couch. It must have been about six thirty in the morning when I heard the living room door open. She walked in, right past me and opened the curtains.

'Hey, what the hell are you doing?' I shaded my eyes from the early morning sunlight.

'Oh, I'm sorry. I didn't realise what I was doing. Habit, I suppose.'

She closed the curtains, left the room and I heard the bathroom door lock. It must have been a good ten minutes later, she tentatively knocked at the door.

'What?' I knew my voice was louder than need be, but I was irritated and wanted to get back to sleep.

'Listen, I'm having pains. I think it's the baby coming.'

That was a real nuisance because I could easily have had another hour or hour and a half's rest. I sighed and hoped she heard me. There was no doubt she'd expect me to get up and take her to the hospital at some point.

She said she was going to have a bath but wouldn't lock the door in case Ginny got up before she was finished. I lay back down. Thankfully, I'd be able to get my thoughts together. I put the kettle on while her bath was running.

'So, when do you need to go?' My voice was sleepy.

'I'm not going in too early. I'll leave it for an hour or two.'

It was then she bent over the kitchen worktop and started doing some strange panting exercise.

'What's all that about?'

'It's what I've to do to prevent the baby from coming too quickly.'

That freaked me out and I was glad when her bath was ready.

When she was out of earshot, I called the hospital and told them what was happening. They said to bring her in, but to take my time driving up. She wasn't entirely pleased to hear that I had called but I thought it was better that she was with the experts. I didn't want to participate in anything that involved blood and guts. By then, Ginny was awake and got herself ready. We headed up to the hospital.

The nurses helped Josie into a wheelchair and took her away, telling me to call in an hour. I dropped Ginny off at my mother's; I wasn't going to do a babysitting job. Back at Josie's, I had a couple of cups of tea and read the paper to see if there were any vans for sale. There was one in the small ads so I rang the guy and got his address. I promised to pick it up right away if it was as good as the ad made out. Then I rang the hospital. Big mistake. I was told to come up immediately. I rang the van guy back and told him I'd follow through the next day. He was fine with that.

Josie had given birth to a baby boy, Jon. I looked at him and could see a resemblance. In fact he looked a bit like my father. I only visited once the following day after I'd been for a pint to wet the baby's head because Josie had said for a second baby, there was an option to leave hospital forty-eight hours after the birth. They would be home soon enough.

The next day, we had to wait for paperwork and a bag of free baby products. After that, the nurses made sure Jon was wrapped up in a shawl Josie had in an overnight case. When we stood up to leave, a nurse handed me the case but I wasn't sure what I was supposed to do with it.

'Your wife has enough to carry with a new baby. You can play your part now and help her out.'

'Of course. That's why I'm here.' She had irritated me, implying that I didn't know how to carry an overnight case. Cheeky bitch.

I wasn't sure if Josie would manage to open the car door because she needed both hands to carry the baby. I was proud of myself that I'd thought about that. She would know I was concerned about her welfare.

We set off and, on the way home, I posed a question.

'I don't suppose you feel up to driving?'

She didn't answer immediately, so I turned to look at her as we drew up to traffic lights. Her eyes were closed.

'No,' she whispered.

'It's just that I was told I could pick up a van from a guy today, but it would mean you'd have to drive this car home.'

Josie looked down at Jon, bundled in a white shawl.

'You could lay him on the back seat.' I suggested.

Clearly, she was emotional after having a baby because I saw her wipe away tears. Women!

To think I had spent ages trying to organise a pickup for the van. Having a second set of wheels, and a van at that, would have been so handy. There were times when I saw or heard of something for sale but I didn't have proper transport to get it home. A van would change that.

I was excited. Here was my opportunity to either use the van myself or let it out to other people. My mum had given me money to get a gift for the new baby but I didn't tell Josie. To me, it made sense to put it towards buying a cheap van. Then I wouldn't miss the chance to bring home not only bigger items for the baby but also heavy tools and bits of furniture.

Because of Josie's selfishness, I missed my chance to pick it up that morning and I had no choice but to pop into the bar once her and the baby were home to see if I could get one of the guys to help me. Thankfully, Archie was only halfway down his first pint and the offer of a second was enough to persuade him to give me half an hour of his time. The van wasn't as decent as the ad had described it so I changed my mind and dropped Archie back at the bar. I never got the chance to buy him his beer.

Josie

Back home and after climbing two flights of stairs, Josie put baby Jon in his Moses basket. He looked so small. She hoped Dave would make a cup of tea but seconds later, she heard the front door close. Dave had gone.

Another mum, Daisy, had said she would pick Ginny up from nursery and drop her off home later that day to give Josie time to settle in. She would only stay long enough for her daughter, Rachel, to see the new baby. Josie knew she had a few hours before they were due to arrive, so she sat down to think through what needed done.

Fifteen minutes later, the door opened and in came Dave, with the two four-year-olds, Ginny and Rachel. He ushered them into the living room, then walked out without saying a word. Now Josie had a baby, and two little girls to deal with. With no thought for her, Dave went to his mother's house to have a sleep.

Josie didn't have time to deal with her emotions, she couldn't cope with little children and a baby so she organised getting Rachel picked up as soon as possible. Daisy was at work, so her daughter had to be delivered there by taxi. Dave didn't come back for hours and, when he did, his mother was with him. She looked at her grandson for a few minutes before Dave said it was time to go. He dropped his mother back at home, then spent the rest of the evening in the bar with his friends. Josie was on her own again. She had come to the point where she didn't find anything surprising. He had an utterly thoughtless character, and it didn't look like anything was going to change that. She stared at her new baby boy and broke her heart, again. The difference was that part of Josie gave up that day.

She was so exhausted she couldn't think through what to do. Life had to go on and everything revolved around the new arrival. The idea of breaking free and moving to another town was becoming more appealing. Her only option, as she saw it, was to escape. Dave enjoyed Falkirk. She was sure he wouldn't want to move miles away. But *she* did.

A new way of operating kicked in. Ginny stayed off nursery for the first couple of days because there was no routine in place. After four years, Josie had forgotten about the number of things needed for a new baby. The place was littered with baby wipes and bottles and the sleeping basket looked enormous for such a tiny person.

Ginny wasn't that interested in her brother. He was too little to do anything with and she much preferred to run about outside with her chums. When they could, the other mums came to visit but everyone was busy and trying to get on with their own lives.

Dave couldn't find anything to do except to spend his afternoons looking around scrap yards to find parts for his car. It would have been nice if he'd made more than a cup of tea when he came over but Josie had to be grateful for the few occasions he arrived with a bag of groceries. Before long, she was able to get out in the June sunshine and show off her new arrival.

Jon was almost the perfect son. Like most babies, he stirred in his basket every couple of hours to remind his mother he needed fed. Josie had expected he would be like Ginny who had got her up five or six times in the night. But, after the first week or two, if she put Jon down around midnight, he never stirred until six in the morning.

Josie had to record Jon's birth at the registrar's office and Moira offered to watch the baby to let her jump on the bus by herself. Josie felt it strange without the children but this was one job she had to do on her own.

Her answers to the registrar revealed she wasn't married to her baby's father so she wasn't able to add Dave's surname to Jon's birth certificate. That wasn't a problem for Josie, so she gave her son hers and Ginny's surname, Cairns. She carefully guarded the documentation. Now that the job of registering him was done, they were a family of three. There was no point in counting Dave in but she wondered what his reaction would be given he had found it hard to believe the baby was his.

Dave

About a week after Jon was born, I spent the night at my mother's because she had made a nice meal for me, thinly sliced steak with three different vegetables. Plus I was tired.

'So, how is Josie coping?' my mum asked.

'Oh, you know what she's like. She's organised. No need to worry about her.'

'But a new baby on the scene. Does she have enough food and that kind of thing in the house?'

'Well, to be honest I would go and get some things but I don't have enough money. I've had to put my car through its MOT because I need to have wheels on the road to take her to the clinic and the likes.'

She handed me a few notes and then I knew exactly what to do to keep in Josie's good books.

I had a great sleep and, in the morning, after breakfast, I left my mum's and spent ages in the local supermarket picking out things I thought might be useful. If I had known what to get for Jon, I would have, but that was a job for Josie. In the chemist, I asked the assistant what I could buy for a new baby but she was less than helpful.

'Is he able to have soap or does he have a mild bubble bath? Does she use talcum powder on him?'

These were things I couldn't answer so I ended up buying myself some bath soak and a new comb so that my visit to the chemist wasn't entirely wasted.

Later that day, I arrived with the shopping and did the usual quizzing Josie about where she had been. She told me about going to register Jon. That was something I hadn't thought about. I asked to see the birth certificate and was completely in shock. My child was named Jon Cairns, Josie's surname.

'What does this mean?' I glared at her angrily.

'It means he's legally registered.'

'No. What I mean is his surname? What's all that about?'

'Well, if you remember right, you said you found it hard to believe this baby was yours. So, I didn't want to embarrass you by asking you to put your name on his birth certificate. Don't you remember? You said if I took legal action, you'd get two of your friends to stand up in court and say I'd been sleeping with them so that nobody could prove who the father was. I'm not going through that so, what's done is done.'

To say I was furious is an understatement. Was there no end to this woman and her ability to hit me where it hurt most? OK, I admit I said I couldn't believe the baby was mine, but she misunderstood me. I just meant I was surprised. It would have suited me fine if I didn't have to pay to support a baby but I had changed my mind about him being mine the minute I saw him in the hospital.

I put the certificate back in its envelope and pocketed it. This was something I had to deal with immediately.

I drove like the wind to the next town and parked in the registry office car park. My breathing was laboured so it was important that I calmed down before I spoke to anyone in authority.

The receptionist smiled. I didn't. Before she could say anything, I had thrown the certificate in front of her.

'I need to get this changed. Who do I speak to?'

'Do you have an appointment?'

Very quickly, she read my glare and realised I was not interested in appointments. I was not a man to be messed with.

'I'll get a registrar to speak to you. Take a seat.'

There was no point in putting the certificate back in the envelope. I'd need it soon enough. By the time the receptionist had made a muffled phone call, I could feel my temper rising again. It must have been a good five minutes later, when a grey-haired woman appeared and ushered me into an office. I didn't smile at her either.

'Right, this needs changed.'

'What's the problem?'

I explained that the paperwork referred to my son but that my girlfriend had been hasty in registering him without consulting me about his surname.

The problem seemed to be that we weren't married. Josie wouldn't have been able to use my name on the birth certificate without either showing our marriage licence, which we didn't have, or me being there in person to sign. There was absolutely nothing I could do. The option to change his name would be his when he was sixteen.

I drove to Josie's, furious. I parked up and rocketed up the stairs two at a time. If her door had been locked, I would have kicked it in. Lucky for her, it wasn't. She was standing at the sink.

'You'll be pleased to know this can never be changed.'

I stood at the kitchen doorway and threw the envelope in the her direction but I had left before it even landed.

Nobody could blame me for my reaction that day.

Chapter 12

Josie

Josie was thrilled when little gifts came in for baby Jon. Dave saw the piles of bibs and mittens and mentioned that he was surprised people were giving so much to someone they hardly knew. Kind neighbours handed in cards of congratulations, and the tradition of putting silver on the baby's pillow in the pram was sweet. Josie collected the money in a round tartan biscuit tin and kept it in a drawer. Between coins and notes, there was a substantial amount for Jon.

One day, Moira suggested they take a trip to the shops so that Josie could pick something of her choice as a baby's gift. This was a great opportunity to get the few extra things she needed for her eight-week-old baby. Just before she left the house, Josie went into the drawer and opened the tin to get Jon's money. It was completely empty. She stared at it in disbelief, then her hand flew to her mouth as she gasped in shock. There was only one person in the world who could have done that.

'Where's Jon's money?' Josie asked as soon as Dave came boldly walking into her flat later that afternoon.

'It's in the bank. I've opened a bank account for him and it's not in the name on his birth certificate. He'll get it when he needs it.' He was practically in her face.

'He needs it now. He needs some clothes and I need to get him a baby buggy within the next couple of months.'

But, although she had snapped at him, deep sorrow engulfed Josie as she wondered what kind of father does that to his newborn child? It was gut wrenching to think his love of money and his desire to steal far outweighed his consideration for the needs of his helpless baby boy. The money was gone, never to be seen again.

What surprised her the most was, although she was upset at him taking Jon's money, after a few weeks, a feeling of resignation took over. She felt nothing. It was as though she was desensitised to his comments, his actions and she took on a zombie like persona. Partly because she was tired looking after a baby and Ginny, but also because she had lost her spirit.

Just when she needed them, Josie found her small network of friends was depleting. Dave's rudeness to them became too much. He and Josie had visited Moira and Ed one afternoon and it wasn't long after that, Moira told Josie she was going on a diet, a very strict one because, since she'd had the baby, she was convinced she looked fat.

She confided in Josie that she had felt miserable after Dave had made a comment about the size of her backside. Moira was slim, with dark hair and dark eyes, extremely attractive. Josie couldn't imagine why Dave would ever have said anything so rude and cruel. As it was, Moira went on her diet and the whole thing got out of control. She ended up becoming ill because she didn't eat or, if she did, it would have been something like a cracker for lunch. It took a long time, years in fact, for her to get over this. Although she didn't blame Dave, she remembered clearly that his comment had struck a chord and made her feel uncomfortable with her body. He had found her vulnerable spot.

Josie told Sheila about this, and it surprised her to hear that Moira wasn't the only one who had been affected by Dave's inappropriate remarks. On a night out before Dave met Josie, he had mentioned to Sheila that it surprised him she didn't know her hair was more akin to a pensioner's style. Sheila also told of when she had bumped into Dave at a party many years before. He had whispered to all the men in the room that one girl was pregnant and to keep away from her. The girl wasn't having a baby and couldn't understand why no one was engaging with her. It was as though he revelled in causing distress.

Then Josie remembered her one and only night out with the girls to celebrate not long after baby Jon was born. She had to organise the babysitter because there was no way Dave would do that job. A group of five friends went to a lounge where there was some music. They spent an enjoyable evening chatting and having a glass of wine. Partway through and in between songs, the guitarist had taken a minute to say happy birthday to someone and then announced that a message had come through from Dave for Josie, congratulating her on presenting him with twins. Everybody in the room looked at her.

'Why would he say that?' she asked the others once the music had started again.

'Well, who do you think is going to come to talk to you if they think you've just had twins?'

But Josie recoiled as her thoughts strayed to other reasons Dave had called in. Maybe he wondered if people would have had a whip round on her night out to help finance her imaginary babies. A little gift that he would surely have helped himself to.

He had whittled down the number of folks she could mix with because it was important for him to know where to find her. Moira, Sheila and Paula were among the few females Dave encouraged her to visit because they invited him in when he unexpectedly arrived at their doors looking for Josie. Of course, if she was there, that meant the end of her visit because he had some reason that he needed her to go with him. He wanted her company at a car auction, a scrap yard or a drive to Timbuktu. The real reason was he wanted to see where she was and what she was doing.

Like some other friends, Paula eventually confided in Josie that she wasn't comfortable with Dave popping in every few days when she was entertaining other visitors or relatives. It was one thing to walk in and put their kettle on, but then, while waiting for it to boil, he would ask if he could use their telephone. Paula said that was, without question, forward for someone who was a guest. Her telephone bill let her know he'd made at least one overseas call. People were becoming tired of his presumptuous manner.

Paula's husband, Alex, would see Dave to the door when it was time for him to leave. She was even less comfortable with what happened then. Every time, the two men ended up talking outside the door of the flat for ten or fifteen minutes. Paula spoke with her husband.

'Look, I'm fed up with Dave. He's arrogant enough to put our kettle on and use our telephone, but why do you need to stand talking to him for ages outside? Have you not said everything you want to say inside? It makes me feel as though you've both got something to hide from me. I'm excluded. What's going on?'

'To be honest, Paula, I don't know. He does that every time. He walks out onto the landing, far enough away from the door so that I have to follow him to hear what he's saying. I can't hold the door open *and* stand beside him. The conversation isn't about anything. In fact, it's usually a lot of rubbish. I want back inside but when I try to end the chat, he keeps on going.'

'Well, I remember the time he brought one ticket for a night out and expected you to go without me. He was putting a wedge between us. I don't like what's happening here and I don't know if he's doing the same again. I can't trust him.'

'Look, the next time he comes round, and it's time for him to go, I'll close the door over as normal. You come close and listen. You'll hear for yourself; the talk isn't about anything. I honestly think the man has no social skills and doesn't even know he's being rude.'

Paula did exactly as Alex suggested the next time Dave appeared. Eavesdropping, she could hear talk of cars and houses, a lot of what they had already spoken about inside. She couldn't fathom it out but made sure it stopped by accompanying Alex to the door from then on. Dave didn't like that and made much quicker exits than before.

Over the next year, Josie tried to be a good mother. Ginny was a super girl and little Jon was a wonderful sleeper, which made life easier. Dave never suggested moving in permanently with Josie and she never brought it up. He came and went at his own discretion and constantly checked up on her under the guise of seeing Jon. There was no denying the child was Dave's. He was his father's double but even so, Dave never contributed money towards Jon's keep.

If he came looking and couldn't find Josie, he would make the usual rounds of her friends' houses until he was successful and insist on her leaving with him or he intruded on girls' events when he wasn't invited. He didn't seem to believe that she could enjoy normal company; he suspected she was up to no good, whether it was ten in the morning or ten in the evening.

Dave

I'd packed in my job two weeks before I decided to check up on Josie one night, to see that she was OK.

The boss was becoming a real pain, expecting me to pick up where other guys had left off. I argued that there was no point in stepping in half way through a job, I couldn't be sure that the men had carried out all the safety checks at each stage and I refused to risk getting the blame for their incompetence if something went wrong. I didn't need to tell my mother or Josie that I was now waiting to sign on at the unemployment office. It was my business. I generally stayed at my mother's house. She left at six every morning for her cleaning job and my father was out for the bar opening at eleven. That's when I got up and had my breakfast before heading down to the British Legion or the Docker's Club. In the end, my mother thought I worked mainly day shift and Josie thought I worked night shifts. My boiler suit was in the back of my car so all I had to do was change clothes and arrive back home around five o'clock for food at my mother's. I told her the new baby was taking up all my money so she didn't ask about payment for board. It was an arrangement that lasted for months.

Then I struck on the idea of telling them both I had been asked to do a shift from eight in the evening to about three in the morning. That meant it wasn't unusual to be sleeping half the morning in either house. A bigger problem was how to while away the time into the early hours of the morning. If I needed to stay out later or come back earlier, I said I was covering for someone, that my back to back had come in before he needed to or I was doing split shifts, all good excuses that neither my mother nor Josie understood.

There was something irritating me about giving Josie freedom through the night though. For all I knew, she could be going out and bringing someone back home with her knowing that I wouldn't appear until what she thought was the end of my night shift.

I gave a gentle tap on her front door one night. It wasn't a surprise that it was locked at two in the morning. What I didn't know was what might be going on behind the door. Rubbing her eyes, she appeared. Dressed in my boiler suit, I made my way through the house, checking every room, then I went into the kitchen and opened the bread bin.

'What are you doing? Why are you here at this time of night?'

This was typical. She was questioning me again.

'One guy forgot his sandwich, so I gave him mine and said I'd come here and make up another one.' I was proud of my explanation.

I grabbed two slices of brown bread and laid a slither of cheese between them. After taking a bite of my sandwich, I made my way back to my mother's house and went to bed. I had been wrong that time. She was on her own with the two children.

It was about this time that I thought of collecting bits and pieces that people were getting rid of. I couldn't believe some of the decent things being binned. My only problem was I didn't have anywhere to store them. Josie's flat was full of baby paraphernalia, so I thought about who might have garage space.

It turned out that my sister Paula in Canada wasn't the only family member who was slightly annoyed with me. My cousin Billy, showed his true colours after an incident that involved storing wrought-iron gates in his garage.

All my life I'd been lucky enough to have friends and family who had workshops or sheds. I remember as a teenager using my friend's lockup to store a bike because it needed a new wheel. His dad was angry when he saw it and asked me to take it away. He said it was taking up too much room in the lockup. OK, some of the things I had stored beside the bike were building up, but all I wanted was a safe place for my bits and pieces. When I went round to see him one afternoon, his dad had piled my stuff outside. It was a real nuisance because nobody was there to help me take it back to my mum's house. I was hacked off that I had to leave most of it

Then, after I finally got my bike home, my mum asked me not to leave it in the hall because my dad had bumped into it when he came home from the bar the night before. It fell over, scraping a piece of wallpaper off. He made such a fuss Mum was forced to redecorate the hall. It took her ages. I couldn't help her. I had plans, meeting friends at a pool competition.

I got used to having to move toolboxes and any bric a brac I acquired from one storage place to another when someone complained and I thought I'd found the perfect solution in Billy. He and his wife had bought a bungalow with a garage and a concrete outhouse to keep things in. They were decorating and had moved a few bits of furniture into the outhouse. When I saw inside it, I got wired up.

'You know what Billy? See if you let me use that empty corner, I could store a small table and a chest of drawers I've got.'

Billy was fine with that and, because he would be out when I was going round with things, he gave me a key to the outhouse.

The first thing I did was take it to an ironmonger and get a copy. It made sense to me to have my own key so that I didn't have to disturb Billy or his wife when I needed in. I never bothered to mention I had the key copied when I returned the original. I knew Billy and his wife were at work when I went round with the dumbbells that were taking up too much room in my bedroom. I kept tripping over them. Because I was going to Billy's anyway, I took a box of tools, a barbeque and my mum's old microwave. Obviously, Billy and his wife didn't mind because nothing was ever mentioned about me moving their two bookcases and an antique looking grandfather clock to make space. It was unfortunate that the glass on the front of the clock cracked when I moved it and it knocked against the side of a wardrobe. It wasn't a big crack and, except for the six at the bottom, the numbers were still visible. The glass might even have been cracked before it fell for all I knew, so there were no worries. When I came across a set of wrought iron garden gates one afternoon on the other side of town, I knew exactly where I could store them.

It was bad timing that the only day I could borrow my mate Phil and his van was on a Saturday afternoon when he normally relaxed with a beer in the bar. Everyone felt sorry for him because he was forced to wear thick bottle bottom glasses due to his extremely poor eyesight. A nice man despite being a bit slow. I was never convinced that he'd passed a driving test but who was I to question him? He had a van and no one else was available. Turning into Billy's street, we saw the empty driveway and, convinced that he and his wife were away for the weekend, I asked Phil to park up and we began to unload the gates. Some rust came off on our hands as we laid the first one against the whitewashed walls which, incidentally, ended up with a few marks.

I heard a car as we settled the second gate against the end wall and by the time I'd turned around, Billy's wife was out of their car. I wondered if they'd had an argument because she looked anything but happy as she stormed into the house. Billy walked towards us.

'How's things?' I greeted him by nodding in his direction.

'I'm a bit confused. What's going on here?'

I told him two things. First of all, I needed a dry place to store the gates and secondly, that I'd do a deal and pass them on to him at half price. If his wife hadn't come marching out of the house, I reckon I might have made a sale but she put a spanner in the works with her shouting and waving of arms.

'Get him, his stuff and his arse out of here, now!'

After that, I couldn't make out what she was saying. Something about an absolutely useless eejit and a motor in the way. I don't think she liked how Phil had parked his van on top of the bedding plants. But I knew these would grow again; Phil hadn't meant it being half blind and all that.

It was a selfish move of Billy's wife. She didn't care that I had kept Phil back from his Saturday afternoon pint. The guy had done me a favour but, because of her attitude, I had to ask him if he'd help me again, not only to put the gates back in the van but also to stack the rest of my things from the outhouse. I admit to being surprised when Billy pointed out the VHS tape player and the collection of picture frames. I'd forgotten all about them, so it was like Christmas again. Phil didn't say a word. In fact he worked so fast to get everything into the van I thought he was going to damage things.

'Watch how you're putting that swivel chair in the van, mate.'

The gates were put into the van first then the other things packed around them. It wasn't easy to keep an eye on what Phil was doing because I wanted to get everything from the outhouse before Billy asked me where the key came from. I needn't have bothered; his wife beat him to it. I heard her before I saw her snatching the key out of the lock.

'You have no social skills, have you? What makes you think you can take advantage of us like that? You are a sponger and a loser. A useless piece of shit.'

That was a bit strong. I was Billy's cousin after all. Now she had my spare key and didn't even offer to pay me for getting it cut.

Phil closed the van doors and we got on our way.

'Let's just go back to the bar, Phil. I might catch big Stu.'

It wouldn't matter if I couldn't get into Stu's shed because my stuff was safe in Phil's van for the time being. In saying that, there were a couple of times when my things took a rattling on the journey. One was when he took a wrong turning and mounted a pavement trying to reverse between a petrol tanker and a hearse in an exceptionally long lay by. Then he failed to see the no entry street sign as we approached the maternity clinic, and we still had three miles to go. I was sure I was going to miss Stu with all the time-wasting.

The stuff was in Phil's van for two weeks before he did the same as Billy and asked me to move it somewhere else. I did. Stu finally gave in to my request for space in his garage but I never spoke to Billy or Phil again.

Josie

The scenario of Dave's nocturnal visit for a sandwich seemed strange to Josie. For a start, he wasn't a man who would have any sympathy for someone else, and there was no way he would have shared anything, even a sandwich, with another worker.

There was no point in saying anything. He was a liar and a manipulator and Josie thought it was a pointless exercise to show him there was a calmer and easier way to live just by being truthful.

His version of the wrought-iron gates story accounted for the friends who didn't want Dave hanging around them or their property. He had no idea how much he inconvenienced people.

With trembling touching every part of her, she made it abundantly clear that he was not to use her cellar at the bottom of the stairs. He would have piled it full of things that would have eventually found their way into the house. She stood her ground, but with much trepidation.

Chapter 13

Josie

Josie stood peering into a kitchen cupboard. Something was wrong; there was more room than before. When she went to make Ginny a drink, there was a space where the soda stream normally sat. After looking in the other cupboards, the mystery deepened. The gadget was gone. She waited for Dave's arrival and asked if he'd seen it.

'I never see you using that thing,' he told her. 'And I don't see you buying the gas for it. My sister will make better use of it.'

He had sold it and pocketed the money. Nothing was safe, nothing was sacred and nothing was his to give away. She felt violated that he was taking her belongings and wondered what she could do to stop him. The worry of his reaction to her complaint stopped Josie in her tracks. Anger and rage brought violence and destruction. Best to leave well alone.

It was difficult for Josie to understand Dave's nature. There was part of his demeanour that oozed self-assuredness, one that implied he wouldn't be threatened by anyone, but another part that showed he had real trust issues. When he didn't have the confidence to conduct himself courteously, Josie wondered what was going inside his head and if he somehow felt intimidated. That became clearer one day when they passed a window display at a men's outfitters.

'I need new socks,' he had said curtly.

She manoeuvred Jon's buggy in and stood to the side while Dave paced behind the customer in front of him. When it was his turn, he approached the shop assistant.

'Socks,' Dave announced.

The man stared at him.

'I beg your pardon?'

'Socks,' he repeated.

His inability to address the situation using normal social behaviour took Josie by surprise.

'What, are you selling them or buying them?' the shop assistant asked.

In that split second, Josie thought Dave would walk out, furious that someone was questioning him. He didn't. All Dave had to do was to tell the shop assistant he wanted to buy socks, but he couldn't.

Here was someone who was responding to Dave in the way *she* should be. Normally he would leave her to analyse what he meant by his one-word statements and ridicule her if she didn't understand them. The shop assistant was being genuine; after all, Dave could have been a socks' salesman. His reaction forced Dave to ask appropriately. He didn't see Josie raise her eyebrows as she grasped he wasn't the confident man she had thought. She suddenly realised he was full of hot air. In front of her, she saw a nervous wreck. His hands quivered as he lifted a pair of socks and almost threw them back at the shop assistant.

'They'll do.' He fumbled for his wallet.

Once they left the shop, she noticed his darkened eyes and twitching lip; he had been outranked. She might have to pay for this later.

That incident alerted Josie to Dave's interaction with others. From then on, she watched what he did when he met other people, known or unknown. It was a surprise to see he rarely made eye contact. He would glance between their face and another part of their body. If he had a cup of tea or a pint of beer to deal with, that gave him another focus rather than looking directly at the person he was having a conversation with. This was another side he tried to hide. She felt sorry for him.

Dave

I dropped into Moira and Ed's one day after I had arrived at Josie's to discover she was not at the flat. It was important that I found out where she was and who she was with because I had to know she was safe. I decided to stay a while and catch up with some of Ed's news. I walked straight into their kitchen and put the kettle on. It came as a surprise when I stepped through to the living room to see a new TV dominating the far corner.

'Huh. Some folks don't let on about the money they've got stashed away for fancy TVs.'

Ed gave an embarrassed laugh. He still had his job on the rigs and must have been rolling in it. His standard reply to any question about money was that he couldn't afford much.

'Did you get a pay rise or something? Looks like a decent TV mind you. So, that's the one that was half price in Murray's window with the offer of paying it up over a year.'

'No, we didn't go to Murray's. We went to the Co-op, and it wasn't half price. Plus, we paid the full amount in cash,' Ed answered.

He did exactly what I had hoped for, gave me information that I could keep on the back burner for the future.

'Aye, well. It was a bargain in Murray's. Pity you missed that.'

I used his words to my advantage to joke with Ed later about buying an overpriced television. I had never seen a bargain in Murray's. My aim was to make Ed think I knew everything. That way I could watch him squirm.

The minute I arrived at Josie's the next Friday night around ten o'clock, I knew something was different. A dark blue Ford Granada was parked at the end of the row of cars. I knew most of the regular vehicles and that wasn't one of them. When Josie answered the door, she was wearing a pink blouse and purple corduroy trousers; colours she suited. She certainly hadn't been sitting around all day wearing *that* outfit. I didn't normally smile at her if I could help it. I kept that tactic for times when I needed to manipulate her. All I had to do that night was to open my eyes wide and focus a second too long on her outfit. I followed her through to the living room.

My immediate reaction was confusion when I saw someone I knew, Daisy, relaxing in an armchair and two men sitting on the couch. Josie introduced me to Mark and Pete. I vaguely recognised Mark but couldn't for the life of me think where I knew him from. I did nothing other than nod my head in Daisy's direction. I had known her long before I met Josie and could see her bulky jumper didn't do her any favours. She was a bit on the round side for my liking and, like a flash, I remembered telling her years before at a bar that some guys liked big girls. Her drink had lain for twenty minutes before she came back to the table, and I assumed by her red eyes, she'd met someone on the way to the toilets who had upset her. Now, with my jacket still on, I stood at the living room door and automatically puffed my chest out. The guys glanced at each other, and without saying a word, stood up.

'Thanks for the tea, Josie,' Mark was obviously trying to play the innocent.

Suddenly, I figured out what was happening. This unknown Pete had been making advances to Josie and more than likely was trying to take my place. In the few seconds it took me to focus on the situation, I couldn't hear any more. I felt a super strength well up inside me and made it my day's work to finish the guy off. Out of nowhere, my fist came up and punched Pete on the bottom side of his jaw. He stumbled backwards and Mark caught him. It was a cracker. His face sat at a strange angle and his jaw and nose didn't look as pretty as they had five minutes before.

'What are you doing?' Josie put her hands on the sides of her head.

I didn't answer. When Pete caught his breath, he suggested they call the police, I began making remarks using a squeaky voice.

'Oh, that's right, we need the police to save us.' I squeezed the words out. 'We're just little kids and can't stand up like men.' I pulled my fist back, ready to land another one on him.

'What are you thinking?' Josie was overreacting and crying, 'Please stop, Dave, just stop.'

Pete held his jaw. It was clear the man was in shock so I let my arm fall. One minute he'd been enjoying a cup of tea and the next it looked like he needed to go to casualty. But I got the desired reaction. Mark ushered Pete and Daisy out, which meant Josie was now on her own. I looked in every room to make sure she hadn't hidden anyone else before I walked out, saying nothing.

I caught the tail end of the Ford Granada turning out of the cul-de-sac. It was then I was able to place Mark; he was Daisy's brother. I tried to make sense of what had just gone on. OK, so if Pete was with Josie, Mark must have been with his sister. It didn't make complete sense but then again, maybe Daisy and her brother were acting as cover for Josie and Pete. I didn't feel like analysing the situation any further. What was done was done and at least they knew I was a force to be reckoned with. Josie wouldn't chance bringing any more guys to the flat unless she wanted them hospitalised. There was a strong chance she wouldn't see Daisy again, better that she was stopped from the temptation of going out too often.

Josie

Josie tried to explain how difficult Dave was making her life. She needed to do normal things and socialise with friends or go to classes and that was why she secured a babysitter a couple of evenings a week. The situation with Pete had happened when she and Daisy had agreed to have a night out at the cinema, then to go for a coffee before heading home. This was a luxury for Josie because the price of a night out had to include the cost of the babysitter. Daisy was luckier. Her mother lived nearby and welcomed the chance to look after her granddaughter. Josie had told her babysitter she would be home by ten.

After the cinema, they wandered into a café where Daisy had spied her brother Mark and his friend Pete. They sat together, chatting and laughing about various things, until Josie reminded Daisy she'd need to be on the next bus home. Mark said he'd be happy to give Josie a lift, then he'd take his sister home. The four of them had piled into the Ford Granada and, as they drew up to Josie's flat, she invited them in for another coffee. They'd had an enjoyable time, and it seemed a shame to bring it all to a close.

While Josie paid the babysitter and saw her to the door, Daisy put the kettle on. The two men sat on the couch with their coffee and the girls curled up in armchairs with hot chocolate. Glancing around the room, Josie thought that anybody walking in now would think that this was a picture of great friends and good company. But the fear tugging at the pit of her stomach would never leave her, knowing that Dave could walk in at any moment and destroy their peace. After his attack on Pete, Josie was more resolute than ever to put as much distance as she could between Dave and her.

Dave didn't know, but the day after his uncalled for outburst, Josie visited the council offices to find out the status of her application for a house exchange. She decided to consider some areas she didn't think were entirely suitable and ticked another box. Within the week she received a few enquiries. None of the responses were acceptable, either too far away from a school or not in the nicest of areas. There was no rush. She knew in time the perfect house for her would materialise. It came in the strangest of ways.

Moira's sister-in-law, Mary, lived about eighty miles north in a town called Forfar and was looking at coming back to the Falkirk area. Moira explained that Mary's house was a two-bedroomed end terraced house. It had a back and front garden and a primary school was within walking distance. Mary planned to visit Josie in a couple of weeks' time to discuss an exchange. If they liked each other's houses, all they had to do was complete the forms and wait for the thumbs up from their respective councils.

Humming to herself, Josie got working on making sure her flat was spick and span. She cleaned windows and wiped down the woodwork. Brushing and washing of stairs could wait until the day before Mary was due to arrive to view it.

Two days before Mary's visit and after a morning at the supermarket, Josie came home to a note through the door. Mary had been and gone. Moira had brought her over on the off chance that Josie was in. It was such a disappointment that she had missed the opportunity to show Mary the flat. Josie dumped the shopping, changed Jon, and made sure Ginny went to the toilet before she trundled down the stairs again and set off for Moira's house. But Mary had gone back to Forfar.

'Listen, don't worry.' Moira reassured her. 'She looked through the letterbox and said it was great and they'll be happy to take it. She couldn't wait for two weeks to see it. That's why we came round.'

Now all Josie had to do to make the trip to see Mary's house. She kept everything crossed because this would be her chance to start a new life with the children. Dave would not feature much in her future; she could leave him, his suspicious mind, and his controlling behaviour behind. She wasn't dependent on him financially, and if she needed extra cash for the removal, there was furniture she could sell.

Moira took Josie in the car to Forfar and when she saw Mary's house, she was over the moon. It was even better than Moira's description. It so happened that Josie's sister, Iona, lived in the neighbouring Arbroath with her partner and two children. To be nearer family was an added bonus. After three weeks, both received positive replies to say they could make the exchange.

Josie sang in the shower that night.

As the steam slowly evaporated from the mirror, she was surprised to see the small lines between her eyebrows. Unconsciously, she was frowning. Josie knew she had to gather all her strength before she told Dave that she intended to bring Jon up in a different district.

She reckoned his calm response was due to him believing if he continued with his usual, *You'll never manage without my* comments, he would try to browbeat her into staying where she was. Over the following days, it was more than obvious to Dave that Josie had a plan. She did a clear out of things that wouldn't fit into a smaller house, offered some of her furniture for sale and looked at removal companies.

One night around eight o'clock, the children were sleeping and Josie had settled down to watch a bit of television when Dave barged in and interrupted her evening.

'So, this will be a new start then?' He opened the conversation.

She sighed and laid her cup down.

'Yes, a completely new start.'

'Look, I know you're doing all this on your own, but I could help you.' He looked at her pleadingly.

'There's nothing you can do for me. I can manage and I'm looking forward to a life of peace with my children. I can't cope with all the drama and suspicion here. You love the clubs and the bars and all that goes on with your mates, so you'll still have plenty to entertain you. I'm going to give my family a fresh start. They deserve to have a calm and happy life.'

He surprised her by getting down on his knees in front of her. Taking hold of her hands, it sounded like he was about to cry.

'Can I come with you? I'm begging you.'

Josie took a deep breath, but the calm shake of her head belied the tension in her stomach. She wondered if he was going to hang around and continue to be an irresponsible bully or become the kind and helpful Dave, the considerate Dave, the Dave that he could be now and again. Josie normally succumbed when he became that person. Not that she wanted help or gifts; she only wanted him to be a partner, a father figure and a companion.

She dreamed of someone that didn't have trust issues, one without anger who didn't need to put others down to feel important. The control he displayed never made him outwardly happy, so, unless he felt better within himself, his unfortunate nature was nothing but destructive. She wondered if his impulsiveness was down to boredom, that underneath it all, his attempts to impress were because he was a tormented soul.

Daisy couldn't understand why Josie wasn't including Dave in her plans to move.

'Even if you don't want him to live with you, why don't you keep him around until you've settled? He can fit carpets and things like that. If I were you, I'd wait for a couple of months, then give him the boot.'

But that wasn't an option. If truth be told, she didn't want him to have any part in her new life, but something inside told her that would not be a straightforward task. He was Jon's father and, if nothing else, that would be the perfect excuse for him to make contact. Having Jon had tied her to a devil. Forever.

The move to Forfar took place without Dave's input and Josie had to make do with half furnished bedrooms and no couch for a week or two. But she was happy. She enrolled six-year-old Ginny in the local school and it didn't matter that close friends and family were eighty to a hundred miles away. Without a telephone, there was no way to make contact except by letter. Josie got writing.

Once Dave had double checked the address with Moira, he made his way up to see two-year-old Jon. As usual, he arrived unexpectedly.

'Well, I see my absence has got you doing something positive.' He looked around the house.

It was so difficult for him to praise without somehow getting himself into the equation. It was as though he had engineered his non-appearance to get her off her backside. Nothing could have been further from the truth.

Although she knew it wasn't her right to expect any financial support for herself, it disappointed her that Dave had an aversion to handing her any money to support Jon. Before she had moved, he brought in things that weren't what a two-year-old needed. With limited clothes and little food on the table, she hadn't been over the moon when he arrived with the latest and most expensive miniature cars and a plastic garage. Jon was just a baby and there were more important things he needed.

Sheila had said to her, 'What is he thinking? You can't eat that with a knife and fork!'

As she unpacked her boxes, he suggested he drive them to a shopping centre. In the past, trips out in the car invariably ended up at a superstore where he would wave some new-fangled toy in front of Ginny and tell her to ask Josie to buy it. She couldn't have continued to live like that, so she refused to let that habit start again and turned down his offer.

The move gave Josie a surge of independence. It was still a demanding job to keep a house and two children with little money or a father's support. She turned things around when her newfound friends offered to help her in any way they could. It was easy for her to join in new company. Even sitting in a café, it was no problem for her to talk to whoever was at the next table and, because she was living in a much smaller town, everybody seemed to know everybody else and her circle of friends grew.

Quickly, Josie learned of groups she could join. The company was stimulating and eventually she made friends with different people for different reasons. She was happy to juggle things around to make sure Ginny could join the after-school club and go to swimming lessons. It took a bit of organising because of how far she was from the centre of town. There was no nearby bus service, but she had told herself she was fit with plenty of energy. She could walk Jon in his pram and get Ginny to her classes. After advertising in the local paper, she had four replies from teenage girls who were interested in babysitting, so she signed up for evening classes in shorthand and typing once a week and planned a few nights out. Finally, she felt as though she was beginning to get control over her life.

Without Dave's negative influence, Josie felt relaxed and able to do normal things. The fear of answering questions about where she had been and who she had been with eventually faded and for the first time in a long time she began to feel safe and even happy.

Over the next few months, she reflected on her relationship with Dave and reflected on how he had never been a support to her. In fact, he was more work than her little girl and her toddler put together. Josie couldn't decide what she had found attractive in him. Maybe it was the attention or maybe it was just that society expected her to have a partner by her side. But really Dave was never by her side. Even with all his talents for doing things around the house and his apparent ability to land good jobs, neither she nor the children got many benefit from these qualities.

Chapter 14

Dave

I never babysat the children to let Josie go out. There was no way I would be taken for a mug, looking after them so that she could go out gallivanting and cavorting. It wasn't going to happen, ever. To be trapped knowing that she was being chatted up was my worst nightmare. There were plenty young girls looking to earn a few pounds babysitting, so she had options. If I visited through the day, I relented a couple of times and stayed in with the children but only if I had something I needed to do in the house. I jumped in first with the offer to fix things before she asked on a couple of occasions to remind her that I was a generous man.

If I arrived late when Josie was out and a babysitter was there, I said hello and stayed in the kitchen reading until Josie came back. The babysitter would have needed paying anyway before she left and that was Josie's job so I let the girl stay even though the children were in bed.

One afternoon, I drew up to find that very scene facing me. Josie came in around three o'clock after having lunch with the mums from the mother and toddler group, or so she said. She took a step back when she saw me coming out of the kitchen. The babysitter was paid and I heard them arranging another session for the following week.

'So, what's the getting dolled up for? The dress?' It was a simple question.

'I got it from my catalogue. I've always wanted this make. The neckline and the way the skirt folds are just my style.' She nervously tugged at her sleeves.

'So, who was all this for?' I pointed towards her sandals.

'Why do you always think that? It's for me. I just want to do normal things and feel good. I never ask you who you get dressed up for. Is there something wrong with you?'

By this time, I could feel the side of my mouth twitching. I touched my throat when it went tight and dry. I could feel the muscles in my neck harden.

I took a step back, looked her up and down, then grabbed the neckline with both hands. In one quick movement, I ripped the dress from her throat to her waist. To be honest, I didn't realise my strength. I grabbed her arm and made her face into the hall mirror. She looked like a scared little animal. Not the Josie I had seen emerging over the last few months. I tightened my hold.

'Look at you! Do you think folk will like you now?' I hissed in her ear.

For a split second, I wondered if I'd overreacted, but then I remembered why that particular dress had made me angry in the first place. I was glad when I saw her shoving a bundle of blue into the bin.

That was the same dress she had worn when I arrived to look for her a month before. I had scoured the town, she made everything so difficult for me. She had been sitting with a couple, Josh and Linda, listening to a group playing at a local venue. I had plonked myself down at the table beside them. At the interval, Josie and Linda went to the bar to order drinks and, rather than standing waiting, they sat on a couple of bar stools. I was only a few tables away, chatting with Josh but I kept my eye on Josie. Two younger men and a girl had been talking to the barman, and I could see them turning to Josie and Linda. They all started laughing and almost falling off their bar stools. I was livid. Here she was excluding me, again.

I looked at Josh but he didn't seem bothered by it all. I could feel my hackles rising even more.

'Wonder what's so funny? Look at them, flirting with these guys. Josie never laughs like that when she's with me.'

I had been watching her and the blue dress. It was quite revealing at the top, in my opinion. She was showing far too much leg and looking straight into the guy's face when he was talking. I'd never seen that kind of concentration on her before.

Josh said it might have been because the noise in the bar was loud so it would be difficult to hear what was being said without getting close. I didn't accept that.

When the drinks came, I asked Josie what was happening at the bar and what was so funny but she dismissed it all too quickly with some feeble story about someone's granny making a mistake and walking into a strip club. Didn't sound that funny to me.

It was all to do with that dress. She actually looked good in it. I had a bit of a rage inside and it had festered from that incident until I let it all out. But now it had ended well. The thing that caused my problem was gone, never to see the light of day again. She went on about there having only been four payments made to the catalogue so, for the next fourteen weeks, she would have to lay out money for an irreparable garment. That would teach her never to wear something like that again.

It was important that I challenged Josie about her friendships because I hoped I was the only male figure in the kids' lives. When I asked them about who visited, they never mentioned any other guys.

One Saturday, I went to see Jon. I arrived as Josie was about to leave with the children. I didn't tell her I wanted to watch a football match, but I suggested I stay in with Jon and that seven-year-old Ginny would be fine playing outside with her friends. If she needed to come home, I would be there. Josie agreed without realising it was all about me getting a chance to watch TV.

'You go and enjoy yourself.' I stuffed a pound in her back pocket.

By four o'clock, I was bored. The game was over. My mind started thinking about what Josie was doing and who she was with. My fists were clenched and my shoulders were tense by the time there was a knock on the door around five o'clock. I rolled off the couch and stubbed my toe on the edge of the coffee table; that made me even madder. Hopping to the front door, I pulled it open with such force that it battered against the wall. It must have left a dent in the plaster but I never bothered to look. Josie was standing outside.

'I forgot my key.' Her face looked bright.

I could feel the side of my mouth beginning to twitch so I grabbed the door and pushed it hard towards her before she could step inside. She must have caught it before it slammed shut because I could hear her behind me, so I did the same with the living room and pushed it behind me so hard that it smashed into her shoulder. She cried out in pain.

She never had the chance to ask me what I was doing because Jon was right over to her side asking for food or something. I hadn't thought to feed him or Ginny.

I had her on the backfoot again.

Although I'd been in a rage, I knew I had to calm down and ask her a favour, or rather talk her into one.

The last time I visited, a guy in the bar had invited me to a stag night which was to take place the following Friday, but I wouldn't be able to accept unless I had a place to stay overnight. It was easy to think of a reason for my temper.

'I'm mad because there's nothing for the kids to eat.'

'What are you talking about? There's pizza and coleslaw and some garlic bread. It's in the fridge. Did you not look?' She was being smart.

Within five minutes, she had the pizza on the go and I was sweet talking her into me staying the following weekend.

'If I come up, we can go to the zoo on Saturday. Let's set off early and give the kids a nice day out,' I suggested. 'I'll sleep on the couch.'

She didn't say no, so that was a yes.

After I ate half the pizza, I left her to do the washing up.

Josie

Another friend came into Josie's life after they met at a charity event. With two children herself, Erynn was struggling with an intensely abusive husband Vinnie, who came from one of the largest, most notorious families in the town and, as a young man, got himself into trouble repeatedly.

Her job was to please Vinnie. He watched her every move and warned all and sundry that nobody dare look at his wife as she perched, bored, on a bar stool. Vinnie always had a job, but sadly, Erynn didn't always have housekeeping. She learned to become a wizard with food. When she opened a cupboard, to Josie's eyes there was hardly a morsel there but, within half an hour, a meal was produced for the family. Most things Erynn and her children wore were second hand because, rather than Vinnie seeing to his family's needs, his bartenders were raking it in from him.

After hearing about a job in a local nursery, Josie arranged for Erynn to child mind Jon three mornings a week while Ginny was in school. The arrangement worked perfectly and Erynn earned a few pennies for herself.

Josie had explained her previous life with Dave and how stressed and unhappy she had been. She told of the violence and the growing confusion around Dave's need for her to be everywhere for him. Vinnie was of a similar nature, he was not a family man and Erynn confided in Josie that he had abused her in so many ways she couldn't even bring herself to put her story into words.

Erynn eventually met Dave. She was visiting one day when he turned up after having driven the eighty miles to see Jon. Given her background, she had learned how to read and engage in conversation with controlling men. She recognised Dave's type of character immediately and struck up a conversation with him that made him think he was the knowledgeable one. They talked about the area, the amenities and the local entertainment. Dave didn't know any men in the area and he asked Erynn to introduce him to Vinnie. It was clear from her demeanour that Vinnie was in charge of the house—no partnership or sharing under their roof—something that Dave approved of. And so, because of that introduction, Dave's circle of friends in the town slowly grew. He dropped in to see Jon more often.

Dave was still an expert at reading situations wrong but Josie hoped he would have learned by then there was no need to control who came and went from her life. Living in the new town was heavenly for her. There were days when her stomach was no longer in knots. Windows sparkled in the sun, women hung out washing and couples chatted over garden fences.

On a bright summer's day, Josie peeked at Jon as he nodded off to the rhythm of the pram. She thought he was too big for a push chair but he still liked a nap now and again. An aura of calmness slowed her walk as she came to a beautiful corner garden.

Oh, that's lovely. My place looks nothing like that, she thought.

The charm of the well-ordered blue and white bedding plants stopped her in her tracks.

'Hello.' A man appeared from the side of the house, hoe and garden fork in hand. 'How are you?'

'Oh. I'm just being nosey. I'm admiring your garden.' Josie pointed to the flowers.

'It takes a bit of work if I don't keep on top of it. Are you from around here?'

'I've moved into Wells Street and inherited a garden. First time in my life. I know nothing about plants.'

Josie's story about her move interested him. Jon didn't stir.

'Come in and meet the wife. She'll make us a cup of tea.'

This was new to Josie. There was a friendliness that she hadn't encountered before. Or maybe situations like this had always been there but had been moved out of her reach.

He introduced himself as Mick and his good lady as Sharon then told Josie to take a seat. They chatted about the area and her new life.

'Mick. You could have a look at Josie's garden and give her some advice.'

Newly retired, Mick had time on his hands. His wife joked that she would be glad to get him out from under her feet for an hour. So they made a plan for him to look over her garden the following Wednesday.

When the day arrived, Jon was rolling around a rug on the grass trying unsuccessfully to build a garage out of an old cardboard box. Josie turned to help him, but her stomach tightened as Dave opened the back gate. He had arrived unexpectedly and did his usual looking her up and down before the questions started. It was important that she stay strong. She had made a promise to herself not to let his mood or comments interfere with her happiness. Within half an hour, Dave had turned her world upside down because Mick turned the corner.

'Hi,' he called out as he stood at the gate.

His manners were in contrast to Dave's as he paused, waiting to be invited in.

'Ah! The very person. Come in. Come in.' Josie smiled over at him. 'Just lift the latch.'

Josie introduced the men and went inside to get a jug of orange juice and some tumblers. She wasn't five minutes in the kitchen and when she stepped back into the garden, all was noticeably quiet.

They must be having a look at the front, Josie thought.

She was making sure the lid was securely on the jug when Dave came back through the gate.

'Is Mick coming for a glass of juice? Is he round the front?'

'He's gone. I told him I hoped he wasn't here to be eyeing you up. So, he left. You won't be seeing him again.'

The feeling in the pit of her stomach almost brought her to her knees. Here he was again, interfering in her life, exerting his control over anyone who crossed her path.

Mick never came back and Josie didn't dare visit the couple for fear of what Dave might really have said. She had lost more potential friends.

With her sister, Iona, and Jimmy in the next town, it was always such a relief to talk to someone who she felt close to. Although there were six years between Josie and Iona, they had grown closer as time went by. Iona appeared happy with Jimmy, but now and again she would let slip about her relationship with him.

He was also in and out of jobs but, as a couple, they liked to join friends for darts or pool nights when they had the money. Something did not overly enamour Dave with Jimmy and vice versa but, when Josie joined Iona and Jimmy, the banter was good. There was a certain amount of security for Josie, knowing that she had her sister nearby. The only cloud hanging over her was Dave and his surreptitious comings and goings. His visits and his presence put Josie's plans on hold once he walked through the door. Of course, the connection was Jon and there were invisible emotional ties that Josie couldn't unbind but she didn't want her son to grow up and be cast into Dave's mould.

She felt she was in control of her destiny, but she wasn't. Now and again she caught herself biting her finger nails or picking the skin on her fingers. Even from afar, Dave manipulated what she did and who she met with. The only difference was that he didn't ridicule her as much. That wasn't surprising, because she was learning what to do and what to say to minimise that behaviour; she often agreed to keep the peace. But there was a part of her that kept fighting back for acceptance, struggling to find who she was as a person and not the stranger he wanted her to be. She had to carry on with things like her evening classes, otherwise she would have gone mad.

Josie had a passion for learning environments, not so much an opportunity to meet people, but more so to stimulate her mind. Every time she enrolled on a course; it took her back to a time when she joined an early evening keep fit class at a local community centre before Jon was born. She had paid for a babysitter for Ginny, and each Monday she made her way to class in her shorts and trainers. A few days after one of her classes, Dave had come round and asked her what she'd been doing that week. Josie told him about the keep fit.

'I know you were there,' he announced.

'Oh, did you see me walking down the road?'

'No, I went to the hall and watched you from outside through a split in the curtains.'

But that had been many years before and Josie felt he was unlikely to continue with stalking behaviour especially as he lived so far away. That was only because something had changed in her. Initially, Dave had to be there to tell her what he expected of her, how she should dress and where she could go. Now he created a type of fear and concern in her that she behaved exactly as he wanted, even when he wasn't there. He could arrive anytime and, despite her not involving herself with too many people and trying to be the best mother she could be, she worried he would find fault or catch her doing something as simple as talking to the postman. He would let her know how he felt through his punishments. Dave told her she made him become violent and it was all her fault. It never crossed Josie's mind that she couldn't make anyone else break her arm or leave her with black eyes.

Dave

Things were looking up when I got to know more people in Forfar and the place became like a home from home for me. It was comforting to know that I could walk into a shop or a bar and recognise people. Having a pint was usually only for my pleasure but sometimes I asked Josie to join me. She knew not to look too long at any man who was talking and never to laugh at anyone's jokes. A weak smile was all that I permitted.

'Don't forget, lip reading is my speciality after working in the engine rooms on ships. Couldn't hear a thing for the noise so that's a skill that comes in handy.' She got the message.

I watched her like a hawk and had no qualms about asking folk what she was up to when I wasn't there.

There was something bubbling under the surface with Josie's friends, especially those who still lived in the Falkirk area. A couple of times I suggested Josie and the children came back with me to see their old haunts. The friends made noises of approval when we visited them and Josie extended an invitation to come to see her new house, even saying they could stay over. I wondered why they never arrived when I was there but miraculously turned up when I was working away. I wasn't intending to take it personally. After all, I was great company, but I wondered if she had a way of letting them know I wasn't around.

With only a two bedroomed house, Josie didn't have spare beds but none of her friends bothered about the sleeping arrangements. Young folk used cushions on the floor or partners slept together in a single bed if there were a few folks staying. She took the kids into her room to sleep and they pretended to be camping with inflatable beds for a couple of nights.

It annoyed me if I arrived unexpectedly to find she had folk staying over. They had clearly been laughing and joking, preparing food and having dinner together. She had been entertaining them but hadn't considered me. Her excuse was that I never told her when I was coming. There were times I couldn't hold it together when I walked through the door and saw a group of them sitting around having what looked like a party. And I didn't like it that the kids were having fun without me so I let her friends know they weren't welcome.

At the last minute one afternoon, I decided to visit Jon. I didn't know what I would catch Josie doing but I was ready for anything. Once I got there, Josie's lifelong friend, Catriona, was visiting from America. I hadn't seen her for a few years so we chatted and drank beers to the point where I was over the limit and wasn't able to drive down the road. Josie agreed I could stay over and sleep on the couch. Ginny had given up her single bed for Catriona and was joining Josie in the double bed.

After everyone had settled in for the night, I went upstairs and, without saying anything, beckoned Josie to get out of bed and come down with me. It was difficult for me to fall asleep. I needed some company. She refused, whispering that she was tired and would talk to me in the morning. I was outraged because she had gone against my wishes. Pointing with my thumb, I indicated towards the door and downstairs.

'Look, we've all had a drink. Just leave it,' she muttered as she turned away from me.

I bent over and whispered in her ear.

'In the morning I might wake up with a hangover, but you'll wake up, still fat and ugly!'

There was no movement. After looking at her lying there, I felt the rage rising. I grabbed her right arm and, with all the strength I could muster, dragged her out of bed. She tried to put her hands out in front of her in an attempt to tell me to be quiet; I slapped them down. I was beyond that, but I wasn't intending to make a noise. Her nightshirt ripped off her like a piece of tissue paper and her ponytail wound easily around my fingers. Walking her across the landing by the hair, I opened the bedroom door to where Catriona and Jon were and threw her into the middle of the room, completely naked. I shut the door on her before she had steadied herself.

That would teach her to refuse me.

Chapter 15

Josie

Dave didn't stop to see if there was movement from any of the beds. Before Catriona could see what was happening, Josie had grabbed the door handle and made a quick exit. She cowered silently while Dave pushed her further into a corner in the hall with his hand firmly on her neck. He made a hissing noise in her face before turning on his heel. Not wanting to waken Ginny, Josie quietly climbed back into the double bed while Dave stomped downstairs. The choking feeling eventually subsided and she got a few hours' sleep.

The next day, Catriona asked Josie if she had come into the room the night before. Josie told a lie; although she acknowledged she had gone in, she said it was to check they were all OK. She never admitted her plight from the night before because she found it difficult to explain. It was all about Dave and another rage. He was burrowing his way back into her psyche again, taking over and interfering with what she had tried to build up for her and the children.

There were many times when Josie became frustrated and couldn't understand Dave's way of working. Some of his ideas were certainly worth thinking about, but sometimes they were not only unreasonable but also downright ridiculous.

A friend gave Ginny a two-wheeled bike so, with her chum, she went out cycling and exploring the area. Jon had a little bike with stabilisers, but it was almost too small for him. Josie went to the dentist one day while Dave was visiting Jon. When she came back, Ginny's bike was in the back hall.

'Right,' Dave started. 'Before you say anything, I've made some changes to the bike. I've sawn a bit off the post that holds the seat so now Jon can use it.'

'But does the seat still adjust? It looks too low for Ginny. Has Jon seen it? It's a girl's bike; he's nearly five, he's never going to want to ride that!'

'You're never happy, are you?' He chucked an oily rag onto the handlebars.

No, Josie wasn't happy. This was Ginny's bike, one that she couldn't ride now. They could have replaced Jon's bike with a more appropriate boy's bike, even if it had been second-hand. Josie got the garden shed key, wheeled the bike outside and locked it away. This was what confused her. He didn't stop to think, only jumped in impulsively, with both feet and, in an instant, could ruin things that weren't his to ruin. His actions meant neither of the children had a bike.

Her punishment for talking back to him and pointing out his error took a completely different turn. On his way out, Dave picked up Josie's keys and spare keys, jumped in the car and drove off. The front door had a Yale lock, so they couldn't open the door from the outside without the key. The back door was a mortice lock with a standard key. He had left it open. The difficulty was it couldn't be locked from inside or outside without the key. That meant they were in a vulnerable position. If Josie left the house to take Jon to school or if she went shopping, the house was not secure. Neither was it secure during the night. She couldn't afford a new lock and so, to keep her stress levels at a minimum, she didn't go out unless it was to the supermarket. Even that was the quickest visit ever. She couldn't take the children out for the day and only managed her evening class because she had a babysitter. To allow a peaceful sleep, she wedged a set of steps between the door and the bottom of the freezer in the back hall.

Dave had found a different way to trap her.

When he came back a week later, she was shaking in her shoes while she mustered up the courage to confront him.

'Do you actually know what you did to us? Do you know how much danger you put us in?'

'You look OK to me.'

He flung the keys onto the coffee table. The sense of relief that flooded Josie was immense, but she vowed to think of a plan to stop him from manipulating her.

Dave

I never made mistakes, or if I did, they were so minor they weren't worth talking about. My policy was to stay positive and see excellent outcomes in everything that went wrong. Neither did I see the need to make any apologies for things that were so badly made, they fell apart as I tried to fix them. Generally, the things I altered weren't mine, but that was because I wanted to help and make life easier for other people. I took ages doing things, often when Josie wasn't around to interfere and to surprise her. But she was never happy.

The school bags the children used looked old-fashioned, especially Ginny's. In my opinion, something that looked more grown up, like a case with a handle, would be more appropriate. One Saturday morning, I arrived just before everyone left to go swimming so I said I would stay in and do a few jobs for Josie. She suggested cutting the grass, but that wasn't my scene. The school bags were lying in the hall and that reminded me of my idea of converting them. Thankfully, my Stanley knife and some other tools were in the back of the car.

The straps came off Ginny's bag easily, so my next job was to make two holes in the leather to insert part of the strap as a handle. I was careful and took my time to get the holes in a straight line. Then I cut the long strap in half and fed it through, tying it inside so that the knot wasn't visible. I left it loose so that Ginny could choose what length she wanted it.

Then I looked at Jon's bag and realised I'd have to do the same for him or he might be upset at not being treated the same. It took ages, but I was proud of my handiwork and left the two school bags sitting side by side on the coffee table.

It was a surprise to me that Josie, Ginny and Jon stared at their tweaked school bags without saying a word. Josie turned and walked out of the room and the children didn't bother to pick them up.

'Well? What do you think?' Neither of them answered me. 'Hold them and carry them around. See what you think.'

Ginny was the first to respond. She picked hers up.

'I won't be able to carry all my books like that. It'll be too heavy for one hand.'

'Well, you can change hands, can't you?' To me, that was the solution. But I was annoyed with her ungratefulness because I knew Jon would take her lead and complain.

'I don't know,' he said. 'Can we change it back to what it was like before?'

I was so hacked off. I took the bags off them, threw them into the hall and told them they were just like their mother, moaners.

A week later, I visited again to see Jon coming in from school with a small rucksack on his back. Ginny had similar but a bit bigger. If that's all they'd wanted, they could have told me and saved me hours of work.

I shook my head and thought, *What selfish children Josie has reared.*

A package arrived at Josie's house for me. Months before, I'd spoken to one of the guys at work who told me the only way to climb the ladder in jobs was to remember things, something that had evaded me before when, at an interview, I forgot to tell the company boss that I had levels one and two in Offshore Safety. It wasn't that I didn't have an excellent memory or had lost my sharpness. I had too much on my mind, having to hold down a job and entertain Josie and the children. Despite all my misgivings about learning, I ordered a memory course that had cost a small fortune; over £100. I had told my mother that if she agreed to pay, I would let her know how it worked and pass on the tricks for remembering. She agreed if it would improve my opportunities for being successful at interviews she would give me the money. It surprised Josie that it cost so much and she reminded me there were many free evening courses on offer at local schools. But I told her this was a unique course and I wanted to focus on self-learning.

With the paperwork spread out on the table, I felt knowledgeable as I sifted through it. The truth was, I didn't know where to start because the first few pages were welcoming me to the course and a lot more bullshit; things I'd heard before on face-to-face courses I'd had to do, courses that had put me to sleep.

Josie came back from her evening typing class to find me sprawled out on the couch. For once, I had sent the babysitter away and surrounded myself with folders and paper handouts. For the first time, I was sporting a pair of reading glasses, no prescription needed. I felt they made me look intelligent. Holding a stapled booklet together, I peered over the top of my new frameless specs and smiled at her. 'Just studying!'

'So, what's all this about?' Josie asked me, as if it wasn't obvious.

'It's a course that helps you remember things by picturing them in sequence and things like that. You wouldn't understand.' I turned back to my studies.

By the time a week had passed, I was only a few pages in. It was difficult to concentrate, even with silence. If I had an hour or two on my own, I would set the folders out on the table, ready to start but by the time I made a cup of tea and put some hooks up in the shed to surprise Josie, I had lost the drive. I told myself there would be opportunities on other days. Time passed so quickly and the folders stayed closed so I put them away. If I looked out my tools for one job before I knew where I was, another job had sprung to mind. There was no point in putting my saws and screwdrivers away so I got into things like moving shelves, taking the lid off the wash basket to make life easier for

Josie or making a picture frame out of the old wood from the shed. The folders hadn't been out for several weeks when Josie said she hadn't seen me studying again and asked me how it was all going.

'Well, the thing is, I haven't done any more because I can't remember where I put the folders,' I replied in all seriousness.

Josie looked at the floor and bit her bottom lip. Unfortunately, that wasn't enough to stop her. The funny side of buying a memory course then forgetting where it was, sent her into peals of laughter. After that, I never wore my glasses or worked with the memory course again. Weeks later, I remembered I'd put it in the car and taken it to my mother's. Josie didn't encourage me to bring it back, so it was partly because of her I didn't get through that course.

Josie

There came a time when Josie was worried about leaving Dave in her house unsupervised. There was no telling what she might come back to.

When she mentioned that an oversized bottle of sauce didn't fit between two shelves, without consultation, Dave prised the top shelf out and drilled new holes to move it higher up. The result was nothing would fit on the top shelf because it was only two inches away from the top of the cabinet. The bottle fitted on the shelf below, but he had completely wasted the space above. Josie wished he would talk about his plans, either that or leave well alone. She might have been able to save some things from destruction or come up with another solution.

Although Dave was happy to do some jobs around the house, he also needed praise and recognition. There was no point in moving a kitchen unit or sawing the garden shed door in half if nobody was around to say how wonderful his work was. A bigger problem was when Dave visited someone and saw what they had done. He revelled in pointing out, with a scowl, that wallpaper looked upside down or they hadn't grouted tiles correctly.

One couple they visited had been renovating their small apartment. Josie told them she loved the colour scheme and couldn't believe that the wife had put up two kitchen cupboards by herself.

'My word, you're a handy woman to have around,' Josie commented.

'But that corner isn't at a ninety-degree angle and look at the door. It's not flush,' Dave chipped in, as he opened and closed the cupboard door three times.

The woman walked into the bathroom, fighting back tears. Her husband pointed out that she had spent the previous day sweating buckets and had been very proud of her achievement which had been extinguished with one sentence. They left before the woman appeared again. Dave had made plenty of mistakes and didn't like criticism but was more than happy to humiliate other people by putting them down.

Their friends were all in the same boat, trying to build a home either by renovating or moving to another property. To guard against potentially damaging comments from Dave when they went to see someone's new place, Josie made sure she passed positive comments before he started.

Dave's much younger friend, Danny, invited them to his new flat. It was in an established part of town and his face beamed as he opened each door and explained what he had done.

'Danny, you've done a fantastic job here. I shouldn't be surprised because you've got good taste. I'm really taken with your couch; the material is so soft. All your colours are matching as well. Your place is super.' Josie offered the young man support.

Not a word passed Dave's lips and they didn't stay for long. Once they were on their way in the car, he screwed up his eyes and spoke to her in a squeaky voice.

'Oh, Danny. Fantastic job, Danny. Your place is super, Danny.' He imitated her comments.

His playground behaviour didn't surprise her.

The following month, Bill and Margo invited them to their new house in Braeness. Bill was an offshore worker, an operations manager. Dave thought Bill was a wonderful guy and everything he did impressed Dave. The couple had two children and lived a comfortable life. Theirs was a sizable house in an estate with a well-manicured garden. Margo had done incredibly well on her own organising the removal and getting the place into order while Bill was offshore. Josie wanted to encourage Margo, but she hung back. She knew Dave would want her to praise every single thing, even if he didn't like it, because of whose house it was. The incident at Danny's house was still fresh in Josie's mind, and she only said one thing to Margo.

'You've done a lot then.'

Dave knew Josie's comment was feeble compared with what she had said to Danny. But she would never say another word for fear of reprisal. It was the very time that Dave would have wanted her to be generous with her praise because these were his special friends. He was silent on the way home. He knew why Josie had limited her admiration and she waited for his reprisal. Surprisingly, none came.

Chapter 16

Dave

Somewhere, and not just at the back of my mind, I wanted a position of recognition. It was my right to be acknowledged for who I was and what I could do, so there was no need to work harder for approval. My family had brought me up as a Catholic, and I admitted to Josie that I had always wanted to be a priest. My reasons were that everyone respected the priests and they were fed and watered without having to do much more than read from a script each Sunday. But I never pursued the priesthood and had to make do with becoming a mechanic and going to sea with the Merchant Navy when I was twenty. That was the first of a long line of jobs where I had tried to better myself.

Josie emphasised why it was vital for me to stay in a job for longer than a few weeks. As if I didn't know how important it was to have steady money coming in. It wasn't a problem for me to secure employment; it was only that now and again it was more attractive to stay in bed in the mornings if the boss had been awkward the day before or when the job became too tiresome. But I wanted to earn big money because the pleasure of driving to work in a Jag, a BMW or a Porsche would have ensured I got out of bed for work. Plus, I knew if I had a house, my own house, I would feel secure and settled and I would stay in a job to pay for it. And I told Josie to have my son around me all the time was crucial. I would feel proud supporting a family. Being a proper father. I was prepared to wait to see if she would see sense in me getting what I wanted and we could become a family.

I had a steady job as a mechanical engineer no less. The work in Thailand paid well so my next goal was a house. Over a couple of months, I viewed a few run-down properties because I liked places that needed some renovation. I could be handy when I put my mind to it. In fact, there wasn't a job I wouldn't tackle.

If I liked a place, I would ask Josie to come with me for a second viewing. She wasn't as skilled at looking at the pros and cons of properties as I was, but she could point out little details I had missed. When she saw me having to duck down to avoid hitting my head on a low doorframe, I listened to her argument. She convinced me that the novelty of such a quaint attraction would soon wear thin. When I took her to a derelict building on the outskirts of the town, she noted the streets were narrow and there was no parking allowed near the house. Granted, I had to leave the car four streets away. It didn't take her long to think that would become irksome through time, creating more stress having to carry groceries and such like across several roads. I got fed up with her negativity.

'So, there's always something wrong with the houses I choose then?' I questioned.

'Absolutely not. They're great and with potential. While you probably can't get everything you want in a property, these are serious problems that I don't think you could live with for very long. They would probably irritate you.'

'Well, I think I know what I want in a house, so just you look at the colour of wallpaper and leave the rest to me,' was my reply.

It didn't take long to find the place of my dreams. I viewed an old property, Laburnum Cottage, near the centre of town and put in an offer. It was a shell of a place. New plumbing and electrical systems were needed, as well as the wide-ranging alterations I envisaged. Plus, I had plans to renovate the cottage from one level to two and create more bedrooms and a second bathroom.

It wasn't difficult to imagine what the finished cottage would look like. Josie, as usual, found something wrong. One major thing that Josie felt was lacking was a parking space or a garage. The house itself was much older than the surrounding properties; it backed onto a newer housing estate. When the cottage was built, no one would have been thinking about cars, probably only horses and carts. From the front door, there was walking access to the main road down about twenty stairs then through an alleyway where three flats were.

With no private parking space available for the cottage, I knew I would have to park somewhere beside the houses on the estate at the back. It surprised Josie that I had chosen a place that didn't have a workshop, garage or parking area within the boundaries of the property. I told her not to interfere. She didn't. She was beginning to understand her place.

I presented the estimates for the modifications to the bank, along with the expected values of the house before and after the changes. I secured a mortgage because I was still working abroad with a good income and the seller accepted my offer. He was lucky to get someone who had enough money to buy such a shell of a property.

It was exciting to think this would keep me occupied and happy for a long time. Most jobs were well within my capabilities. That was except for the roof, I wasn't going up there to deal with slates. My original plan was to save money by doing it all myself but my job in Thailand took me away for six weeks at a time, then I was home for three. In the end, I had to employ tradesmen to help. I knew I wouldn't have time to shop for materials and do the work. It had to be done within a matter of months because it was April and one drawback would be the Scottish winter. If it was raining or snowing, there would be problems when bags of cement were left outside and the roof would have to be secure to stop the elements coming in. The workmen would need to get the jobs done quickly.

All went well and I was delighted with my house purchase. Within the first few weeks, I had called in the companies that had given me quotes and arranged times to make a start on walls and ceilings.

My work gave me the date of my next trip away and Josie came down with me to look at the cottage again because, as I saw it, it would look very different by the time I came back. We looked around inside, then walked outside to survey the cottage. Looking up the hill at what was my first house purchase, I felt my lip twitching.

I was annoyed, in fact, I had been on the verge of bursting for almost three days. I needed her to offer to organise the workers and keep an eye on them. That offer wasn't coming.

'I think it'll look great when it's finished.' Josie must have realised I'd picked an amazing place.

'Well, all I need now is some bastard to look after it for me!' That was it, it was out.

Josie looked stunned. She must have known she was the bastard I was talking about and that it was really her job to make sure everything was going smoothly when I was away. There was no retaliation so the following day I gave her a set of keys.

'Look, all I need is a normal life. Someone to do the normal wife things. That's what makes a man happy, and that's when things work between couples. That's not asking too much, is it?' There was more than a subtle inference behind my words. 'My sister in Canada. She always takes care of her husband's needs and he produces diamond rings, expensive watches and stuff like that.'

It surprised me when Josie told me the lifestyle she craved was a million miles away from fancy jewellery. All I could say was, 'You're never happy, are you?'

The workers did their jobs when I was away, but the progress was much slower and cost more than I expected so I offered to help when I was home. Needless to say, the tradesmen were difficult to work with. They explained that they wanted me to prepare cement or plaster and I obliged but they complained when I walked away to buy a newspaper or a tube of grout.

Despite their grumblings, I still had a goal. I felt upbeat and Josie seemed happy. The cottage wasn't liveable in the short term, so when I wasn't working away, I stayed with a couple I met through Erynn and Vinnie, but during the day I went to Josie's to see what she had in the fridge.

Josie

Dave saw problems creeping into the renovation plans. It didn't take long before he was falling out with contractors, not paying the bills and generally being awkward.

Josie's next-door neighbours were a family with two children not yet of school age. The husband worked locally and had been in the same job for several years. The wife was a stay-at-home mum and they were happy to do the usual family things like sit in the garden, play with the children or go for picnics at the weekends. They owned a compact car and didn't have any aspirations to move away from their council property.

'In all honesty, I wish I could be like Eric next door,' Dave announced one day.

'What do you mean?'

'Well, he's got a simple life, and he's content. They don't have a lot, but neither do they want much. He's happy with the job down the road and doesn't need any more than that.'

This was a new side to Dave; it seemed he knew now that *normal* wasn't always reaching for the stars at every turn and there was happiness and contentment to be had from the unpretentious things in life.

To coincide with the near completion of Laburnum Cottage, Dave brought up the subject of he and Josie getting together on a more permanent basis.

'Why don't you let me make an honest woman of you?' he proposed.

Josie wondered if that would be the answer, to agree to a permanent family life now that he was sticking with a job and building a home. After a few weeks of pondering, she said, 'Yes.' After all, he had assured her on numerous occasions things would change once they were married. A ceremony was to take place then Josie and the children would move into Dave's cottage.

They announced their wedding. Josie made all the plans and friends and family wondered if this was the answer. Maybe now the couple could be at peace if all Dave needed was for Josie to have a ring on her finger. The wedding wasn't to be a lavish one; a little country church was all that Josie had ever dreamed of. She took her time picking out invitations, knowing she had six months to prepare things as best she could.

Dave went back to work in Thailand and, although the men had finished most of the jobs at the cottage, Josie said she would monitor how the work was progressing and wrap things up. She co-ordinated plumbers, electricians and roofers so that by the time Dave was ready to move in, all that would need doing were some small internal jobs. The garden would have to wait because there were plans to excavate earth from one side of the cottage to create a path.

The children were pleased. They were soon to be moving into a house where they could have their own bedrooms. With tentative plans about where things would go, Josie was happy to see the children looking forward to a future with two parents living in the same house.

Dave

Why Josie was so annoyed about a fireplace, I'll never understand. We hadn't even moved into the cottage when it all started. The original fireplace in the living room was dated. Granted, some fixtures and fittings have their place when trying to preserve the old-fashioned look of a house, especially a cottage like mine. But the fireplace had rusted and the grate was too small to get a roaring fire going. It had to be replaced somehow. I met a man in the bar, Shug, who was out of work and looking for something to do to earn a few pounds. After he agreed to have a look at the work, I took him to the cottage to show him jobs I wanted done. Josie had been banging on about the red and black decorative tiles between the surround and the fire itself. She wanted to keep them.

'These are amazing. Bet they are the originals from a hundred years ago. They are going to blend in perfectly with red flocked wallpaper. I love them.'

I agreed, they fitted in and it would have cost us a fortune to replace them, that's if we could have found anything similar.

I had originally said I would help Shug to remove the old parts of the fireplace, but by the time he arrived to start the job two days later, I had been thinking about going to see another bloke, Doug, about helping me out. I wanted to catch him before one o'clock and persuade him to let me use his welding equipment later that day.

'Shug, something's come up. I need to dive out for half an hour. You know what you're doing, eh? All I want is the surround removed. The rest can stay.'

'So, the hearth is to go as well?'

'No, leave that. Just the surround.'

I indicated the whole of the fireplace with my hand and didn't wait for him to answer.

Time ran away from me at Doug's workshop and the minute I got back to the cottage, I shouted out a greeting to Shug and dashed up to the toilet. I heard Josie arriving and by the time I got downstairs, she was waiting at the old kitchen table with her head in her hands.

'What's going on in there?' She nodded in the direction of the living room door.

'What are you talking about? Have you found something else to blame me for?'

'Go and look at the fireplace. Have you actually been helping him like you said?'

The living room was full of dust and smelled like damp houses that hadn't been lived in for years.

Shug was kneeling, making little piles out of stone and debris. The surround was on the floor along with a couple of fire bricks and I reached out to the heap of smashed black and red antique tiles. Only then did I realise Shug hadn't understood what I had wanted. My instructions had been more than clear. Remove everything that surrounds the hearth. Anyone with half a brain would have known that didn't include the tiles.

'Oh, I thought when you waved your arm, you were meaning the whole lot.'

OK, I hadn't specifically told him to leave the tiles, but it wasn't my fault they were gone. He hadn't done a good job at all.

Josie went on and on about them for days and challenged me about my ability to give instructions, asking how on earth I had been given a supervisor's post. She was such a bitch sometimes.

I had a lucky escape that day because she never knew I'd left Shug alone for almost the whole morning. In time, we got replacement tiles but I never asked Shug to work for me again. Anyway, Josie never did anything. She could have offered to come to supervise him. Such a lazy cow.

Chapter 17

Josie

The Christmas prior to moving to the cottage was to be special. There was a bit more money to go round and having the opportunity to treat the children made Josie reflect on recent Christmases when she struggled to buy even one new toy.

Many a time, the children woke up to a second-hand pram or bike. They would never have known it had been used, but Josie knew. She watched as her friends bought hundreds of pounds' worth of goodies and hung extras on their Christmas trees. Jon and Ginny had to make do with whatever decorations they had made at school. But there was fun in making their own Christmas cards with cut outs from a previous year's card or creating wall decorations from tissue paper.

The sad part in the past was when the children went shopping with Josie. It seemed like everything they pointed to or asked for was followed by the same answer.

'We can't get that this year, maybe next year.'

But they looked for bargains and baked cakes for the big day. Agreeing on a desert was always a joint effort and inevitably someone was disappointed, normally Josie. The children just wanted chocolate and more chocolate, nothing if not creative. There were times when they each had different things for all the courses. It depended on what was in the fridge.

Also in the past, Josie thought she might have been too strict with the children when they wanted to wrap presents and she had to remind them that there was only one or two sheets of wrapping paper each. They couldn't make a mistake with the scissors. Small gifts of home-made paper baskets with a few chocolates were lovingly wrapped and set aside.

Although the occasion was tainted slightly because the children got what they needed instead of what they wanted, they still had fun writing to Santa in the hope that he would have extra in his sack.

Ginny could keep a secret, not so Jon. One Christmas, Josie had bought a pair of slippers for Ginny and Jon helped her wrap them. He was sworn to secrecy but after two days he couldn't help but let the cat out of the bag.

'Jon, I am so angry with you. You have spoiled Christmas for Ginny because now she knows what I've bought her.'

He never said a word but slinked upstairs where he had hidden his gifts for Ginny and Josie. A few minutes later, he came down with chocolate on his lips but Josie didn't ask what was going on.

On Christmas morning, Josie opened her present from Jon, a bar of Fry's mint chocolate. It took her all her time to keep her face straight when she saw a hole in the end of it.

In anger, he had stuck his finger into the chocolate and ate some to get back at her for scolding him.

Dave

Before we moved into the cottage, Josie had been going on about Christmas coming up and how we might want to focus on the children instead of each other. That suited me fine and we agreed to spend no more than £20 on each other.

It must have been about four weeks before Christmas that my mother said she didn't want to spend the festive season with my dad. It was true he was a complete idiot with a drink and Christmas and New Year were prime opportunities for him to stay drunk for days. I told her that if she wanted, she could come and spend some of the time with us.

The cottage was not quite ready, but one more person wouldn't be a problem for Josie to cook and clean for. My mum agreed and Josie sorted out the bedrooms in her council house.

Mum was always proud of me and happy to see that I was settled and about to be married. She didn't have a clue how much it was going to cost to run a house and a car, not to mention the cost of raising two children. I wanted her to see I was successful and finally bringing in big money.

She settled in two days before Christmas and helped with the decorations. Thankfully, she was happy to come up by bus which was a blessing because I couldn't be bothered driving the three hours there and back to pick her up. She assured me she could manage her suitcase by herself despite being well over seventy.

I struck on an idea that would surprise Josie and reassure my mum that I was the epitome of a good provider.

Josie was in the middle of making table decorations when I left. There was no time to tell her I was going out because I was in a hurry. It had been a long time since I had let Josie buy new clothes and I remembered her pointing out something in a shop window: a stylish jacket. I parked up and wandered round to the shopping centre. The gift I had in mind was still there.

I told the girl behind the counter it was to be a surprise and I was ninety-nine percent sure I had gotten the size right. She reassured me if it wasn't suitable and returned within seven days, I would be able to change it or get a full refund I left the shop with the neatly tied up Christmassy looking box.

I waited until the correct moment to bring it into the house without being noticed. I had paid for most of it from what my mother had given me for presents for us all and a small amount from my bank card.

I hadn't told Josie about my mum's contribution to Christmas. I needed to keep that a secret if she was to get her special present.

On Christmas Eve, my mum and Josie were busy preparing food and doing things for Christmas Day, so I went out for a few pints knowing full well she would never open the box even if she found it. She would think it was the £20 gift we had agreed on, albeit in an oversized box.

The following morning, the children were up early and unwrapping their presents from Santa. I had made a great choice with Jon's Star Wars figures and the Millennium Falcon, that would keep him occupied for ages.

Ginny was delighted with her jewellery box and necklaces. My mum thanked us for the chocolates, the book and other small things. She would have been grateful for anything. It was enough that she was away from my father.

Then my moment arrived.

'Time for our presents. Here's yours,' Josie announced.

I opened the red and white striped paper and meekly smiled at the multipack of socks and the stupid star shaped air freshener for the car. The Elvis tape I didn't mind so much.

I made sure everyone stayed put while I ran upstairs. I admit to being excited when I thought about the reactions to my gift to Josie. She put her hand to her mouth when she saw the size of the box.

'Here you are. Especially for you. Great soon to be wife and lovely mother. Have a happy Christmas.' I bent over and kissed her on the forehead.

Everyone looked on in amazement as she pulled the dark green leather jacket from the tissue paper that had protected it. I sat down and watched her reaction.

'You're joking,' she whispered. 'I thought—'

I indicated for her to be quiet.

'Now that looks like a beautiful leather. Can I touch it?' my mother asked as she reached towards the box. 'Oh my word. That's so soft. What a beautiful gift, son.'

Josie was stunned and I knew why. She tried in on and it fitted perfectly.

'Well. Do you like it or not?' I looked at her.

'Of course. Yes. It's lovely.' But I could sense the uncertainty in her voice.

She obviously decided not to say any more and went fussing about with the finishing touches for the meal. I poured a wine for us all and sat chatting with my mum while the children played near the Christmas tree.

When it was time to eat, we sat down and pulled some crackers. The children wore the paper hats and niggled about where they wanted to sit. Everyone commented on the size of the prawn cocktail. It was massive and delicious.

Once we had finished that course, Josie suggested we wait at least half an hour before she served up the main meal.

Josie's living room was small, but there was an alcove where the table sat. A few times during the first course, I saw her looking across the table at me.

'What?' I stared at her.

'Just checking that everyone is happy.'

'You've done a grand job.'

My mum looked over at Josie.

It was then I realised I hadn't said anything negative about Josie or her efforts. That's maybe what she was waiting for. But my mother was with us so I could keep any adverse comments for another day. Anyway, I didn't want her to think there was a problem and that we were going to end up like her and my dad. She had made a bad choice with him and this was one Christmas day she would be free from his antics and drunken stupors.

The second course arrived. I insisted on carving the turkey while Josie poured some champagne for us. The children got bubbly of some sort, without alcohol.

The whole thing was incredible and none of us could face the trifle and cream until hours later.

Finally, it was half-past nine and my mum was the first to turn in. The children went to bed and I was alone with Josie.

'You really shouldn't have done that. The jacket is beautiful but we can't afford luxuries just now.' Josie just had to mention my special present.

'But you said before you didn't have a decent jacket.'

'I know, but I would have been just as happy with a cheaper anorak. But I love it. I can't wait to wear it. Thanks for being so kind.'

'Don't wear it until we have a night out. You'll feel great in something new.'

My plan was unfolding perfectly.

My mother left on the 27th, the day after Boxing Day. When I put her on the bus, she asked if everything was OK between Josie and me. It was all to do with Josie's paltry gift and me going out of my way to get something expensive and unique for her.

'We're alright, Mum. Don't you worry. I know how to treat a woman.'

It was early the next day when I recovered the box and made sure what was left of the tissue paper was protecting the jacket. I set off while everyone was occupied. The same shop assistant was serving, so I waited patiently in the queue in front of her counter.

'You might remember me?'

'Eh, yes. I think so. Didn't you buy the green leather jacket for your girlfriend? Did she like it?'

'Actually, that's the problem. She liked the jacket but not the colour. She's seen another one so are you still holding up your side of the bargain? Can I return it? She only tried it on. It's never been worn.'

'Yes, that's OK. Let me have a look.'

After careful examination and me giving her a few chat up lines, I walked out with £200 back in my pocket.

The first thing I did was to drive down to the bar. The guys started telling me about their Christmas experiences and what their wives had produced for Christmas dinner.

'So, what did you buy your other half for Christmas, Dave?'

'Well, this year was kind of special. I paid attention to what she was hinting at and I finally decided on a leather jacket.'

'For God's sake. Don't tell my wife that. She'll go nuts. She wanted a winter coat but it was almost a hundred. No way could we have afforded that,' Matt said.

'Ah, you see. You've got to be in the good jobs to get the good money.'

I was proud of how my life was turning out. I was almost where I wanted to be.

I patted the wad of notes in my inside pocket to make sure it was still there and, since three of the company put their jackets on and walked away, I asked the one guy still sitting if he wanted another pint. He was the manager in the local Volkswagen garage. A man worth knowing.

Once home, I told Josie I had to speak to her. I told her that all in all, Christmas Day was a success. My mother had enjoyed it and the food was great.

'Yes, the children had fun. I'm glad it went well.'

I knew what I was doing, making her feel good so that the next part of my conversation wouldn't deplete her completely.

'I've been wakened most of the night. I can't believe I was so stupid and you were right. The leather jacket. It's out of our price range at the moment and it was when you said you'd have been happy with an anorak I knew I had made a mistake. So, I took the jacket back this morning. Here's £20 that was to be the value of our Christmas presents. Much better that you chose the jacket you want.'

I could tell she wasn't pleased, but that was just too bad. I had managed to do the right thing and finally end up with some cash that I would put towards getting a new radio and tape player for the car. Something we would all benefit from.

Josie

Dave left to work abroad a couple of days before New Year so Josie invited Iona to come and stay. By this time, Iona was heavily pregnant and couldn't bear the thought of going out for Hogmanay. It was agreed, she was to arrive on New Year's Eve after dropping Jimmy off at his mother's house.

The children were allowed to stay up until the clocks stuck twelve and another year began. While they waited, the dips and crisps were demolished in record time. Nobody had any celebratory drinks because Iona wasn't having a wine so there didn't seem much point in Josie having one on her own.

Throughout the evening, they had so much fun that Iona told the children to stop joking around. Her jaws were so sore from laughing. Jon must have been delirious with tiredness and started imitating the men in the family. He had them all down to a T. But, once he sat down, he was trying to figure out the strange concept of waiting up until the next day started.

'Is it tomorrow yet?' he asked in all innocence.

'No, it's yesterday tonight,' Iona answered.

That sent everyone into peals of laughter again trying to work out how to explain that the new day hadn't dawned yet.

While the rest of the world had a long lie on 1st January, Josie sat crumpled at the kitchen table and was unable to come to terms with what Dave had done regarding the leather jacket. It was confusing and hurtful. She often felt her worth diminishing and that anything she did wasn't good enough. For one brief moment she'd believed she was of value to him only to have it snatched away. She didn't want to dwell on it and spoil the festive season but the whole thing didn't seem right.

Once the rest of the house woke up, she put it to the back of her mind and focused on the roast beef and trimmings they were to have for dinner.

Chapter 18

Dave

It was a disappointment to me that Josie wasn't comfortable around animals. Ever since I had known little Ginny, she showed great affection for cats and dogs. Josie didn't know how to cope because she hadn't been brought up with pets. She told me she'd had a childhood experience where a German Shepherd had chased her when she was about seven years old; that had scarred her as far as dogs were concerned. Moira and Ed had a series of dogs and, if they didn't jump up on her, Josie could cope. Personally, I think she was attention seeking. She could have managed around animals.

After reading a newspaper ad one day, I came up with a great idea but didn't say a word to anyone. This was to be another wonderful surprise. I went over to Josie's and said if they were ready soon, we could head off to Perth. It all sounded good so, because the journey would take over an hour, Ginny and Jon picked out a couple of toys and books while Josie made sure she had a fold up shopping bag in case we visited a farm shop. I threw a couple of cushions in the back of my estate car, something that Josie commented on.

'Now, that's a good idea. If they get tired, they can doze off comfortably.'

She never asked about the rug that was tucked away in a corner. I don't think she noticed it.

It was lunch time when we stopped at a services station where there was a café/restaurant with seating inside and outside. Ginny and Jon were running back and forward to the buffet, filling their plates with whatever they wanted; chicken nuggets, chips and beans, anything but green vegetables. With beaming faces, they stuck chocolate flakes in their ice cream.

Once further into the countryside, I consulted my piece of paper with the scribbled directions. It looked to me as if we were near the place I was looking for.

'Where are we going?' Ginny asked.

'You'll see soon enough,' I told her.

I turned up a narrow side road and drove for about a mile. In the distance, I could see what looked like the start of a forest. We had barely hit that point when we came to the entrance of a double-gated, tree-lined driveway which seemed to disappear into the forest a couple of hundred yards further on. The gate was wide open, but I was unsure if this was our final destination. I took a chance. A minute later, we were confronted with a massive house surrounded by trees and bushes.

As I pulled on the handbrake, a young man appeared at the carved wooden front door that wouldn't have looked out of place in an old castle. He took a couple of steps towards us and even the way he walked told me he was full of himself. It was clear to me this guy was stinking rich. It took me all the inner strength I could muster to get out and speak to him; I wasn't completely out of my depth in this environment but it took a lot out of me. We spoke for a few minutes and it turned out I had taken the wrong turning. With much waving of arms, the young man gave me directions; I wasn't far away.

Ten minutes later, we were parked in front of what looked like a palace. Josie and the children sat memorised and didn't dare move until I told them. Once again, I got out and approached an older man sitting on a bench against the house wall. He lifted his hand in acknowledgement as I got closer.

'Am I at the right place? Huntington House?'

'Yes, you've arrived. Dave Alexander, I presume?'

His accent told me he was in a different league from me. Probably private school educated. He oozed confidence.

Seconds later, a litter of puppies came running out of a side door and into the cultivated garden which resembled a well-cared for field. Ginny and Jon screamed. I could hear them behind the closed car doors. They didn't stay shut for long. The two of them were out of the car and over to the five bearded collies in a matter of seconds. An adult dog sauntered up the garden towards us.

Josie stayed in the car even when a woman and a young boy joined our group. She'd be thinking there was no need for her to get out. This wasn't her thing, and she would be afraid of approaching not only the dog but also its puppies. Ginny knelt on the grass and let the puppies jump over her. Jon hugged as many as he could in one go. I chatted to the couple and repeated what I'd said on the phone.

The man took me to look at some paperwork. Inside, the hallway seemed to go on forever and groaned with antique furniture, sideboards, dark wooden tables and the odd well-padded carved chair. Five minutes later, I was out again. By this time, I had the papers and a packet of dog food. I walked towards the car holding a puppy with Ginny and Jon at my heels. We must have made a lovely family picture. After I had opened the boot, I asked Ginny to hold the puppy while I spread the tartan rug over the floor and pulled the two cushions into the middle. Jon was more than excited when Ginny placed the black and white bundle on the rug.

'We're getting a puppy! Look, Mum, we've got a puppy and we can take her home!' He almost screamed.

Josie was silent for a few minutes.

'What's happening?' she found her voice.

I looked at her, my eyes narrowing, and shook my head.

'What do you think is happening? You can see, can't you? I've bought them a puppy.'

Because Ginny and Jon were by then sitting in the back seat, listening, I was certain Josie wouldn't start putting up objections. Questions must have been popping into her head, but it was too late. The children were kneeling and looking into the boot, leaning over to touch the puppy. There was no way she could spoil it for them now. If I'd gone to see the dogs alone or only with Josie, she would have objected but this way the children were already involved and I was being the man of the house, the one who made decisions

The children garbled on.

'What's her name?'

'Can *we* give her a name?'

'She's so tiny.'

'She looks a bit scared.'

'I love her so much!'

'What about Tiny as a name?'

'She's not always going to be tiny.'

'Right then, names.' I needed to take control. 'What about we call her Rags? It's a great name and she'll grow up to be a scruffy-looking dog with straggly hair.'

'Oh yes. She suits Rags.'

Back at Josie's house, we tripped in. Jon held Rags while Ginny guarded the packet of food and the certificate of pedigree. The puppy had a good sniff around while I laid the tartan rug under Josie's stairs, then fashioned it into a bed. The children were fussing over the puppy, I had made them really happy.

Josie

It became clear to Josie that, despite Dave having planned to view, and most probably buy, a puppy all along, he hadn't thought through what essentials it needed. Apart from the packet of dried food the breeders had given him, there was nothing. No dish to put the food in, no bowl for water, no bed and not a single thing for the puppy to play with. Without a collar and a lead, it wouldn't be going very far.

Josie hadn't been taken into consideration. When she went upstairs to put the children to bed. Dave put his coat on and walked out without saying goodbye and without taking his puppy.

By this time, the cottage was at a stage where Dave could sleep there, but there wasn't anywhere to leave things and really no sign of a proper bedroom or kitchen. Workmen were all over the place.

All he had was a bed made up in what was eventually to be the living room. It was basically uninhabitable and nowhere ready to house a family.

The whole thing about the dog was crazy. Dave had nowhere to live and neither did the dog. The following day, Josie did her best to explain she couldn't deal with a puppy and how he had put her in a compromised situation.

'I won't be able to go out to the supermarket because I can't leave a little thing like that alone in a strange place. The children don't know how to care for an animal without adult supervision and you're going away. Why are you doing this to me? And why are you doing this to a little puppy? You can't care for it, so you need to find somebody who can.'

'Are you joking? Look at how disappointed they're going to be. You never stop being a selfish mother, do you? Don't make me question what I did. It was for them,' he shot back.

'Listen, Dave. You worry about the dog. I'll worry about the children.'

Josie was in a state of flux. She was trying to find a solution to her predicament. She didn't want to think this was a ploy to keep her tied to the house while he was away. Surely he wouldn't create havoc, then walk away? But that's exactly what he was up to, again.

The children were upset when Josie told them it would be impossible for them to keep the puppy at their house. They saw their mum couldn't handle it.

When someone came to the door, Rags rushed ahead of her, escaping down the two steps into the big, wide world. Toilet training a puppy was beyond her and, short of enticing it out of the house, none of them knew the procedures to get Rags to make use of the garden. But, providing they could still see the puppy now and again, the children accepted the situation.

Not so Dave.

He still didn't understand why he couldn't bring a puppy into a house that wasn't prepared for an animal and where the main occupier was afraid of dogs. He also expected to walk away and leave it for weeks while he was working with no thought of how it was going to be cleaned, groomed or trained. Over the coming weeks, he talked other families into taking the puppy. And so, Rags was in and out of houses with different forms of training in each one. The dog only appeared when Dave was around, but that wasn't a sustainable situation and not fair on the puppy.

Around the same time, Josie's alarm bells started ringing when the house paperwork was being prepared to be split into payments of a loan and a mortgage. Dave had told her what was happening and how much he would have to pay; it was all more than manageable as far as he was concerned. All he had to do was convince the bank manager.

Josie knew she wouldn't be able to contribute financially to the house, but she still had her dream of getting some qualifications and securing a decent job in the future. She had enrolled to start college after the summer. Her secretarial skills were excellent but, unlike the youngsters leaving school, she didn't have certificates to prove her abilities and that was becoming more important to secure a job. Given a year, she felt she would be confident enough to offer her services to an employer and help to pay some of the household bills.

Dave mentioned that he'd have to visit the bank manager the following day to thrash out what was needed.

'I was wondering,' Josie began. 'Is there any chance my name could go on the paperwork for the house, the title deeds, the mortgage and such like?'

Dave stopped what he was doing and looked her up and down, slowly, twice, with a sneer on his face.

'You?' he whispered mockingly and shook his head. 'You?'

That was the end of the conversation.

Dave

It seemed to me that this woman was out to destroy my married life which was to begin in a couple of weeks. The rule about wives being in submission to husbands applies to all females. She must have felt she was above that. No matter what I wanted to do or buy, Josie always had something to say about it. House didn't have parking, garden didn't have proper access, cars weren't big enough for a family, things for the house didn't match, the dog wasn't able to stay. The list was never ending.

She wasn't so great at what she was put on this earth to do. All I needed was a bit of support from time to time. It beggared belief that she could be so negative about the puppy. I knew she had an aversion to animals, but if she'd stuck with it, she would have got over her fear. Maybe in the long run it was for the best. Somebody would have to take it out, bathe it and groom it and no doubt that would all have fallen to me. I didn't have time for that.

I suppose the most frustrating part was when I suggested Josie wear things I liked or saw on other people. She always took that as me not liking what she wore. But it wasn't that. It was only an idea that it might look good on her.

When we were out and passed either a shop window or saw clothes on someone, often Josie would start a conversation about it.

'Now that's nice. I like that colour.'

'Nice hat she's wearing.'

Comments like that got me thinking and sometimes I bought her something that was the same colour as she'd liked. But no, that was wrong. She'd only liked it because it was a dress and it was not so nice when I got her a scarf the same shade.

Even the hat I brought in. I could see she was stifling a laugh. That wasn't fair because I didn't know hats came in different sizes. I stopped buying her things and it was her own fault. She was just ungrateful.

Chapter 19

Josie

Moira and Ed had agreed to be the witnesses at the marriage ceremony. There were no plans for a girls' night out before the big event. Josie felt Dave could have ruined it by turning up or sending some cryptic message on the night. However, Dave decided he should ask Ed out for a pint two nights before the wedding. The day after his evening with Dave, Ed spoke to Moira.

'I've got something to tell you, but you must promise you'll never tell Josie.'

'Oh, really?' Moira sat back. 'OK, I promise. This sounds exciting!'

'Well, it's anything but exciting. I'm concerned for Josie. When we went to the bar last night, Dave became a different person. He was chatting up the barmaid. She wasn't interested, but he kept on and on. He was calling her *doll* and *babe* and crap like that. He even asked her what time she finished work, you know, like an invitation to meet up later? I've never seen him like that before. Then, when she told him she wasn't interested, he started on the female next to him when her man went to the toilet. In one way, I'd like Josie to know about this, but in another way, I wonder if it was him being like "I'm getting married, but don't think I'll be trapped." Maybe something like that. I don't understand it.'

'Wow! I'd never have imagined. Wonder if he thinks being married is old hat, and he's trying to prove himself as still being a catch? Macho man. That's strange though. I'm sorry for him because I know for sure Josie would never, ever be involved in sweet-talking anyone else.'

'Remember, you promised.'

Dave and Josie tied the knot in a quaint country church and twelve-year-old Ginny and eight-year-old Jon felt special with all the attention they received on the day. Josie was happy and relaxed, hoping her life was taking a turn for the better. She wanted to make things work with Dave and enjoy the security that she felt came along with having a husband and a house. The possibility of a comfortable future was a bonus.

The ceremony was far from being a grand affair. Josie borrowed a full-length blue dress and Moira and Ginny were in reduced price bridesmaids' dresses. Jon was wearing jacket and trousers, not completely matching. Josie had done everything on a budget, but it surprised her to see Dave arrive at the church sporting a new suit. She hadn't expected him to spend money on something that he was unlikely to wear again. However, he looked the part.

One thing that had been important to Josie was to have them both repeat their marriage vows in full. It appeared fate was against her because, hours before the ceremony, she lost her voice and could only speak in a whisper. When the minister met her at the church door, he heard her struggling and presented them with shorter vows without consultation. He didn't want Josie to strain her voice more than necessary, so she agreed to become Mrs Alexander under a croaky cloud that she hadn't expected.

Because she had organised the ceremony, she suggested Dave take charge of the honeymoon. She only had one stipulation, that he planned something nearby, only a couple of hours' drive at the most. After a day of getting to the church and having a meal with close family and friends, Josie knew all she would want to do was relax in a surprise location. Ginny and Jon had been farmed out and so immediately after saying goodbye to everyone, the newly married couple headed off, not quite into the sunset.

Dave

We were about twenty miles into our journey when I mentally checked what had been packed.

'Did you bring your sports shoes, the trainers, like I told you?' I asked.

'Oh no! I forgot to pack them. Never mind, it's not that important. Or had you planned that we run a marathon?' Josie laughed.

'It's certainly not funny. I especially asked you to bring them. Now that's my plans ruined. A simple thing to pack. Do you ever listen?'

My anger was rising. Here we were, not even married five minutes and she wasn't doing what she was told.

We continued in silence which gave me a chance to thrash out the importance of a pair of trainers in my mind. All I wanted was to have a couple of games of badminton or squash. I liked the idea of looking as if I was a bit of a pro playing the kind of sports people were talking about. Going to the gym and keeping in shape was right up my street. It wasn't only about keeping fit, it was a chance for people to see me dressed in the right gear. I had wanted her to look the part too. Now that had been scuppered. I sat fuming for ages until I had a think to myself. If she needed to buy something, then so would I. Maybe I could get new trainers as well, a sports top, jogging bottoms or a pair of swimming trunks. Or maybe all the above. I calmed down at my idea of a shopping spree and focused on the road.

Passing by familiar towns and cities, we headed south, avoiding the turning to the airport. It was clear we weren't going anywhere near sea, sand and sun. By that time, we had been travelling for well over two hours but that wasn't too long in my opinion.

'Obviously I don't know what you've got planned, but if we're able to stop for a cup of tea, that would be great,' Josie suggested.

Six miles further on, I turned in at the next service station. From that she knew we weren't near our destination, otherwise I would have continued driving. We went straight to the self-service counter where Josie ordered food after she saw me asking for fish and chips. It was almost nine o'clock at night by the time we set off again.

A couple of surprises were awaiting her; where we were going and who we would be with. I continued driving until it was cracking on for ten-thirty. Thankfully, she didn't remind me of her one and only request not to be travelling for too long. By that time, five hours into our journey; we were in Wales. We turned off the main road and I consulted my map. I had to turn around twice before I was forced to ask directions from a lone couple. It took another half hour to find the place.

At a pleasant hotel, we drew up and parked. I lifted the cases out and Josie peered through the trees and the darkness, trying to figure out what was beyond. Because of the late hour, the main door was locked so I had to ring the bell at the entrance. As we approached reception, something made Josie turn around while I checked in.

A couple were sitting on a couch reading newspapers held high to obscure their faces. But Josie did a double take. Suddenly, they both lowered the papers and there were Moira and Ed. Josie was delighted to see her bosom buddy there. We had a very late drink and turned in for the night. My surprise had been a welcome one for Josie. I was good at that.

The following day at breakfast, we had a good laugh. All four of us had got lost the night before and couldn't find anyone on the streets so late on. We made tentative plans about what we would do over the weekend. I was keen to get a game of badminton in and started talking about singles and doubles. Neither Moira nor Josie were that interested in sports although they were happy to join in for the fun of it. I made several comments about Josie not having trainers but Ed pointed out he had seen some shops in the hotel foyer; beauty products and sports equipment were on sale.

'Well, I suppose we'll have to buy some since her ladyship here forgot to pack hers. Everyone else has got everything they need, except…' I nodded in Josie's direction.

'Let's go round after breakfast because we don't know what time they'll close,' Moira suggested.

In the shop, Josie said she didn't want to waste anybody's time, then went straight to the trainers to have a browse with Moira. I spied the racks of t-shirts, shorts and swim wear and quickly made my way over to them. Josie took a while but finally picked up a cheaper pair of trainers and headed to the counter. But I had got there first in the hope that I'd be served and away before she saw me buying new sports socks, designer shorts and matching t-shirt.

'Are you OK, Dave?' Ed had asked me while I was waiting to pay.

'Yes. Why? What do you think is wrong with me?'

'It's just that your hands are shaking and you look worried.'

It annoyed me that he had sensed my anxiety. Lots of thoughts were swirling in my head. To begin with, I didn't want Josie to comment on me buying stuff after going on about her forgotten trainers. Even without that, shopping wasn't a comfortable experience for me. I often went into shops knowing what I wanted, only to find out I had to make important choices without warning. Waiting in an unexpected queue hyped up my tension. Normally, I'd have my heart set on something only to find out it wasn't available. If I was told it was out of stock or not in my size, that posed another dilemma for me. Should I place an order or go to another shop? What if it was the same in the next shop? Then the pressure was on. When I had to walk away without the thing I had been dreaming of, I was so deflated I wanted to kick something or someone. Paying was another stressor. I hated parting with cash and I hated the embarrassment of being told they had refused my bank card.

I managed to get my new clothes and we had a few games of badminton together. That almost ended in disaster because we played against Moira and Ed, but Josie was far too relaxed. She and Moira weren't competitive at all.

It was a disappointing excuse for a honeymoon and after the badminton experience, the only time I left the bedroom was to go for a swim or for food. Moira and Ed took Josie for walks in the woods and into the village for coffee. That wasn't for me because there was a TV in the room.

Four days later, we said our goodbyes and headed home. I had a week before I was due back at work in Thailand, then I could leave Josie in charge of the remaining workmen and deliveries. I intended to enjoy travelling and my stay in a nice hotel en route to work.

A few days before I was to leave, I suggested we go into town because I had an appointment with the bank manager. Josie must have been surprised when she was called into the office along with me. After some small talk, the bank manager handed me a new cheque book.

'OK, so this is for you, Dave.' Then he turned to Josie. 'And this is for you.'

He passed over a second cheque book in joint names.

'If you'd like to give me a specimen of your signature here please, Josie,' he added.

And so, it came about that, within minutes, we had a joint bank account, something that Josie hadn't expected. I was becoming an expert at giving her surprises.

After a few months of me working away for six weeks at a time, Josie and the children were settling into the new house. Things were taking shape. Josie told me the workmen were finishing up and handing in their invoices while she was waiting around for deliveries and installations. When I got home, it was pleasant going to the supermarket with the children and buying treats now and again, but Josie was cautious with money. She had always watched the pennies and she told me that wouldn't change. She kept her eyes open for bargains. The difference was that she didn't always have to look at the sales racks when buying shoes and stuff for the children.

Josie had always been a saver, even if it was only spare coins, so I knew she would build up a few pounds and use it for emergencies. She wrote to me while I was away and gave me news and gossip. In one letter, she told me practically all our bills had been paid and we now had four figures in the bank. That might have pleased her, but it didn't please me. I felt we should have had more.

After that trip, I began talking about changing the car. Josie was used to this because it was something I did regularly. I looked around some salesrooms and pondered over the private ads in the paper. There was a white Jaguar for sale in the next town; I made an appointment to see it and took Josie. The minute I drove up and saw the car sitting outside a block of flats, not only did I know it was the car of my dreams, but I was sure it was also financially within my reach. We took a trial run and I was smitten. It wouldn't have been the first time Josie had seen my eyes glisten and sharpen as I surveyed a decent car. I haggled a bit with the seller.

'OK, let's do it. Nice motor. I'm happy with it and if you knock a hundred off, I'll sign a cheque right now. It'll clear within three days and I'll come back to pick the car up.' I knew I was almost drooling.

Likewise, I could see the seller was pleased to have a buyer because he agreed with the price I offered. I turned to Josie and patted my pockets.

'Oh no. I've forgotten my cheque book. Write one out for £900.'

She did, and I became the owner of a Jaguar Mark 2.

Occasionally, Josie couldn't see the point in what I was trying to do regarding changes inside the house. For example, the stairs.

Much time and effort had been spent in building an internal staircase. It was erected immediately inside the front door and had an attractive bannister leading to a landing upstairs. After a few weeks of coming and going, I suggested the staircase would be better if it was moved to the other side of the hall so that the view on opening the front door was of a spacious hallway instead of stairs. I told her it would look impressive. I was set on my idea even when Josie pointed out that, if moved, its position would force them to walk further to get up the stairs and prevent light coming into the kitchen. But, after great upheaval and along with a mate who was unemployed, the staircase was dismantled and moved.

Two weeks later, I got fed up with the master bedroom now being directly at the top of the stairs instead of at the end of a corridor, as it didn't have the same privacy it had before.

Two workmen agreed to help out.

'Why are the joiners back?' Josie asked.

'I've decided to get them to put the stair back to its original place. It's no good where it is.'

This didn't please Josie and she took great pleasure in pointing out that the new carpet had already been cut around the stairs, and the hall was, yet again, going to be in another upheaval while the men repositioned the staircase. Then it was the usual, going on about the cost and asking how would we pay the joiners. But all that was unavoidable if we were to get things back in order.

Josie

Josie gave up her council house for good, taking all her furniture and belongings to Dave's cottage, despite a nagging doubt. Sometimes she found herself welling up with tears but she didn't know why and never told anyone.

Josie had told friends not to bother with wedding presents. It wasn't as if they needed people to go out and buy things; they had enough. Some hadn't listened and ended up giving them gifts. Josie's friend Erynn came round to visit not long after the wedding.

'I've waited because I want to speak to you both about a present. I know you said not to bother, but I'd like to buy you something special and I need to talk to you together,' she explained.

Erynn had an idea to buy them a brass name plate for their front door. It was a lovely gesture.

'So, what I need to know is what you want on the nameplate. Do you want Alexander or do you want Alexander, Laburnum Cottage?'

Josie was about to say something when Dave demanded, 'I want David R Alexander, Laburnum Cottage.' He smirked.

Erynn fumbled over a few words of reply because he was making it clear it was *his* house and not the Alexander *family* house. Josie felt a wave of disappointment wash over her; she and the children weren't to feature in *his* name plate; she wasn't to feature in *his* house. She let it go and Erynn ordered the name plate of his choice.

The minute they had moved into Laburnum Cottage, Dave took to having long baths, as usual lasting an hour and a half. On the odd occasion he had taken a bath at Josie's flat but, because there was only one bathroom, he hadn't been able to stay in there long before someone needed in. Now they had an upstairs bathroom. He could indulge as long as he wanted behind a locked door. Josie didn't think it was that unusual. He had already told her he liked lying there and topping up the water as it cooled down. She remembered the incident in the bed and breakfast when he was prepared to lock her and toddler Ginny in a bedroom while he luxuriated in bubbles at his leisure. What *was* unusual was that every time Josie went to the toilet, she wasn't in there for thirty seconds until he came rattling the door handle. She couldn't get peace for a moment.

He had started to do that in her flat near Falkirk and it was a habit that had continued. It annoyed Josie. She couldn't use the toilet, have a shower or even put on some makeup before he was at the door handle. Initially, she had hurried up and opened up, but it had never been that he needed in; he only wanted to know what she was doing. His need to have access to her at every turn was suffocating.

Chapter 20

Dave

Building a home was something I tried to do in conjunction with Josie but, increasingly, she sulked when I made spontaneous decisions. Her moans became commonplace when I brought in wallpaper or ceramic tiles, ones which I thought she would like. I wanted it to be a surprise for her. One weekend, I went shopping without telling her and arrived a couple of hours later with three oversized bags from a Do-It-Yourself store and proudly emptied the contents of one bag onto the dining table.

'I'm not taken with the cork wallpaper for the kitchen. I think it's too plain for a room that size.' That was her starting.

She picked up a roll and saw there were eight more in another bag. It was dark, plain and, in her opinion, dated.

Yet another bag held accessories for the bathroom. A few months previously, I had asked Josie what she thought about a cream-coloured bath. She said that was the kind of thing that was ideal. I was delighted that she had finally agreed with me and she qualified her reasons. Go for simple colours for the fixtures then brighten the room up with coloured accessories. A cream bathroom suite had been installed. Now in front of her were different-sized towels and accessories for the shelves. Everything was in various shades of yellow.

'Was that the only colour they had? Try it against the colour of the bath and see. Maybe we can exchange them if they don't suit.' Here she was, complaining again.

'I don't care if you like them or not! I've picked them because *I* liked them. You're not taking them back. Don't you realise you're married to me now? I've told you before, that means you're in submission to me. What I want is what I get!' I stared straight into her eyes.

Once I emptied the bag with the bright yellow accessories, Josie saw I had bought a single toothbrush; it was still in its packet. I took everything through to the bathroom and found a place for them. She said the things weren't the best quality, so it wouldn't be long before they became stained or broken.

The following week, Josie came in from the chemist's shop and I spied three toothbrushes in one packet.

'What's this?' I demanded, holding the packet as if it was contagious.

'Toothbrushes!'

'So, what you're saying is you bought toothbrushes for you three but didn't buy one for me?' I was offended.

'Well, yes. But you don't need one because didn't you just buy one for yourself last week?'

To be honest, I had forgotten all about that and I didn't feel like answering her.

It was about this time that I became frustrated with not having my own private parking area. Depending on when I arrived at the cottage, I often struggled to find an empty space. The front area was out of the question. The garage and the spare ground belonged to Mr Berwick's flat. If his car wasn't around, I didn't see the problem in me parking there. But he was mad when he came home from work to find my car in his spot. He came up to the cottage and asked me if it was my car parked at the front and, if so, it had to be moved.

I was more than slighted. I felt I was entitled to park wherever I wanted; after all, I had communal access across his land. Berwick was being smart when he told me that was only walking access. This created ongoing bad feelings between the two of us and parking became a major issue for me. I continued to park my car there, saying it was only for a few minutes. To preserve his space, Berwick took to leaving his car out rather than putting it in his garage. He was laying claim to his piece of ground. That was the beginning of the end of the cottage for me. I began to speak about moving. We hadn't been in the house for a year and I had lost interest all because of Berwick being childishly territorial about his land.

Josie

While Dave had been working away for a few weeks, Josie was surprised to get a call from the people who had taken Rags months before. They asked her to come and collect the dog because she wasn't blending in with the other pets the folk had already. The children were over the moon but, as Josie had to explain again, this would only be temporary because a new home would have to be found. Ginny and Jon said they'd take her for walks and do the doggie things until Dave came home. They kept their promises and took her to the local park to run around. Josie felt the strain though because the children had to go to school and at the end of the day, they had friends they wanted to go out with. Josie was left with the dog because Dave was working away. She was glad she had told the children this was only a short-term arrangement, despite Ginny doing her best and taking Rags to dog training classes.

Dave arrived back and Rags was all over him. He thought it would be possible to keep her because she was now house trained. Also, he pointed out the children were older and could be more responsible for the dog when he was away. Josie waited a couple of weeks to see what transpired. As she predicted, it didn't work. The dog needed to go out last thing at night, but Dave tried to get out of taking her. Much earlier than normal, he would appear at the top of the stairs, ready for bed. The message was simple. He wasn't taking the dog out; he'd *forgotten*.

Josie put her foot down; she told Dave he had to find another home for Rags. But, while they were waiting for an answer from a couple, Rags came into heat. While the children were at school one afternoon, Dave, once again, couldn't be bothered to take the dog out. Josie couldn't handle her, especially when other dogs came over to have a sniff around. Dave had put her in the back garden and she jumped over the wall. It had been the first time she'd been so brave, so it surprised them both. But she finally made it home half an hour later and came in wagging her tail as though she'd been for a little stroll.

Dave went manic.

'If there are any puppies, there'll be hell to pay,' he screamed at the top of his voice, pointing his finger at Josie.

He ordered the dog into her makeshift bed in the hall and, with an almighty kick, he booted Rags in the belly. The dog whined, but Dave didn't stop. He kept kicking.

'No! No! No! Stop it! Stop it!' Josie cried and screamed as she stood halfway up the stairs. 'Leave the dog! Stop it! It's not the dog's fault! Stop it!'

He stopped but, like Josie, the dog was a trembling wreck. Josie mustered up all her will power and moved towards the dog that was looking up with huge, sad eyes and giving a feeble wag of her tail. Even though she was scared to death, Josie was determined to stroke Rag's head.

'Don't you *dare* go near it or you'll get the same!' Dave growled.

It dawned on Josie that he had addressed Rags as *it*. She was no longer an animal with feelings and he didn't care if he had injured her, possibly permanently. The dog wasn't allowed to move for almost two hours until the children came home from school. As soon as Dave was out of the house, Josie contacted the Guide Dogs for the Blind Association to see if they would take Rags. She was collected a few days later while Dave was in the bath. Josie braced herself for repercussions, but none came. The dog had fallen out of favour so Dave had no emotion but anger towards Rags. She was much safer out of the house.

The organisation was to train her to be the eyes for a blind person and the children were happy that she was going to be loved elsewhere. However, a call came in from the centre a few weeks later. They had news of Rags. She had failed her training; she was too nervous, so they had to reject her. Josie took the children to the centre to collect her but the trainer who handed her over, looked at Josie and scowled. The woman couldn't speak, and her face was getting redder by the minute. It was while she was driving home that Josie realised the woman would have picked up that Rags had been abused. The staff might have thought by Josie.

Iona and Jimmy loved animals and said they would be happy to have Rags. Dave came home the following week and offered the dog to Jimmy if he would build a wall in the back garden. Even though Josie couldn't cope with animals, she was heart-broken knowing that here was an innocent dog, a whim of Dave's, being passed around from pillar to post instead of having a stable home from day one.

One thing that Josie knew from old was that Dave never used the words *please, sorry,* or *goodbye.* He would use *thank you* now and again, but for that, he used a put-on squeaky voice, normal polite exchanges were alien to him. When he answered the telephone, it was always with an abrupt *hello*. He never said it in a welcoming manner and never gave the telephone number on answering, as was commonplace then. But that was his way and people were used to *right* or *OK* when he bumped into them or walked into their houses. Although Josie felt she could teach him some social etiquette, after trying a couple of times and listening to the condescending retorts and smart remarks that followed, it wasn't worth the bother.

Dave

We had some enjoyable times together, sitting round the fire having a chat, but after half an hour, I usually sent the children upstairs to do their own thing. They were fine with that until Josie started making noises about the way I was treating them.

One Saturday morning, I came down to find Ginny watching TV. She was still in her nightdress and watching teens' stuff.

I needed a newspaper to read with my cup of tea so I got some change.

'Right Ginny. Here's money. I want you to go to the shop and get me a paper,' I told her.

'Awe no! This finishes in five minutes. Can I go then?' she pleaded.

'I'm telling you to go now.'

She got dressed, then, reluctantly, went for my paper.

'Is the paper so important that she couldn't have had a few minutes more to watch the end of the program?' Josie asked.

'Look, I pay for all this,' I swept my arm around the room to remind her I was the financial provider. 'Is it too much to ask her to get me a paper?'

She said that wasn't the point; it was the immediacy of it that wasn't necessary. The paper shop was only minutes away. She even suggested she could have gone if I was so desperate. I wanted them all to obey me and I didn't see the problem. But Josie never let up.

Once a year, fairground attractions came to town for a week. Thirteen-year-old Ginny counted out her pocket money and asked if she could go with her best friend, Arlene. That wasn't a problem. Ginny didn't have much money and, what I didn't know at the time, she had mentioned to Josie that if she had fifty pence more, she could have three rides.

Seems Josie had suggested she ask me because, as she explained later, she was hoping to see me do something *fatherly* for Ginny.

Ginny's face had been tripping her when she went back in to tell her side of the story to Josie. She'd said I wouldn't give her the fifty pence because she hadn't asked for it properly, which was true. She wasn't at all polite to me.

'Where is she?' I asked, appearing a couple of minutes later.

'Ginny? She's gone to the fair with Arlene. Why?' Josie had said.

'Oh, she's gone? She asked me for fifty pence, and I was going to give it to her.'

'Too late.' Josie smiled. 'What happened?'

'She came out and said, "Can I have fifty pence to go to the fair with Arlene?" I told her she could have it if she asked for it properly.'

'What did you mean?' Josie asked.

'Well, she never said *please* after she asked me.'

'Do you always say *please*? You're not exactly the best role model. She's not saying please because she doesn't hear you saying please, so she likely thinks that's the way to ask for things.'

That put me in a right bad mood. How dare she try to put me down?

But she kept on about how I dealt with the kids and reminded me of a time when I was so careful about letting Jon go out. She said I had been treating him like a baby. She was wrong. I only wanted to make sure he was safe.

The story was Jon had spoken about going to his friend's house and Josie said of course he could go. She helped him to find the toys he wanted to take, but he was only nine years old so I asked what was going on, her letting him go out on his own.

'I'm going to Simon's because I want to play outside with him and my cars,' Jon explained.

I sat down and got him to stand in front of me so that I had his attention.

'Right, make sure you walk straight up the road. Don't go through the park,' I told him.

Jon nodded and went to move away, but I pulled him back.

'Listen to me. When you get to the main road, you've got to cross at the lights,' I went on.

Again, Jon nodded, then said, 'OK.'

I pulled him back once more. 'And the minute you get to Simon's, tell Erynn you've to use the phone to call us and report in.'

Jon stood for a second or two more, waiting. His shoulders dropped and his face fell but I knew he had heard my instructions.

'When you go outside to play, you've to stay right next to his house. Don't go to the park.'

Jon laid his cars on a nearby table and almost stood at attention while I continued.

'When you want to come home, you've to call us again to say you're leaving.'

It was then Josie walked into the room, but she must have heard all that I had said.

'And tell Erynn that you've got to be home by five o'clock, so she can shout on you when it's time.' I finished.

Then Jon walked towards Josie, leaving his cars on the table. He looked at the floor.

'I've decided I'm not going to Simon's.'

I had no idea what had changed his mind.

'I'll walk to the end of the road with you if you want,' Josie had suggested, but he refused. It looked like his day was spoiled but he could still have gone and had fun with his friend. I wasn't stopping him from doing that.

Chapter 21

Josie

It wasn't surprising that Josie had grown used to the comments Dave continuously repeated to demean her. That didn't mean she was any less hurt, but she had stopped showing her feelings. They became buried deep inside. That wasn't always what Dave wanted, though; he needed to see her squirm now and again. Using the children was certainly one way of destroying her happiness. When he put Josie down with his comments and Ginny or Jon were in the vicinity, he involved them in the conversation.

'Look at your mother's shoes. Would you not think she was going to play football in these?' He pointed and wiggled his forefinger.

The children smiled and looked at Josie's face to see if she was taking it as a joke. He would persist until he got the answer he wanted from them or saw them laughing.

One Sunday lunchtime, Josie pulled out the leaves to extend the table in the living room and set four places. The roast chicken would be ready in half an hour, and the potatoes could go on in ten minutes. There was nothing more to do in the kitchen, so, still wearing her apron, she poured a glass of wine and sat on the rocking chair in the hall. The children asked about food. It wouldn't be long. Josie watched Jon happily lining up his cars under the hall radiator. Dave appeared from whatever he had been doing, hovered around for a few seconds, then glowered at her.

'Look at you. You tell me you're busy, that you've always got something to do in the house and here you are, doing nothing but sitting with a wine glass in your hand.'

It was clear by her apron and the smell of food that something was happening in the kitchen, and it wasn't him who was making dinner. Josie couldn't understand what was going on in his head, but he cut her ten minutes of relaxation short. She stood up and went back to where he felt she now belonged, at the kitchen sink.

Once they sat down to eat, Ginny realised she didn't have a knife.

'Oh sorry, Ginny, I thought I had put everything out. Wait a minute,' Josie said as she pushed her chair back to get up.

'It's OK, Mum, I'll go,' Ginny offered and was back in an instant.

They spoke about different things during dinner.

'I can't wait for my birthday,' Jon announced.

He talked about the latest Star Wars figures and dropped heavy hints about which one he preferred.

'Oh well, that's good to know,' Josie said. 'What about you, Ginny? Any idea about what you'd like for your birthday?'

'I think some music tapes.'

'And what about your *mother*? What should she get for *her* birthday?' Dave sneered at no one in particular.

It wasn't anywhere near Josie's birthday. She wondered why he had brought that up. The conversation had been about the children, but now it had turned to her.

'I don't know. What would you like, Mum?' Jon piped up.

Before Josie could say anything, Dave had commandeered the conversation.

'What about a haircut? She needs that for sure. Maybe even a face lift!' He laughed and pointed at Josie with his fork. 'Look at her, look at the state of your *mother*! Sitting there like Lady Muck and looks like someone has dragged her through a hedge backwards. She doesn't even try to look decent these days.'

The children looked at Josie and laughed as she smoothed her hair.

'She's fat too, isn't she?' Dave continued. 'That'll be her new name, Fatty.'

He pointed at her, this time with his knife.

'Fatty, who can't set a table.'

Josie was a size twelve and at five feet three inches, she was anything but fat. Her hair was shorter than before, but her curls still sat on her shoulders. Not even in her mid-thirties, there wasn't a wrinkle in sight. It wasn't Josie's body that was heavy; it was her heart.

While the children were laughing, Josie was aware of them glancing between her and Dave. They knew, especially Ginny, he was roping them into being on his side; but they didn't have the skills to deal with the manipulation. Neither did Josie. He was doing his best to isolate her and use the children to gang up on her.

The threat of violence hung in the air every day. Josie automatically winced when Dave came within striking distance, especially if he moved his arm quickly. And, completely out of the blue, he continued to say things and make comments about Josie that were unnecessary. Demeaning her was his game.

One night, she deliberately left the bathroom door open slightly while brushing her teeth. It was her way of stopping him from rattling on the handle. He put his head around the door and looked at her reflection in the mirror. In two strides, he was by her side and lifted his hand to her face. She flinched and let the toothbrush fall into the sink. He guffawed.

'What are you doing? I only want to show you something,' he whispered.

His action wasn't to be a slap or a stroke of her cheek; it was to stretch the skin at the corner of one eye with his thumb and forefinger.

'My goodness. You'd look so much different without wrinkles!'

Josie's body practically went limp with relief. He hadn't done any more than hurt her feelings.

The cottage was on a hill and faced down towards the main road. Dave found it convenient that there was a bar on the corner, visible from the front of the house.

He did very little to help at mealtimes and often went to have a pint while Josie made dinner. One afternoon, he left her with a verbal list of instructions.

Call to order two bags of cement

Open the doors of the stove in fifteen minutes when the logs are lit.

Put a box of soap powder in the window when dinner is five minutes from being served

He could see the kitchen window from the bar and would have time to finish his drink before leaving when he saw the box.

It was becoming obvious to Josie that something as simple as not carrying out his instructions could lead to an argument, threats and even punishment. So, that evening, once she had put the lasagne in the oven and prepared the salad, she called the building supplies company for cement. She was on the phone longer than expected and, by that time, the fire had been going for over twenty minutes. When she bent down to open the stove doors, the intense heat made her draw back. Through the glass on the cast iron doors, she saw the logs burning too fiercely. There was no way she could touch the red-hot handles.

Josie took the oven gloves and tried again, but the handles were stiff. It was an impossible task. The flames would burn the logs to cinders, and that would cause an argument. Her fault, of course.

She paced the floor, not knowing what to do. Then she remembered the lasagne had been in the oven too long. Panic. She took the food out and put the salad on the table, then tried the fire doors again. They were stubborn and immovable.

Suddenly, the packet of soap powder sprung into her mind. Dinner was ready, and she was supposed to warn Dave five minutes beforehand. Everything was going wrong.

With the packet now in place, the lasagne and salad on the table and the fire burning like a furnace, Josie shook and her stomach churned.

She called on the children and they waited for Dave. Josie was wringing her hands when she heard the front door open. Now was the moment of truth.

'I couldn't open the doors. It was too hot,' she blurted out, pointing to the stove.

'Oh, that's OK. I'll see if I can do it. It's not the best design.' He opened it on his first try.

Standing with her eyes wide open and her bottom lip trembling, Josie wondered at his understanding manner and asked herself why she had been so worried. Something dangerous was happening to her; she was now terrified of his reaction to anything. If things didn't go well, she might have to suffer. The waiting was just as torturous as the punishment.

Her relief was short-lived when, once dinner was over, Dave began again with his snide remarks.

'So, what can we say about that?' He nodded towards his empty plate.

Nobody answered.

'Think your *mother* should go to cookery classes!'

The following evening, Josie made dinner. She set the table for four and called to them, saying their food was ready. As they took their places, Josie lifted her cutlery and looked at Dave.

'I hope you enjoy your meal. I'm not joining you because I'm going to eat in the kitchen. I'll come back to this table when you at least try polite conversation and drop the name-calling.'

She turned on her heel and left them with their mouths hanging open. She enjoyed her food, and they ate in silence.

The next evening, Dave came up behind her as she was cooking.

'Are you joining us tonight?' he whispered.

'Are you going to stop insulting me?' She kept her eyes on the cooker.

'I didn't realise you were so sensitive. OK, I get the message. But I was only joking.'

Dave

I got fed up with making humorous remarks about Josie. There was nothing wrong with her teeth, but once she had a crown put in, I started to call her Fang. Nobody could see the funny side of it, so I curtailed my comments over the next few meals and turned my attention to Ginny.

I had noticed that Josie encouraged the children to show affection. I hadn't been used to that as a young boy, but it looked good, especially in front of other people. A small peck on the cheek at bedtime was a comforting gesture, and Josie had kept it up since they were babies. Once I got to know Ginny, and if I was around at her bedtime, she included me in a goodnight kiss.

One evening at the dinner table, Ginny dropped food on the floor. She had said she didn't like the carrots, and it wasn't clear whether the pile of orange under her feet was a deliberate act or an accident. But that wasn't important. She needed a good scolding, but Josie said nothing more than, 'Well, pick them up then.'

At bedtime, Ginny and Jon went over to Josie for a final chat and a goodnight kiss. Then they moved towards me, lying on the couch. I let Jon come close to peck my cheek, but when Ginny approached, I turned my head to the side.

'No. You're not getting a kiss. You made a mess at the table. No. That's it. No kisses tonight.'

Ginny lowered her outstretched arms. She looked confused and later on Josie just had to mention it.

'Who does that? Who turns away from a young girl who wants a dad?' She had missed the point completely. It wasn't anything to do with not wanting to be her dad, it was about punishment for making a mess.

I tried to make amends when Josie bought Ginny a new pair of shoes. She held out a pair of school shoes and told me her feet had grown.

'Oh well, you'll be known as Flipper from now on,' I joked.

When Jon tripped over her outstretched feet that evening, I saw my moment to refer to her with her new name.

'Right, Flipper, get your feet out of the way.'

Josie stared at me.

'And what have you got to say about things, Fang?'

They just didn't have a sense of humour. I mean, I was trying to give them a pet name. Lots of people do that.

There were other things that I felt Josie was far too lenient about. By the time Ginny had been in secondary school for over a year, she had got to know students within a twenty-mile radius. I didn't know them all but I heard lots of names being bandied about. One day, she came home from school gabbling with excitement.

'Guess what? One of the girls is having a party on Friday. Can I go, Mum?' Ginny didn't ask *me* so I wasn't being given my place. Josie answered her.

'Yes, of course, that'll be fun. Who's all going?'

Ginny rhymed off a few names. Josie said she knew most of them and their parents, but I didn't. Then Ginny told her the party was in Newport, a small-town miles away. I sat quietly, pretending to read a magazine.

'I can go home with Jenny and her mum straight after school on Friday and we'll be staying at Jenny's after the party. The only thing is, how will I get back here on Saturday?'

'Don't worry,' Josie answered. 'We'll sort something out. I'm sure we can have a day out over in that direction. If not, we'll find out about trains.'

I looked up to see Josie smiling at her.

'What's going on? What's all this about?' I had heard everything but I acted dumb.

Ginny outlined the plan again.

'No way. You are *not* going to a party miles away then staying out all night.' I was forceful.

'But I know these kids,' Josie told me. 'They've been here before, and I've spoken to their parents. What's the problem? We can take her and pick her up later on Friday if you'd rather she didn't stay at Jenny's until Saturday.'

'Nope. She's not going. I'm not driving all that way on a Friday night or a Saturday morning.'

Ginny walked away, obviously in tears and not looking forward to telling her friends she wouldn't be going to the party. I had to control her movements and let her know who was the boss.

I didn't completely forget to use short remarks to remind Josie of how easy it was to lose her looks.

I'll get you a cup of tea, you don't look well or *Not that I'm criticising but are you really going to eat all that?* or *That's a nice dress. Didn't think you'd be brave enough to wear that colour.*

I did this to show her I could look after her and give her compliments, but I didn't want her to become too full of herself.

The best place to keep control and show she belonged to me was in public. In the supermarket was best and especially when we were waiting in the checkout queue, I would fold my arms and lay all my weight on her shoulder.

It was a protective gesture, a signal that she was mine to do what I liked with, sending a message that she wasn't moving unless I allowed it. I wasn't pushing her the way she implied.

An even better tactic to make me feel good was to creep up behind her in shops and wrap my arms around her waist. Then I squeezed her as tight as I could. It wasn't supposed to be a loving gesture, it was a bit of a joke listening to her struggling to breathe. It probably looked to other customers that I was hugging her and whispering in her ear. I didn't care that it annoyed Josie. I thought it was funny when she was gasping.

'What are you doing? You've hurt me. Leave me alone!'

Her natural reaction was to push me away. First of all, I would laugh then stand back like a wounded animal while folk looked at Josie as though she were a cold, cruel woman.

But I kept my physical strength hidden when there were family or visitors around. I had other ways of showing I was He-Man.

Like the time when Bill and Margo appeared on a surprise visit one Friday afternoon with their two children. After an hour, I suggested we men go for a pint.

'No, we can't. I've got to get down the road. It's Friday night and I'm meeting a few guys later,' Bill announced.

That was something I didn't want to hear so I let the words go over my head.

'Oh, forget that. We'll have a couple across the road.'

I walked out of the room to get my shoes from the cupboard but I could hear Margo explaining to Josie that they needed to leave soon because they were facing a two-hour car journey.

'That's OK. I understand,' Josie said. 'You'll be down the road before it gets dark. It's a long drive with a couple of kids.'

Margo obviously agreed and they began to make other plans.

'Yes. Look, why don't we organise for you all to come down and stay over? We can go to the new Chinese restaurant Bill was talking about. It's fantastic.'

At that, I appeared from my eavesdropping place, holding my shoes.

'Are you going out?' Josie asked me.

'Bill and me, we're going for a pint!'

Bill gave a short laugh and said again that they would be leaving soon; there wasn't time for a drink.

Josie shook her head.

'Why are you doing this? Bill has told you he doesn't want to go.'

I couldn't believe she was encouraging them to leave and spoiling my plans.

I was furious. There was no way I was letting her ruin my night. I was going out no matter what, and I wasn't going to back down in front of Bill.

We all left together. Bill, Margo and their family heading home and me heading out.

Sitting in the bar alone put me in an even fouler mood because I didn't know any of the folk who were in, it was too early for the regulars so Josie would have to learn not to interfere in the future.

Chapter 22

Josie

Josie began to see how sly and cunning Dave could be when it came to money and other people's property. She also reflected on what he and others had told her about his life before she met him. From simple misdemeanours to being involved in a darker, vicious side of life.

At the cottage and when Dave wasn't working away, he would hang around the house in the morning, have a bite to eat at lunchtime then suggest heading out somewhere. The problem was that Jon was home first from school just after three o'clock which meant Josie couldn't go with Dave otherwise they had to rush home in time for school closing.

Winter was approaching, and Dave wanted to invest in a wood-burning stove for the kitchen/dining area. It sounded like a good idea, so they set off to look around heating showrooms. Jon had started going to school lunches which gave Dave and Josie the freedom to plan more or less a whole day out. By the time they left, it was touch and go whether they would have time to visit a few showrooms. After Dave had spoken to the salesman in one supplier for almost half an hour, Josie reminded him they'd need to leave within the next ten minutes.

'OK, let's go for the red one,' he burst out to the salesman without consulting Josie.

'I'll get the payment through and take your address for delivery,' the salesman said as he made his way towards his desk and filled out a form.

He handed it to Dave for signature.

'Right, pay the man.' Dave looked at Josie and nodded towards the salesman. 'I've forgotten my cheque book.'

Josie wrote out a cheque for over £300 for the stove, delivery, and a yearly maintenance fee.

Josie scratched her head. Within a short space of time, between the Jaguar Mark 2 and a stove, she had written cheques for over £1,000. Something wasn't right, but it was there in black and white. Her signature was on the cheques and their bank account was rock bottom. The penny dropped when she found the same thing happening again.

A couple of weeks later, they headed out to a garden centre. The plan was to have a coffee and look at garden statues and fountains. As they drew up, Dave felt around in his pockets.

'Oh no!' he said. 'I've forgotten my cheque book.'

She briefly rummaged through her handbag. 'Isn't that funny? So have I!'

He laughed. The game was up, and she was onto him. He had been making sure he could explain his innocence if the bank manager questioned him. He wasn't signing for things. *She* was.

It wasn't just money he was cunning with. Josie thought back to when Danny had come to visit with his girlfriend.

Dave was out getting petrol and Josie had put on a tape, humming to the music when the doorbell rang.

'Hi Danny. Hi Melissa. Lovely to see you again. He'll be back soon.'

They sat in the kitchen/dining area, waiting for the kettle to boil.

'I'm just listening to that music. Is it the radio?' Danny asked.

'No, it's a tape.'

'Can I see it?'

Josie stopped the tape machine and let Danny examine the handwriting on the label. He handed it back to her and shook his head.

'That's mine. I copied that tape. Dave must have taken it out of my car the last time he was down.'

'You are joking!' Josie was practically speechless.

'Funny, I wondered where it had gone.'

He didn't have to wonder anymore. Josie put it in its plastic case and handed it to him. She waved her arm as if to say get it into your pocket now, then she put on another tape. She never mentioned it to Dave and he appeared not to notice it was gone.

His manipulation also extended to what questions she could and couldn't ask. After a weekend away, Dave came home with a white, electric, digital clock. It was a trendy piece of equipment, not in a box but wrapped in tissue paper. It was about six inches long and four inches deep, a neat little item.

'Thought you might like this. Just take it and don't ask questions.' He gave a quick nod of his head.

Naïvely, Josie thought he must have got a bargain, maybe from a shop display or it was a very good second-hand model. The digits were large and there were no difficult settings. It told the time and had an alarm, all very simple, so Josie plugged the clock in. It fitted perfectly in the bedroom and sat at her side of the bed. A few weeks later, Dave came downstairs one afternoon with the clock in his hand.

'I want you to get this out of the house. I don't care what you do with it, give it away to someone, but it's got to be out of here. Give it to your sister if you like.'

There was no explanation, and Josie knew he wouldn't answer her questions. She gave the clock to Iona, revealing no real reason for its exodus from Laburnum Cottage. Josie guessed what had happened. He had been in someone's house, noticed the clock and pocketed it. And there could only be one reason he wanted rid of it as quickly as possible. Whoever it belonged to had made noises about coming to visit Laburnum Cottage. But no one came and there was never a hint about who originally owned the clock.

Who was this man she had married? For sure taking a tape or a clock wasn't a criminal offence, but it wasn't right to steal from friends. This led to her thinking about other things he had told her he had done to either get what he wanted or avoid what he didn't want.

The history of this, according to Dave, started at the end of primary school. He reckoned his intelligence was far superior to that of his classmates. That was the time of junior and senior secondary schools and a class test in the last year of primary, the eleven plus, allocated pupils according to their ability. Dave reckoned his friends had no chance of passing sufficiently to get into senior secondary, but he did. Once there, pupils were expected to gain high-level qualifications and follow a career path once they left school. Junior school pupils were steered down a more practical route with mechanical and technical courses. Dave wanted to be with his friends and so deliberately flunked the test. When he told Josie, she had at least one question.

'So, where are all these special friends now?'

She wouldn't have been surprised if he'd failed the eleven plus, but made out it was a deliberate act to save face.

He also told her of times at work when he was prepared to create mayhem to avoid things he didn't want to do. Despite Josie never seeing any paperwork to prove Dave's qualifications, he made out he was proud of them, and, given that he boasted about his achievements, it surprised her he never waved any certificates in front of her face. She had read him as that kind of man. This left her thinking maybe he wasn't the clever mechanic he purported to be. Another story caused her to doubt his abilities.

In one of the first jobs he secured with a petroleum company, his boss gave him a task. It was to take him a couple of days but Dave wasn't pleased to be given what was a menial job in his eyes. In the changing area, he noticed a few guys from the labs had left masks and caps lying around, so he picked up a set and stuffed them in his pocket. He waited until lunch time when there would only be a skeleton staff in the whole plant and made his way to one of the chemical labs, a place that was out of bounds for him without a special pass. That didn't bother Dave. Wearing the mask and cap, he went upstairs, getting entry to the restricted area as one of the technicians walked out.

He lied and told the chemist his boss had asked him to collect a bottle of acid. The man handed over the bottle. Dave signed for it, but his signature was such a scribble they would never have known who it belonged to. Neither would they have recognised him under the cap and mask. Back in his work area, he opened the bottle and poured it over his left hand. It didn't take long for the skin to blister and for Dave to call someone to help. He said he had found the bottle and wondered who had left it there. Explaining that as he opened it to see what it was, the bottle had slipped from his hand. He tried to catch it, but the liquid had splashed on his hand.

Someone took Dave to the medical room for treatment, but the nurse felt it was better to get him to a hospital. He was off work for over two weeks and never had to do the job his boss asked of him. There was something about his story that made Josie wonder if he would have been able to do the job in the first place. It seemed a dangerous ploy to avoid work and could have resulted in permanent damage. But that was Dave's story, and he stuck to it.

Another avoidance tactic was not getting to the workplace on time. When he was working away either offshore or in Thailand, it was extremely important that he caught the flight. Otherwise, the knock-on effects for his travel arrangements were up in the air. The small Dundee airport was a twenty-five-minute drive from the cottage and he had plenty of notice about the time of departure. After the first couple of trips, he left his packing until the morning of the flight. No longer was there motivation to get going. Then he started doing some unnecessary jobs around the house a few hours before he was due to check-in. It was when he said he was going out for the morning that Josie wondered if he was doing everything possible to avoid getting to the airport on time. Finally, it happened. She travelled with him to Dundee to bring the car back only to find out that his flight was taxiing and he had missed it. He would never catch the connecting flight so there was no alternative but to turn around and go back home.

All in all, he missed almost a week at work and didn't like the ticking off he got from his boss. He left that job.

Josie recalled years before Jon was born, Dave took them to the south of England in the car. It was a long journey so a couple of times they stayed at bed and breakfasts. En route, they tended to travel on B roads to see the scenery and stop at out-of-the-way cafés. On a winding country road, Dave was forced to hit the brakes because a Land Rover, complete with a horse box, pulled out from a side road. The driver didn't even slow down and ploughed into the side of Dave's car. No one was hurt but the nearside of the car was badly damaged. The driver admitted he was responsible, gave his insurance details and, because both vehicles were driveable, they set off without the need to call the police.

Once home, Dave finally admitted his car insurance had run out and so he wasn't covered. He was sure there was going to be a report by the other driver whose insurance company might dispute who was to blame. He dug out an old cover note and spent ages trying to obliterate the original date and carefully wrote in a new one. It looked like at the time of the accident he was covered.

Dave had to report to the local police station with his driving licence and car documentation within seven days and boldly made his way there. He came back with the story that the policeman on duty was a young guy so all the time he was taking note of the details, Dave kept talking to him and successfully managed to distract him. He never examined the cover note for any discrepancies. Dave didn't make a claim against the other driver who must have wondered what had become of the private car he had damaged. His no claims bonus would remain intact.

But there were other, more disturbing stories that came out either through Dave or inadvertently through his few friends. Josie didn't want to believe she might be living with a dangerous man, one who could extend his cruelty to more than bullying a woman, beating a helpless man or kicking a dog.

Dave and another man, Steve, who lived in the next town, eventually worked together. There was a promoted post up for grabs and both said they were in with a chance. But Dave was nervous before the interview. Josie could tell he wasn't as confident as he made out to others. One evening, he left with his overnight bag without saying where he was going. Josie and the children went to visit Iona and spent the night there.

On their return the next morning, Josie was surprised not only to see Dave back but also that he had lit the stove in the kitchen. It was the middle of July and there was no need to fire up the radiators. A small pile of clothes sat at the side of the fire and as they walked in, Dave opened the top of the stove and stuffed the clothes in.

'Why are you doing that? Is that not the jumper your mum bought you for Christmas?'

'It doesn't fit me and I can't stand clothes with emblems on them. I don't see why I should advertise for companies.'

'But you could have given the things to a charity shop. Was that a pair of jeans as well?'

Dave scowled and told her to mind her own business. She did. He didn't want the clothes, and that was that.

Steve never applied for the job, and Dave was successful because he was the only candidate. In fact, he didn't mention Steve again other than to say that he'd spent a short while in hospital after receiving an unexplained head injury. The man never returned to work. Something irked Josie about that situation.

Dave

Back in the days before I ever met Josie, I was eager to help those who were building or renovating old properties. It was an opportunity for me to get to know people who had workshops and tools for me to borrow and to learn the tricks of the trade. I wasn't sure if I had made a mistake in telling Josie the story of Louis. We were doing a job on a garage roof. Mick had employed four of us and within two days, it was clear that I clashed with Louis.

A few coarse remarks were passed between us, and one lad, Danny, said he'd never seen me so agitated. At one point, we were up on roof beams, moving stones and broken metal, while Louis and Gaz worked on the ground. Danny heard the crash. I looked down to see a cloud of dust amid yells. A massive boulder had fallen from the area where I was and somehow caught Louis on the side of his leg and above his knee. Gaz had jumped out of the way and was dusting himself off when Danny looked down.

Louis was yelling something about getting help when Gaz shouted up at me.

'What the hell are you doing? Are you stupid? You're supposed to be thinking about safety.'

'What?' I laughed. 'It never touched *you*. It must have been teetering on the edge.'

'No, but it's hit him. You're a pillock.'

'He's already seriously mentally damaged, mate. Don't think this is the job for him. Tell him to go off home like a good wee boy and cry to his mammy.'

Louis was lying screaming by this time, and before long I saw Mick come running out of his office to see what the problem was.

Apparently, the men were convinced the boulder had been secure and Gaz was looking at me, saying that it had injured Louis and I was the only one within striking distance.

Louis went home, badly shaken. He gave up that job and me and the other two finished up, one man down. I didn't tell any of them that I had bumped into the boulder with a lever. It was an accident. I could have shouted out, but I didn't see why I should warn a guy that was making my life miserable.

Josie

Of the many tales Josie heard about Dave's previous life, there was one that she never mentioned to anyone. She hoped John, his friend from years ago, was exaggerating, although there was no reason for her to think that was the case. Josie had only met John twice but he arrived unexpectedly two days after Dave had left on a trip and they got talking over a cup of tea. She never knew why he started to chat about life when they were young, but she listened intently.

John and Dave had been part of a group of five young men who hung about together. They had each other's backs. It was the days of men being tough and alcohol fuelling fights in bars, normally over girls.

John had been in a bar in another town with his cousin when a young man mouthed off at him. Territory was important and the man didn't take kindly to a couple of well-built, imposing strangers, waltzing in as though they owned the place. Unnecessary comments flew back and forth until the man picked up a pint glass, smashed it on the bar and stuck it into John's chin and face. He immediately went to have it stitched. True, he had a scar to prove it and since then, had grown a full beard to cover as much of the disfiguration as he could.

When he came back from his cousin's house, he relayed the story to Dave and the other three guys in the group. The five of them came up with a plan to get back at the man. They didn't want to visit his local; he likely had a lot of support from his cronies there. It was agreed that somehow, they would find out where he lived and pay him a visit.

It was almost three months later when Charlie, one of the five, and Dave announced their surveillance had paid off. They had found out the man's address.

One morning, four of the five set off to find him and get revenge. After parking their car out of sight, they approached the back stairwell of the building like police officers, silent and synchronised and only using hand signals. Each had been told which part of the young man's body they were to attack. With no weapons, nothing would identify them. The plan was to stand out of sight while John rang the bell. He knew who he was looking for. The signal to attack came when the man opened the door.

What John hadn't bargained for was the man had answered the door while holding a baby of about six months. Hugging the child to his chest, everything happened in a flash. The man couldn't drop the baby or do anything to protect himself and his child while John and three others pummelled into him up against the wall with complete disregard for the helpless baby that he continued to hold. When the man fell to the ground, they each gave him a couple of hard kicks where it would do the most damage,

John said that a woman was screaming in the background.

'The baby! The baby! The baby!'

It was all over in a matter of a minute. The man lay on the floor, bent over in a foetal position, moaning and bleeding from the blows John had rained down on his face. The baby rolled out of his arms, no longer crying but whimpering, while the baby's mother continued a primal scream of indecipherable words.

John gave the signal to stop. He was the only one who took a split second to look at the carnage. The others hid their faces and left. They ran down the stairs and what sounded like the whine of an injured cat echoed around the silent stairwell.

The four of them left the building without running. There was little chance of anyone following them. They had devised a plan to meet up. Only one of them was to go back to get the car, picking the others up at designated points. Josie asked if Dave had been involved, but John's look told her that he would never reveal which other three men had taken part.

'We never really spoke again about the fact that there was a baby involved. That was something we didn't factor in. Since then, we've had a kind of code of silence about the whole thing.'

'So, the young man must have been seriously injured?' Josie asked.

'I would think so, but I've no idea. He would have struggled to have another child after that kicking, but there's one thing I *can* tell you. That baby would never have been the same again.'

After Josie heard that story, her nightmares began. How could any sane person be involved in that kind of behaviour? But, to a certain extent, it explained the need for him to have a baseball bat sitting behind the back door. It was out of sight but within easy reach. The children, and Josie, had been warned never to move it.

They never did.

Chapter 23

Dave

After my fifth trip away, I asked Josie about our bank balance.

'Of course there's money in the bank. And that's the boiler serviced and the hob is now paid for,' she explained.

'No, no!' I closed my eyes and shook my head. 'I should come home to much more than that. When I left work two days ago, some guys were talking about changing their cars this time back home and others were booking a holiday. I want to do that. This isn't working. I'm going to deal with the money from now on.'

Taking over responsibility for paying the bills was to be my job from then on.

'It's a bit late for that. Most things are paid now,' Josie reminded me.

'I'm going to take over the money, and that's that.'

My tone told her I was on the brink of flying into a rage. But she couldn't let it go and told me I had the wrong end of the stick. She sent me into a darker mood by pointing out that the men I worked with had healthy bank balances because they had been years in well-paid jobs and likely their children had left home. They could buy cars at the drop of a hat. She reminded me that I had only started earning regularly the year before. She didn't have to remind me we were renovating a house and supporting two children.

'Give it time. It'll all fall into place soon. Sure, we haven't got any big bills now and that means the savings will mount up.' She was almost pleading with me.

The stupid woman was saying things I didn't want to hear, so I looked her up and down. She breathed in as though she was mustering up strength from somewhere. I waited for the next onslaught. A minute later she began.

'OK, you do what you think is best, but I'm going to tell you something. If you take control of the money, never come to ask for help when you get into trouble. I'll let you decide, but I mean it. I can't drag us out of overdrafts and ward off debt collectors. The choice is yours.'

She was talking rubbish. There was no way I was ever in debt to anyone.

When I was due to go away on another trip to Thailand, I told Ginny and Jon I was going food shopping. I asked if they wanted to come. Of course, that kind of outing with me delighted the children. They loved throwing as many treats as they could into the shopping trolley. Josie stood back as I loaded up with what I knew they'd need for the next few weeks. Ginny and Jon kept looking at the cakes, biscuits, and chocolate breakfast cereal in the trolley. Jon picked up one of the multi-packs of crisps, practically drooling over them. Ginny wanted to carry the family-sized bags of chocolate bars. It was like Christmas because it was me making them happy.

As we got nearer the checkout, I turned around to look at Josie and her long face.

'Well? OK? Are you happy with what's in here?' I didn't agree with her that my tone was sarcastic as I nodded in the direction of the groaning trolley.

'Yes, that's fine. Maybe a few things so that I can make soup, also more pasta and rice if this has to last more than two days. They're going to need some shampoo and we're just about out of washing powder, toilet rolls and washing up liquid.'

I glared at her. She was trying to be her usual awkward self. There was no more room in the trolley. This was crazy, but if that's how she wanted it, I would say nothing. I turned the trolley around. On the way to the aisle where the shampoo was kept, Ginny asked for shower gel and Jon asked for a Superman facecloth. They didn't get either; the fun was over because of Josie.

Back home, I decided to unpack everything at once. There wasn't a single space left on any kitchen surface. Ginny and Jon were hungry, but Josie said there was nothing they could eat at that moment except for a couple of slices of bread.

'Don't we have any rolls?' Ginny asked.

I walked out of the kitchen because I could feel chaos descending when I heard Josie barking at Ginny. That was the wrong thing to do. She should have started by sorting out the foodstuff I had left on the worktops.

The children ate a snack and Josie got started on making space in the cupboards for things she said she couldn't see much of a meal being made from. And she couldn't stop at that, seems the shopping bill had been enormous; much more than she would ever have spent. Rubbish.

'Look, Dave, you'll need to leave enough money for Ginny and Jon to have school lunches over the next few weeks.'

I didn't answer.

Later that evening, when the kids were in bed, I chucked a magazine I had been reading onto the floor, jumped at her and dragged her up the stairs.

'You need to do your job here! You can't even pick enough food for the kids' lunches.' I snarled in her ear as I once again threw her into the bedroom and slammed the door on her, unbuckling my belt as I moved towards the bed.

She had a lot to learn.

Josie

There was increasing restlessness and unhappiness about Dave; it filtered through to everyone else. The cottage was not the be all and end all Josie had thought. There were lots of jobs outstanding, but Dave was past caring about them and his toolbox lay dormant. Nothing about the town appealed to him anymore. It bored him because he hadn't reached the dizzy heights he had imagined he would and wasn't being included in the exclusive social circles he hankered after. Into the bargain, he still had nowhere to park his car.

Josie had taken some piano lessons before she married Dave and, although she found playing a challenge, she whizzed through the theory. Her teacher, Mrs Bell, asked if she would take over teaching the theory of music with the younger children and so they joined forces. Along with Mr Bell, they had the making of a small music school.

On one of the days she had her practical lesson, Dave was showing more signs of discontentment and revealed a few reasons for his dark mood.

'I don't know what's gone wrong. I'd always dreamed of coming here and getting involved with people who play golf or squash or are members of the Round Table and organisations like that. I don't know where to start because the only folk I know are the ones who drink in the bar across the road.'

Josie felt he had answered his own question. If he needed people to introduce him into salubrious environments, he'd need to frequent the same places they did.

He was bored and boring.

At her music lesson, Josie couldn't concentrate and apologised to Mrs Bell. She told her she wasn't sure if she could commit to their dream of a music school because Dave had hinted at them moving from the area. The words were hardly out of her mouth when a huge tear rolled down Josie's cheek. Mrs Bell made a cup of tea and they abandoned the class. When Josie revealed one of the reasons behind Dave's restless demeanour, that he wanted to spread his wings and meet more people, Mrs Bell told her she and Mr Bell would be happy to introduce Dave to the golf club. She also knew of friends who were part of local charities and he could make inroads there.

As another attempt to support Dave, Josie came home with the good news that he could have a round of golf with Mr Bell. The fact he didn't own a set of golf clubs wasn't a problem; he could borrow a set from Mr Bell's son.

The following Saturday, Dave set off early. Josie was naïve enough to think a round of golf would bring Dave back down to earth. After the game, he told her the golf was good and that Mr Bell was a very good golfer. But, and there was always a *but,* he didn't have the right clothes for golf. He wasn't able to talk to Mr Bell about much because they had different interests and the golf club was an intimidating place because he didn't know anyone.

'But that all takes time,' Josie reassured him. 'It's not to say you'll enjoy Mr Bell's company, but through him, you're likely to meet other people.'

His restlessness manifested itself in other ways. Something happened one afternoon before Jon and Ginny had returned from school. Josie had finished ironing and was putting it away when she passed the back door and, not for the first time, she saw his overnight bag against the wall. This time, she challenged him.

'What's that for?' she queried Dave.

'I'm going to see my mother and I thought I might have a game of squash with Brian, so it's just shorts and stuff. I'm not sure whether I'll stay over,' he told her.

His mother and cousin, Brian, lived eighty miles away, so Josie didn't know what to say. She couldn't go. Jon was due home, and Ginny wouldn't be back for well over an hour. He wouldn't wait for them so that they could go as a family. Anyway, the children had school the next day, so they couldn't stay overnight.

Josie laid Ginny's freshly ironed clothes on her bed and heard the back door close. No goodbye, only silence. Was this him finally turning his back on the town, the house and the family he appeared to have craved? Josie felt the mixed emotions of both fear and relief.

That evening, Josie and the children watched a film and had supper in front of the television. Jon loved the change in routine and cosied up on the sofa with a blanket. Ginny hugged Josie in the oversized armchair. It was just like old times. Dave stayed away all night.

Each time Dave went out of the country for work, Josie was aware of the calmness that descended on the house. Everyone was free to come and go, no questions asked. Ginny had friends come to stay over; Jon brought his chums into the garden and almost covered it with toy cars. Josie was conscious of her friends only coming to visit when Dave was away, but that wasn't all that odd. It was an opportunity for the women to get together and chat over coffee and biscuits without interfering with any plans their men might have made.

But from the depth of her tortured soul, Josie knew her personality changed when Dave was home. There was no point in putting on decent clothes because then he asked which man she was meeting. She walked around with her head bowed, as though she wasn't worthy of even looking at where she was going. Her mouth became dry when he asked her a question because she wasn't convinced she could give him the right answer. She asked herself on several occasions whether life was worth living if she really was the disappointing human being he called her. His walking out with his overnight bag proved he couldn't stand being in the house with her and the children.

When Moira visited Josie after a couple of months, she was stunned and angry at what Dave had turned her into. She had been brave enough to say she only put up with Dave because of Josie. It was then that Josie noticed everyone waited for Dave to go away until they invited her and the children to their houses or out for a meal.

As it drew closer to the day of Dave's return from work, Josie and the children grew increasingly tense. They left no stone unturned. They prepared as though a king were coming to visit. While Josie knew other women were excited to have their husbands come home from offshore or foreign lands, she dreaded it. The criticism and insults began the minute he walked through the door.

When Dave and Josie first married, Moira had a few words of advice for her, probably misplaced guidance.

'Josie, I know you are really tidy, but you'll have to remember it's Dave's house as well now.'

'What do you mean?' Josie had asked.

'Well, for example, let's say Dave starts a job in the house the day before he's due to leave for work and he's got his toolbox out.'

'Oh yes! That's exactly what happens every time. I can't understand why he starts a job he knows he won't be able to finish. I've got to put all the stuff away and clean up,' Josie replied.

'That's what I mean. It's Dave's house too. If he wants to leave his tools out, then maybe you need to give him that right. He'll be picking the job up again as soon as he's back.'

Josie pondered this suggestion. Moira could read people better than she, and maybe Dave had said something to Ed about her putting tools in the wrong place. She went along with Moira's idea.

Sure enough, the day before Dave was due to leave for six weeks, he brought out his toolbox and, in the kitchen, chipped away at a bit of wall behind the table. He wanted to move a socket. As was normal, the job didn't get finished and off he went the following day to the other side of the world. Josie didn't touch anything he had left lying around. She was giving him his place and couldn't bear another explosion.

Dave

When I got back from one trip, I hadn't even laid my case down when I looked through the French windows into the kitchen. I couldn't believe it and I stopped in mid-stride. My toolbox and some tools were sitting exactly where I had left them weeks before.

'What the *hell* is this?' I was as calm as I could be. 'Did you not even bother to tidy that up? Has that been lying out all the time I've been away?'

'I thought you'd be using it as soon as you came back.' She was only trying to excuse herself because she knew she was lazy.

I couldn't help myself. I had to point out how she was incapable of looking after a home. She had to be reminded that it was her job to make sure I came home to a tidy house. It didn't take me long to find other faults.

At the bottom of the stairs, I stood holding out my index finger.

'What's this!' I demanded.

'Eh, a finger?' Josie almost sounded genuine.

'No! It's dust.' I ran another finger over the wood between the spindles of the bannister and held it up to her. 'You're supposed to clean.'

She was so slow she couldn't even see the dust on my two fingers.

It didn't even take a minute for her to start defending herself. Her excuse was she always cleaned the house before I came back, then did nothing other than the usual washing, ironing and cooking when I was home. I know she was trying to make me feel good by saying the idea was to spend more time with me. Basically, she was trying to weedle her way out of her inabilities as a housewife.

I got the chance to show her how to do things. There was a problem with the car so I had to wait a few days until it was repaired. I took the opportunity of being confined to the house to give Josie a few lessons on how to wash pots and light a fire. Next thing, she screamed at me.

'You know what? Why don't you leave us alone? We're sick of you, and nothing seems to please you. It's not as if you're Mr Perfect, is it?' She stood with her hands on her hips, looking defiant.

My surprise was evident. I lunged at her and dragged her up the stairs by the hair. She half landed on the bed and fell off, bringing the bedside lamp and a pile of books with her. Her face brushed the side of the bedside cabinet and I caught a glimpse of some blood trickling down her cheek.

I pushed her chest down on the bed and held her there.

'Just you stay there until you calm down!'

That was a lesson she wouldn't forget in a hurry.

Chapter 24

Josie

Josie missed her old friends from when she had lived in her flat near Falkirk. Moira had carried on their friendship despite the miles between them. Normally, they called each other and there was the occasional trip that Moira made when Dave was away. When they stayed over at each other's house with the children, there was much hilarity and spontaneous outings for picnics and country walks.

But Josie became stressed when Dave was home; in fact, she was visibly shaking when she knew he was due to arrive back from a trip. When she finally dared to contemplate her situation, she could see that she had given up everything to become involved with a seriously controlling man; a man who ridiculed her looks, her hair and everything she did. He never said anything directly about her dress sense anymore, it was the way he ran his eyes over her outfit while shaking his head. She knew she had made a huge mistake when his outbursts resulted in him tearing blouses and dresses from her body. When he dragged her upstairs, she prayed the children wouldn't come out of their rooms. She took the punishment rather than let him take it out on Jon and Ginny. He was a big bully to them all.

Something Josie had found odd was Dave's constant mistrust from day one; the accusations about where she had been, who she talked to and the reasons behind her normal everyday plans. He appeared to know all the tricks people invented to cheat on their partners. But there were things he did that made Josie think twice about *his* faithfulness. She wondered if he was accusing her of the very thing he was doing.

One weekend, they went to a party in a friend's house, every guest brought some food or drinks to lighten the load for their hosts. With ten people there, the spread was enormous. The ladies dealt with the food. The men were in charge of drinks and mixers.

While Dave was dealing with the pre-food drinks, she noticed he asked everyone in the room what their preference was. But there was one lady there that Josie didn't know. She'd been introduced as Sally. Her partner, Ken, wasn't familiar to Josie, but she'd heard Dave referring to him now and again when he had spoken about cars and garages. Dave passed out the drinks and handed one to Sally. Josie had been watching and noticed something strange.

Dave never asked Sally what she wanted, but he knew her drink was a Bacardi and coke. A telling sign, maybe. He knew more about the woman than he was letting on. She stopped herself from going down that road. She didn't want to become suspicious like Dave.

Josie knew she could only have a few weeks' respite at a time before he was home, and that was unless he packed in the job and came home unexpectedly. Her stress and his control started sooner than anticipated.

During July and August, Dave's rota meant he would miss almost six weeks of the summer at home, but he was going to Asia where the weather would be fine. He left two days before schools broke up.

Josie made plans to go to Braeness as soon as possible to visit Margo, her son, Daniel, and her daughter, Catherine, and join in the town's gala day. They loaded the car up and the children sang and told jokes during the two-hour journey. Then, after they made a comfort break, the children wanted to know the plans.

'So, I'm going to Nana's for two nights, then you're coming to get me so that I can go to the Braeness fair?' Ginny was making sure she understood.

'And I'm going to play with Daniel and Catherine for two days, then I'm going to the fair as well?' Jon double-checked he wasn't being left out.

'Yes, then we'll all stay at Margo's for a few more days and I think we'll be able to go to the zoo. After that, we'll visit Moira and the dog before we come back home. And we can go to the seaside with your cousins. Dad won't be back for six weeks, so we will still have time to do much more.'

The town of Braeness was overtaken on gala day. No one wanted to miss the fair; people came from miles around in their finery to see the festivities. Margo and Josie preened the girls and groomed the boys, then set off. At the fair, the children ate hot dogs, drank fizzy orange and ran around to look for the best rides.

On one street as a parade passed, Josie had an uneasy feeling; it was as though someone was watching her. She turned around but could only see hordes of people, children holding balloons and fathers balancing children on their shoulders.

They followed the lorries adorned with garlands and, at one point, they stopped for a few minutes because Daniel's shoelace had come undone. Margo tied it while Josie leaned against a fence. It was then that she saw Dave. He was standing a few feet away with his arms folded. She had to do a double take to make sure she wasn't hallucinating. He should have been in Asia but he was there, in Scotland.

It surprised Margo to see him standing there as she tapped Daniel on the back, showing he could return to the others. She smiled.

'Dave! My goodness, what a surprise! What? Where? How?' Margo tried to get her head around what was happening.

It would have taken him ages to sort out tickets and travel, so he could only have been working for two or three days before he did a complete turnaround.

Josie couldn't speak. Here was the impulsive Dave, the Dave who arrived unannounced, the Dave who would now expect them to pack their cases and head home.

A holiday ending.

He wouldn't join in and he would want his car from home. She knew he would have hired a car at the airport intending to pick them up and make sure he firmly ensconced them in the house, then take himself off to appear somewhere else unannounced.

'I'd be delighted if Bill came back and surprised me like that.' Margo tried to understand.

'I don't think you would be, Margo. I know what this means; he hasn't got a job now; he won't have a reference to move on and we won't have any money to pay the bills. We're back to square one again. And, by the way, we'll be going home. Our time with you and the children is over.'

Dave

Sometimes I liked being in the cottage especially when it was empty and quiet. One afternoon, I got my Exchange and Mart magazine, made a cup of tea and reached into the fridge to get my Cadbury's milk chocolate bar. It was gone. Wondering if I had made a mistake and put it in the freezer, I rummaged through everything. No, it wasn't there. The orange juice spilled over the lettuce and tomatoes, but I didn't care. Someone else could clean that up. All I wanted was my chocolate. I had to make do with a dry tasting bit of shortbread. Absolutely no comparison. I couldn't read my magazine with my head bursting with anger.

When Ginny came in, I asked her if she'd seen my chocolate.

'Ah. Jon found it and we shared it.'

To say I was livid was an understatement.

'Just get to your room and don't come out until I tell you, not for anything.'

That was what my dad had said to me when I ate his chocolate snowball. That was lesson enough for me nearly forty years before so it would work for Ginny. Jon was told the same.

'But we thought it was for us because sometimes Mum puts chocolate there for us.'

'Well, you were wrong, weren't you? Room! Now!'

But I still fancied chocolate. After a few minutes, I went upstairs and put it to them that they could get something for themselves if they went to the shop for more chocolate. So ten minutes in their rooms was all the punishment they got. We were all happy. I'd seen a five-pound note under the clock the day before so I wouldn't be paying for chocolate if I could help it.

Well, that seemed to work until Josie came home and harped on about the money she had left sitting out. I shook my head when she asked where it was. I saw her confusion, but she probably thought her precious children weren't as honest as she had imagined.

Josie

Ginny's father had always paid a small amount each month as child maintenance and, along with the family allowance, Josie kept the money in a separate account. She knew she might surprise Dave with it one day either to get a job done in the house or, if she could let the amount grow, it might have stretched to pay for a weekend away. In the entire scheme of things, it didn't amount to much but it was hers to choose what to use it for.

Once Dave had taken control of the housekeeping, Josie realised she needed to keep that little bit she had set aside in case there was an emergency. She changed her mind about buying any more for the house or giving Dave a treat, it was to be for her children in a time of need.

Even in the past, after Josie had paid the workmen's bills and let money build up in their joint account, she was sure Dave would want to use their savings for himself. He wasn't careful at all with cash and his idea of buying something worthwhile was to buy another car, or at least a part for the one he had. His habit of getting his mother to pay off hire purchase agreements had worsened his lack of money management skills. Spending at the supermarket got completely out of hand.

Ginny went to secondary school in another town, and it wasn't workable for her to take a lunch box as well as the books and gym kit she carted back and forth practically every day. Jon's school wasn't far from the house, but his friends went to school lunches and the highlight of their day was messing around in the playground after they had wolfed down whatever was put in front of them. Packed lunch was the best. They got out of the dining room quicker. Despite Dave being in charge of the money and shopping, there was no consideration given to their school lunches.

She thought he would get fed up with the comments from the children.

'There's no orange juice.'

'Why is there no cold meat?'

'Do I need to have tuna again?'

'Somebody stole my apple. I put it in the bottom of the fridge.'

And so, the arrangement continued until Dave realised shopping trips were taking up too much of his time. He hadn't appreciated that previously Josie had stocked up and cooked before he came home, so there was no need to go for a full shop when he was back. It was a pleasure to go for extras but not for the mundane task of filling the cupboards, especially when there had to be enough for a few weeks. The novelty wore off, and Dave ended up handing Josie some cash now and again, but he never put housekeeping in the bank for her.

Dave took her bank card away a few days before he had an appointment with the bank manager. He was ready for awkward questions.

'Ok Dave. What seems to be the problem? There's more money going out than there is coming in. Can I help in any way?' the manager asked.

'Well, to be honest, I'm glad you discovered that. It's my wife. She keeps spending even when I tell her to stay away from the shops. I think the only answer is to take the cheque book off her. I've stopped her from being able to withdraw cash but I'm at a loss as to what I can do next.' Dave put his head down as if in shame.

'Most of the time we can see how the money is being used and for a family of four, there's a lot being spent in supermarkets. I know you need to eat and it's tempting to overspend now that supermarkets are selling everything from tea to trainers. Maybe you could look at that with her? We need to sort this as soon as possible.'

After some harsher words from the bank manager, Dave left knowing there was nothing he could do. Josie was hardly spending anything now because the days of him conveniently forgetting his cheque book and getting her to sign a cheque were long gone.

Convinced Josie would have an answer to the problem, he told her. But she only shrugged her shoulders while he continued.

'I asked if I could take out another loan to cover the overdraft and he laughed at me. Stupid man. He's supposed to be there to help with my finances.'

Chapter 25

Dave

When I arrived home from work and announced that Josie was never to buy a car while I was away, she looked confused and surprised.

'What are you talking about? That's not something I would ever do! And I can't get any money out anyway.' I knew she didn't have enough for the petrol, never mind a car but I wondered if she would ever take a loan out in my name.

This was in my mind because a man at work had arrived home to find his wife had surprised him with a new car. I never knew the full story behind the purchase. But it was my worst nightmare that I might be excluded from being involved in buying a car.

Josie kept saying we didn't have enough to buy anything and I was bored of being skint. For weeks I had listened to what the guys at work were hoping to buy this time home and that was when the notion of another car grew on me. More car magazines and brochures appeared, and I felt compelled to share my preferences with Josie. She knew nothing about cars, except that they depreciated quickly, but she mentioned she liked the shape of the Volkswagen Golf. I nodded and continued looking.

One day, I took off without saying where I was going. I wanted to surprise Josie. Two hours later, I walked in and asked her to come down to Mr Berwick's parking area at the front, the one that apparently didn't belong to me.

'Wait until you see this.' I beamed.

There, in all its glory, I had parked a silver car. A Lancia.

'I'm thinking about this one. It's between this and a BMW. It's the colour of the BMW that's bothering me. You might not like it.'

She said she didn't like the idea of another car never mind the colour. I knew she would try to deflate my excitement, but I was determined not to let her.

'It's an orange BMW. I have to take this Lancia back, so why don't you come with me and have a look?' I wanted her to be part of the decision making.

It wasn't a long journey to the garage in Arbroath where Iona lived. I had another look at the car. It was a beaut. The salesman walked over.

'So, you're back. What did you think of the Lancia?'

'Nice machine, but not enough room. We've got two kids so I can't see it working.'

'I think you've got your heart set on the BMW. It's all up to this lovely lady, is it?'

'Well, yes and no. We both drive, so we've both got to be happy with it.'

After a bit of chat about miles to the gallon and automatic gearboxes, the salesman suggested I take it for another spin to let Josie get the feel of it. It was complete luxury to climb into the oversized leather seats. The control panel lit up and the whole experience made me feel like a film star.

I drove a few miles down the Montrose Road and mentioned how well the car was handling when I picked up speed. A car park came into view so I said I would turn there. Instead, I stopped the car and got out to have a look. I showed Josie the size of the boot and stood back to take in the view of the whole car.

'Look in the back. See how roomy it is.' I encouraged her to give it the once over.

She said there was nothing wrong with the orange colour as far as she was concerned, so I reckoned it was a done deal if I could agree on a price and get a monthly payment plan in place.

I wanted to take the BMW back to the garage on my own, so the plan was to drop Josie off at her sister's house first. When we arrived, we sat in the car for a short while until I had said what I needed to say.

'I like the car. It's a great bargain. Can you see a way for us to get it?'

'In a nutshell? No. Dave, we've got enough on our plates at the moment and I don't think we need to take on any more commitments.'

'How can that be? I've got pay coming in. Surely we could do without something for a few months to get a decent car that's not going to give up the ghost within a week? He's going to take the Granada as a trade in so that's perfect.'

'Well, yes. There is a way to do it. Once you pay off the loan that you got for renovating the garden but used it to buy a TV for every room, that would be a payment less each month. So, of course, there would be scope to replace the loan payment with car payments,' she explained. 'But the BMW will be expensive to run. What about the Mini Cooper you were talking about? That's a nice car, small, cheaper to run and easier to park.'

'If you think I'm letting *you* run about the town in a Mini Cooper—'

She got out of the car.

Josie

Iona was delighted to see Josie, but all she saw of Dave was the tail end of his car.

'So, where's he off to in such a hurry?' Iona asked.

'He's been looking at cars and he's seen one he likes.'

Josie sighed.

'What's up?'

There was no way to make her situation sound better than it was. Iona wasn't surprised that Josie was struggling a bit and not just because of Dave's spending. She had watched her sister slowly sink into a preoccupied, depressed woman. And she had lost weight when there was no need to. Nothing seemed to be going right for Josie and she knew it was hard for others to be jolly and fun loving around her when she brought so many negatives with her. She sat hunched in an armchair, her timid and tense expression was not lost on Iona.

'Life with him isn't quite what you expected, is it?'

'Not really. I'm just hoping he takes on board what I've said about not getting another car,' Josie replied. 'The only thing is, I know him too well and if the salesman allows him to take out a loan, Dave won't be able to resist it. I've told him we can't afford it.'

But that wasn't entirely true; she hadn't said that in these words. While most people would have got the logic of paying off one loan before taking on another, Dave didn't. As Moira explained to Josie later, all Dave would have heard would have been the *yes* and *there's a way*. He knew Josie was good with money and if approval came from her in any form, that's all he needed to hear. If Josie could see it was possible, then it was a signed, sealed and delivered deal in his mind.

Moira burst out laughing when she heard about Dave not wanting Josie to drive a Mini Cooper.

'Look, it's a neat car, maybe even a collector's item for some, so folk might stare at the car and see you, the driver. In his mind, he'll be thinking you'll be drawing attention to yourself.'

'This is crazy. Here I am, with glasses and curly hair. Two children into the bargain. If I'm out in a car it's to either pick up the kids or go shopping when he throws me a couple of pounds. He's nuts. People could still look at me when I'm walking along the street. I have no power over that.'

'You've got to get it into your head. He needs to control where you go to reduce the risk of other men seeing you.'

Moira said that Ed had been the same when she had suggested getting a Volvo. She had read it was a safe car to drive but Ed had almost hit the roof.

'What the hell are you thinking? You imagine I'll let you drive around the town in a big car like that? You can get that idea right out of your head.'

He agreed she could have a Citroen until Dave started calling it a sewing machine. Then Ed bought a Volvo.

Dave

Two days later, I was positively elated driving the orange BMW into the public parking area at the back of the cottage.

Josie shook her head. 'I don't know about this.'

But it was too late. I had signed for it and the Granada was gone. I never told Josie but the salesman had given me five days to change my mind. That wasn't happening.

'Don't get onto *me* about it. *You* started it all by talking about a Volkswagen Golf. I was happy looking through my car magazines and dreaming, but you were the one who instigated all this.'

It was her fault we were in more debt. My words sent out a signal telling her she needed to keep her mouth shut. I didn't need her opinion on cars.

Even though she didn't have access to our bank account, she said she knew there wasn't enough money to make the payments I had agreed to. She had sat beside me while I wrote out the monthly cheques only a few days before. I had taken that job away from her too because I wanted to see where the money was going. By the time I got past the electricity bill, the gas bill and the outstanding coal bill, I looked at the pile in front of me with a slow blink. I flicked through them and asked if any could wait.

'The only ones left are the rates, the washing machine repair bill and the invoice for the tiles you ordered for the bathroom,' she sat straight-faced. I'm sure she was being cheeky. 'But don't forget, the mortgage and the home improvement loan will come off automatically.'

I was confused. All I wanted was to be like the other guys I worked with and get a decent car. The only way I could see to pay the first instalment of the car was to avoid paying something else. Josie had been juggling all this for months; she had paid everything and saved for us so there was no reason why I couldn't do the same. I was entitled to whatever I wanted, whenever I wanted.

Sometimes daily living bored me and that partly accounted for the stream of second-hand cars I bought. I had to change something to give myself a boost. Often, when the only thing left to do was to fix something in the house, I couldn't face it. It was better to drive somewhere and visit some of our friends.

One Saturday, we were on a day out to a superstore of household items. This never enthralled the children unless they could choose from a limited supply of goodies. Outside the store, I reminded them we weren't that far from Bill and Margo's house and I took a turn onto the motorway heading towards Braeness. After we were almost at our destination and as I drew in to fill up with petrol on the outskirts of the town, Josie looked at her watch and told me it was a quarter past five.

'And?'

'Do you realise we'll be hitting Margo's house bang on the time for food? This is probably when she'll be cooking.'

'So, what's the problem?' I didn't have a clue why she was telling me that.

'Lock, I know you come down here on your own and I suppose it's not unusual to invite a surprise guest to at least have a cup of tea, but four of us? I know if they arrived at us, we wouldn't be able to feed them.'

I knew she was trying to spoil the day for us all but I let her go on. 'She won't want us dropping in. Prove me wrong and make a quick call to Margo. Tell her we're in the area and we'd love to see them. Ask if we should come now or wait for an hour. If she tells us to come now, then I'm mistaken and she's obviously happy to have a hungry family arrive while she's trying to make and serve a meal for her own brood.'

I stopped at the next phone box and spoke to Margo for a few minutes, using the exact words Josie had suggested.

'That would be great if you waited a while. I'm just about to serve up the dinner so we'll see you once we've cleared the decks.' Margo stunned me.

I couldn't believe Josie had been right and all I could do at that moment was raise my eyebrows. All because of her we were going to be stuck for an hour when we could have been up at Margo's and at least be enjoying a cup of tea. I had to buy fish and chips and we ate them in the car while the rain pelted down. The windows steamed up like my temper. Josie would definitely have to suffer for this eventually, but I let it go by filling my mind with more important issues. I had to think about leaving for my new job in Holland.

I set off a week later. It would have been a great feeling to be offered a permanent job by the company instead of temporary work through the agency but I had no choice.

A few of the lads had Level One in certain areas and knew that their only hope of promotion was to spend time doing the stupid courses. Some of them were so desperate they offered to go to training centres on their two weeks off. That certainly wasn't something I was prepared to do. By chance, I overheard one guy, Tom, saying he was going to approach the boss to ask about an upcoming course running in company time, so I reckoned if I got in there first, I'd get to do the course instead of working.

A few days in, I found out the boss was staying at the same hotel as us lads. I'd seen him sitting alone at the bar with a pint of Guinness more than once while our lot headed out to the more exciting bars after work. Sure enough, I got the chance to corner him as he walked into the almost empty bar the first Friday after I'd ordered a pint of Guinness. The others had done their usual and headed straight out. This might have been my one and only chance with Alan. There was one way to get him on side and show him I paid attention to detail.

'Ah, my man. You look like you need a pick me up.' I indicated to the barmaid that she was to give the pint I'd already ordered to Alan and continued, 'And the same for me, sweetheart.'

His pint was right there in front of him before he could blink. I had shown him how kind I was and, without saying more than a few words, we were buddies. Alan wasn't the kind of guy who would say thanks and walk away.

'Something I wanted to ask you, Alan.'

I told the lass to bring my Guinness once it was poured and walked to a table in the corner. From my vantage point, I could survey the whole room and see who was coming and going. He followed.

Within two minutes, I'd come straight to the point. A couple of my certificates needed renewing. He must have read my CV. I told him a bit of a white lie. It was true that without them I was stuck, but I told him I had been on the point of enrolling, ready to pay for them myself when the call had come from the company offering me the job. I didn't want to let the them down, but I was really giving up my chance of promotion to help them out. I wondered how he felt about putting me on the next available course.

While he was contemplating my suggestion, I interrupted his thoughts.

'Look, I know there's a course coming up and sending me on it would give you an extra body with damn good skills. I'm not going to name names, but a certain person has been talking about how shit a boss you are and crap like that. He doesn't appreciate the responsibility you've got. He's telling the crew that he can talk you into sending him on courses for the duration of the trip so he'll be able to skive work for weeks. You've got an important decision to make, Alan.'

He knew who I meant because apparently, the guy had already officially requested a meeting. I had got in there quickly and unofficially. Alan finished his pint.

'Leave it with me.'

We headed off in different directions; Alan to his room, me to join the lads.

First thing Monday morning, I hadn't even changed into my work gear when I got the message that Alan wanted to see me. The others asked me if everything was OK. I could truthfully tell them I didn't know.

All Alan said was, 'You start tomorrow on the first course.'

'Thanks Alan. You won't regret this.'

Once I heard the news from the horse's mouth, I could relax. I punched the air the minute I closed Alan's door behind me, then headed back to the changing room.

I could hardly believe my luck when the first person I met was Tom's buddy. He took a step back.

'What are you grinning at?'

'I've been head-hunted. Boss man thinks I'm the perfect candidate for the one vacancy on the course that starts tomorrow,' I said, hoping that Tom was within earshot.

I walked round to my locker and there he was, sitting with his head in his hands. He looked up.

'I can't believe you. You've well and truly stitched me up, haven't you?'

'Oh, come on. That's life in this kind of job. The best man won and that's that.

I meant it as a joke but he took it far too seriously.

Out of the corner of my eye, I saw him jump up, so I put my hands out in front of me. I like that gesture; it can be taken as trying to calm someone down or make folk think it's an action of self-defence but I was ready to take him down verbally.

'Look man, you've either got it or you haven't.'

It was a shame really, because Tom was one of these blokes who saw the good in everyone. But Alan had made his choice and I had come off better for it. I was the best man after all.

The course began at nine o'clock sharp and I took a seat at the back of the room. On each desk was a notepad and a pen. I listened intently on the first day and followed the others who took notes now and again. Until lunchtime, it was simple enough, filling in forms and looking over a few handouts. Food was provided, no one complained although, in my opinion, the beef was tough. I made sure I got the same seat for the afternoon session, tucked away in a corner. The teacher was boring. He was spouting off procedures and practices that I'd never heard of and, before long, I was drifting. There was nothing for it but to keep my mind on which car salesrooms I could visit once I got home. Finally, we packed up. I scratched my head and thought about how I could avoid the classes. It's true I could have done the same as before and called in sick, dropped out or explained about some problem at home but the certificate at the end of this course was important.

Only once before when I had dropped out of a course did I ask to see some of the lads' certificates when they came through. None of them noticed when I slipped Bert's under my magazine. It took me just over twenty minutes to change the name to mine. I tucked it away as proof that I had passed. This time wasn't going to be so easy.

Imagine my surprise when I spied Bert at the front of the class on this very course. I didn't want to admit I had met him two years before. It was important to feign complete ignorance. He must have got a replacement certificate because here he was, in all his glory. I knew I'd have to attend each lesson, well I might have got away with skipping two or three in a row providing my reason was good. For the time being, I planned to wear sunglasses in class, lean against the wall and float in and out of a dream like state. All I needed was the certificate, not the knowledge. I knew most of it anyway.

I was back home every three weeks and the job was going well. At the end of one of my trips, the four men I had been working with were complaining as we waited to be signed off for home leave. I made sure they heard me saying to no one in particular that I was going to our hotel bar after I had my tickets, then I headed to the toilet. I knew one thing for sure, some other guy would get the round in first. What I really wanted to do was to bring up the conversation we'd had the day before. I was keen to wind them up.

They said they were being treated abominably. To begin with, we all agreed that the woman on the end of the phone in the office was a condescending bitch. Every one of us had been left feeling useless and she never dealt with our problems quickly enough.

The next issue was one of the bosses on the job; he had his favourites and five of us had missed out on half-decent jobs because we weren't arse lickers. I suggested the lads should call the agency and report bad working procedures. It needed to be done the day after we left, before midday and before the boss left the site. A report about lack of safety procedures and how two people had been injured should put him in his place and turn things around.

These guys were in awe of me when they realised I had been working in the industry for years. When I told them where I'd trained and how I'd worked for numerous agencies and companies, they knew I was the voice of experienced reason. I exaggerated a bit but only to keep their attention. I said instead of them getting into bother if they complained, it would be the boss. After all, the buck stopped at him, that's what he was getting paid for.

'So, how do we go about this? Dave, you seem to know the procedure.'

'All you have to do is tell them you're putting yourself at risk every shift. Give them a couple of examples. Tell them you've asked the boss if a report could be put in about that idiot on the crane and that you can't do your job properly because you're keeping an eye on him and an eye on what you're supposed to be doing. Probably good to remind them you're not getting paid danger money.'

I hated that crane driver. I had sat for ages, pondering over how I could drop him in it. If truth be told, he was OK at his job, but he was full of it, ordering us about and shouting out to all and sundry when I left mid-task. It's my human right to go to the toilet whenever I need to. And he earned a damn sight more than the rest of us; that irked me. Now here was an opportunity to get more than two birds with one stone.

'I'll be on a train for hours tomorrow. I won't be able to call. Can anyone else?' Brian looked around.

Every one of them had an excuse not to call the agency or the company. I think they were scared to speak to the big bosses. I was the best qualified, so it didn't surprise me when one of the guys looked at me sheepishly.

'You're good with words, Dave, and you know how to land somebody in it without making it obvious.'

That was enough for me. I was elected spokesperson and double checked the office numbers. These guys needed me to be their support.

When I called, the main man was available right there and then and it only took me five or six minutes to lay it on the line about Jake the on-site manager, the crane driver and a couple of other guys who had bad mouthed me. These kinds of dudes were so jealous of the jobs I've had that they couldn't hold it in. They'd taken every opportunity to make me feel like an outcast. But it hadn't always worked because I'm made of tougher stuff. Anyway, I managed to get their names noted in my report.

I told the agency boss I had been elected as representative for the five of us and that we were all concerned. He was obviously impressed with my succinct report because he only asked me a couple of questions. I skimmed over what I didn't want to say and put the boot in when I got the chance.

Shortly after that, I realised I had been taken for a mug. I got a call from the agency to say they didn't need me for the Holland job anymore. I was well hacked off and wondered if it had anything to do with the grievance. I called one of the other complainants and he sounded surprised that I had been given the boot. But there was something about his voice. I could have sworn he was smiling at the other end of the phone.

I had told the agency I was available but after two months of nothing, I called them. No work. The same reply came every time I approached them. When I bumped into one of the supervisors on a night out, I mentioned that I wasn't getting any work.

'Were you the one who called to complain about the woman in the office and other things? Did you know she's big Jake's daughter? Somebody told me the complaint was about the crane driver as well. His brother is Operations Manager. Bit of a mistake there, eh?'

I stared at him for a second too long then shook my head.

'Jake? Who was site manager?'

So that had been their game. I had been duped into becoming the spokesperson for four others and complained to the wrong person about the wrong people. But I learned from that mistake and made sure I collected more important information on anyone I wanted to dig a hole for in the future.

Chapter 26

Josie

After the orange BMW appeared and while Dave was away, Josie drove the children down to Moira's for a long weekend. Coming off the motorway, she took a corner too fast, and the car spun out of control. They ended up in a field.

'Is anyone hurt?' Josie finally spoke.

She couldn't open her door because of an enormous tree trunk. The eerie feeling of being in the dark in a car that was pointing downwards in a field wasn't a comfortable one. She felt scared. With no cars going by on the country road, they were out of sight of most passing motorists. But luckily, a car stopped and a couple helped them to climb out of the passenger door. They said they had seen the headlights shining at an awkward angle. Once Josie and the children were out, the couple took them to Moira's; she called a garage. Police came round and said they wouldn't charge Josie with reckless driving because they knew Moira and it wasn't as if Josie had been driving under the influence. The next day at the garage, Josie cringed when she saw the car, Dave's pride and joy, looking like a plant pot with branches and bushes poking out of the bumpers.

'If you'd been in any other car, this could have been more serious for at least one of you.'

But Dave was Josie's biggest fear.

When he called, he listened to the tale. Josie was surprised at his response.

'Is everyone OK?'

She thought his first comment would be about her almost wrecking his car, but no. He appeared to be showing his caring side.

On the way home, the children made claw marks in the back of the leather seats and kept asking about the speed Josie was doing. She drove at a snail's pace for hours.

Months passed. After telling Moira about some ideas Dave had and how it was impossible to sustain their way of life, both financially and emotionally, Josie sank into a pit of despair. What she wouldn't have given for her old life. All the orange BMWs in the world weren't going to change her miserable existence. There were many things Josie didn't know how to handle.

One example was that bills came in Dave's name and offers and ads came in both their names. An understanding between them was that she would open everything because often the deadline for paying an account coincided with him being away. Josie didn't have many letters addressed to her, but there was the occasional letter from Moira or Sheila and the odd prospectus on courses. If he got to the mail before her, he had taken to opening all her letters and throwing out the prospectuses. Josie didn't like this but didn't know how to change it. When she tried to address it with him, he cut her short. Holding up his hands in front of her face, he argued she opened his mail. Not that there was anything to hide, but Josie felt he was intruding, and she didn't even get control over her own post.

It hadn't escaped her that his comment 'If you don't like it here, you can go' was becoming more frequent and her mood was lower than ever.

She had to visit her GP to ask about a persistent cough that was giving her sleepless nights and when she was there, she found herself in tears, telling him she wasn't happy at all. Her marriage wasn't what she thought it would have been and her husband criticised everything she did. To begin with, Dr Boyd gave a little laugh. He suggested it might all be down to the upheaval in her life, marriage, a new house and that she might eventually settle in. In a feeble voice, she explained she had survived before on very little and brought up two children. Now that Dave was around, she felt inadequate and useless, while in fact she had been, in her eyes, keeping them above water. After asking a few more questions, the doctor realised Josie was in a dilemma.

He prescribed anti-depressants for her and said she was suffering from a deep depression. He pulled out his notepad and drew a graph of how such a condition manifests itself, the difficulties and the probability of coming out of it naturally. He reassured her she would bounce back, but he couldn't say when. For this reason, the treatment would bring her back to a level of stability where she could enjoy life again quicker.

Josie's reluctance to take tablets meant she didn't pick up the prescription right away. The next day, the agency called to see if Dave could stand in immediately for a colleague. The trip to a rig was to last for two weeks. He left the following day.

After the children had finished their evening meal, Josie took a tablet just after six o'clock and reckoned it would kick in about nine when she could go to bed. The drug hit her immediately. At seven o'clock, she tried to stand up but fell back onto the couch. She had to get to bed.

'Listen,' she said to the children. 'I'm not feeling well. I'm going to lie down for a minute.'

This was not what she wanted. Something to lift her mood was one thing, but practically collapsing in front of her children was another issue. The effect was dangerous. It didn't matter that Ginny was almost fourteen. That was far too young to be dealing with a ten-year-old brother and a mother who appeared to be on some hallucinogenic drug. Somehow, she managed to drag herself to bed.

Dave

When I came back from my two weeks away, I brought some gifts, including a bottle of wine and two beautiful, long-stemmed wine glasses. I'd had great fun at the airport shops. The cash I got from my work was burning a hole in my pocket. Normally, the company did our washing for us but there had been a problem with the contractor and we were given an extra day's pay every week, in cash, for doing our own laundry. I never mentioned that to Josie, after all, it was my money. The truth was a lot of us didn't bother to do the washing at all because we wore overalls, so wearing the same t-shirt for two or three days meant we only had to give small things one quick rinse through each week. The rest we put in our cases for our wives to wash once we were home.

After the children had gone to bed one evening, Josie came clean and admitted she wasn't happy at all but couldn't quite put her finger on why. She told me she was taking prescription medication to see if it made her feel more positive. Later, I opened the wine, and we sampled it from the new glasses. After admiring their shape, I agreed with Josie that we find a safe place to keep them; they were tall and only fitted into one cupboard. These were special glasses and not to be used for any old reason.

Two days later, I wanted to fit door handles. Josie had to go to the post office, and the children didn't want to go with her. She contacted a couple of friends to see if they could meet for coffee after she picked up her parcel. I told the kids to stay in the living room while I did a couple of jobs.

What I didn't think about was the tennis ball Jon had taken in with him. Five minutes later, he came to find me and said he had thrown the ball in the air but hadn't caught it in time. It had knocked one of the new glasses over; it smashed and I was livid.

When Josie came home, Jon was crying because I had yelled at him and sent him to his bedroom. Ginny was sitting with her homework on her knee and didn't know where to look.

Out of the earshot of the children, Josie wanted to talk to me.

'Can I just ask?' Josie began. 'Why were the glasses out in the living room?'

'Don't turn it around as if it was my fault. I was looking underneath to see if there was a name on the bottom because one of the guys at work wanted to know.' I didn't need to explain myself.

'But you didn't put them away and they were sitting out while you went to fix the handles, knowing the kids were in the living room with a ball?' Josie couldn't see that it was all Jon's fault. Here was I, getting the blame when it was nothing to do with me.

'Listen to yourself. *He* threw the ball; *he* broke the glass. Anyway, have you taken your tablet today?' I reminded her she was the one with the mental problem.

'This is exactly what's wrong. You will do anything to discourage and demean me,' she said.

Her voice was breaking, so I knew this was the time to kick her, when she was down. The children didn't need a mother with that attitude.

'Just remember, if you don't like it here, you can go!'

I used the same sentence a couple of times more over the next few days when she was dragging herself around rather than being her usual busy self. I saw she was different; she wasn't reacting the same.

Josie

Even with medication, Josie couldn't drag herself out of her depression. She didn't expect any sympathy from Dave. All she needed was a bit more mental strength to recognise the crossroads she was at and make some life-changing decisions.

'Listen, why don't you go to Moira's later today? Spend the weekend there,' Dave said one Friday morning when he saw Josie hadn't got dressed.

She couldn't believe it. Not only was Dave suggesting she go for a break, but he was also going to look after Ginny and Jon.

'That would be great. I'd love that. Just the chance to catch up with her.' She became motivated at the thought. Her train journey there was a mix of going over the bad times with Dave and then talking herself into a more positive frame of mind. But there was always a dark cloud hanging over her.

Moira was excited at seeing her chum again and, because Josie didn't have the car, they met at the train station. Moira was now living in a remote village near Eyemouth in the south of Scotland. Ed had persuaded her to move to a country house, thinking he would isolate her with limited friends. But Moira discovered life there was a combination of relaxation and activity.

The village people were accommodating and welcomed their new neighbour and her visitors with cups of coffee and home-made cakes. Bars didn't adhere to closing times and lock-ins were common. Restaurant owners and shopkeepers gave attractive discounts to the locals and their friends. So it wasn't possible to be isolated or in the dark about what was going on.

Josie and Moira caught up on the news about the children and the friends they had met. Josie told her about the medication and mentioned the rather callous comments of *if you don't like it here, you can go.* Moira almost laughed when Josie told her that, five days hence, Dave would be going on another trip to the rigs.

'Well, when he says that to you, why don't you retaliate by telling him, "It's OK, I only need to wait five days and *you'll* be gone!" See how he likes that.'

Chapter 27

Josie

A light bulb went on in Josie's head. It was true he'd be going to work, and she wondered why she hadn't thought of such a retort. Her responses had been slow; her ability to think beyond the next hour had all but disappeared. Part of that was to do with the anti-depressants which hadn't kicked in to lift her sprits. But her focus was still on *his* responses and how she could keep *him* happy.

Her time with Moira was productive. The train journey was uplifting and her decision to follow her instincts for a happier life came to fruition. It was one thing to keep Dave happy but the cost of pleasing him was too high. She hadn't had the strength or the inclination to stand up for herself, it was as though she was living in the dark ages where women were not considered worthy citizens.

Moira hadn't influenced her, but she gave Josie strength. She had only pointed out that Josie was a human being, a mother and a wife, so she deserved to be treated as more than a doormat.

Josie had to change trains in Edinburgh. With half an hour to wait, there was time for a snack and she practically skipped to the table with her scone and cup of tea. The smile on her face was visible to all. She was going home, prepared to change whatever was waiting for her with a new lease of life.

Dave

On Sunday evening, I was in the bath when Josie arrived home. The door was partially open so I could hear the conversation. She was greeted by a thrilled Ginny and Jon.

'Oh, that's a lovely welcome! Have you two been busy?' she asked.

They didn't say very much and I could only hear a few mumbles. I had to cut my bath time short as I needed to get out there and see what was going on. I wrapped a big towel around my waist and popped my head out the door.

'I'll be out in a minute. Don't move.'

'Oh, OK,' she answered.

'Now, you're going to get a surprise when you go upstairs,' I told her when I came out.

For a fleeting moment, Ginny turned her head away and back again as I appeared.

'Oh well, I hope it's a pleasant surprise. Right, let's go up and look. Who's coming with me?' Josie waited to see who was joining her.

As we climbed the stairs, the first thing Josie mentioned was that all the bedroom doors were closed. I directed her into Ginny's bedroom. It had been rearranged and the bedroom unit Josie had brought from her council house was no longer the full-sized cream wardrobe with drawers and shelves. I had been busy with my saw. All that was left was the wardrobe section, the shelves and a pull-down part were gone. Josie looked at Ginny's jumpers and underwear sitting in piles on the floor and put her hand up to her mouth. I couldn't tell if she liked my idea. She walked onto the landing.

The door to Jon's room didn't open properly because his chest of drawers was stopping it, only by a few inches. But once inside, she could see the other half of Ginny's bedroom unit where the drawers used to sit. The pull-down section with two drawers underneath were fine but the four shelves that had been attached to the wardrobe weren't fixed to anything yet. I hadn't got around to doing that so they couldn't be used at that moment.

Josie appeared speechless when I said now the children had part of a unit each, but she wasn't. It was then that she started to berate me.

'Before I moved here, I saved up and paid for this unit and there wasn't a mark on it. Now it looks like a piece of junk not fit for a second-hand shop.'

This didn't surprise me. She never acknowledged any of the work I did.

'Don't complain. You disappeared for the weekend, so I got busy.' It was her fault for not being there.

She hadn't seen our bedroom so I was sure that would cheer her up.

The room stretched the breadth of the house and had a window at each end. On Josie's suggestion when we first moved in, we had chosen light-wood furniture to bring even more brightness into the room. The two bedside cabinets had matched the tallboy and the dressing table. We had temporarily used a built-in cupboard as a wardrobe but I was fed up with that and it was on the *to do* list to buy a proper wardrobe.

I opened the door in dramatic style for her to see the changes I had made.

With her hands together, she lifted them, prayer-like, to her chin. She quickly looked around but it didn't surprise me that she ignored the bedroom suite and walked over to the bed first, focusing on the mattress. She'd said often enough a decent mattress was the answer to a good night's sleep. She covered her mouth again and spoke through her fingers.

'Where did this come from?' she almost whispered.

'It was for sale in the paper. I went to see it on Friday afternoon. It belonged to an old woman who'd had it for years, like a family heirloom.' I was proud that I'd got a good deal.

'Have you lain down on the bed?' She didn't look at me.

'No, why?'

'Just try it. It looks small.'

I lay down and tried to manoeuvre myself into a comfortable position but I couldn't. When I bent my knees to avoid the footboard, I almost fell out.

'We don't have bedding to fit this.'

'Well, we can buy some,' I told her.

'So where are all our clothes?' Josie asked, pointing to where the previous chest of drawers had been.

'In there.' I pointed to the right-hand door of a dark wood wardrobe. 'Look, there's even a key to lock it!'

Josie

Josie couldn't believe her eyes. All the positive vibes she had mustered up at Moira's and on the train disintegrated in an instant. She thought she had walked into a pitch-black dungeon. Standing opposite her was a dark, old-fashioned wardrobe only ever seen in retirement homes. It dominated the room, and it took her a few seconds to move her eyes away from the hideous article. She turned her head to the left and saw a matching dressing table. The three drawers at each side had peeling veneer and the entire unit sat in front of a window. An old, damaged mirror with black spots concentrated on the upper right-hand corner, sat so high on the drawer section it practically covered the window, blocking out the light. Josie almost collapsed when she focused again on the bed. It had a headboard and a footboard. But it wasn't a double bed; it was three-quarter sized.

It was at that moment that Josie knew it didn't matter what Dave tried to do from now on. He was really a silly little boy in a man's body with no insight into life. He wasn't a thinker and never would be. Leaving the spending and the cars aside, he had ruined the unit she had paid for, just as he had with other things, including Ginny's bike, an expensive garden bench and an antique desk. Now he had disposed of their bedroom furniture and she hadn't featured in his decisions. Somehow, he had bought and arranged delivery of things that were unbelievably ugly and unsuitable. She tried to think of positive words to say but surprised herself by staying calm and silent.

She thought, *So this is why he wanted me away for the weekend!*

'I hope you get a good sleep tonight.' She smiled at him because she pitied him. She wouldn't be joining him.

That was the last straw. There was no point in trying to make things work in the cottage. Not because of an old set of bedroom furniture, but because Josie needed to be on her own with the children. Something had come to an end.

Josie decided she would have to get out. Apparently, so did Dave.

Chapter 28

Dave

'*It's not happening* for us here, so I'm going to make enquiries about selling up and we can move back down to Falkirk,' I announced one afternoon after I'd had a few pints with the boys.

'But you can't sell yet. The council grant for renovating stipulates that you must keep the house for five years, otherwise you need to pay the money back,' Josie reminded me.

'Well, that's the thing. I was speaking to a guy today, and he said that's all changed. There's no penalty now if you sell early. They've scrapped that rule. I'm going to check it out and if it's right, we can move. I don't want to be trapped here any longer.' I became animated.

I didn't go golfing again or try to integrate with the others I'd met. I'd had enough. And I found out the message was correct about not having to pay back the renovation grant, so that gave me a new focus. I wanted to put the house on the market.

'So where will we go?' Josie asked me.

'Back down to Falkirk, back to where we came from. I told you that already.' I looked at her, surprised that she didn't know that was the only place in the world I wanted to be.

The following day, the sun was shining, and Josie took a deck chair out to the back garden. It wasn't the most pleasant place to sit; I'd never had time to finish it. There were still massive holes that needed filled, a wall to be shored up and the rubble from the excavated earth was still in piles. It was a surprise to Josie when I joined her.

'Oh, I thought you were busy,' she said.

'Well no. Nothing that can't wait until another day.'

'Dave, can I ask you something about this idea you have to sell up? What is your thinking? What is it you want and what don't you like about what we have here?'

I was calm when I answered and told her I always dreamed of having a picture-perfect life, a house with two-point two children and a dog. I wanted a decent car and some recognition. The reason I wanted to move back to the Falkirk area was because every time I visited and walked into a bar or a café, someone would acknowledge me, ask how I was and what I'd being doing work-wise, like we were old friends meeting after a long absence. That didn't happen in Forfar because it seemed nobody was interested in me anymore. Josie suggested that the warm welcome I might get down south would also wear off in time because people would become accustomed to me once they knew what I was doing. She said life was like that. But that was stupid. People in Falkirk would always want to know what I was doing. I had an interesting life when I was upbeat and happy. Forfar was basically a boring place with boring people.

Josie also told me she would be concerned about the children having to uproot from their friends and schools. They had done that before and Jon was already in his second school and he was just finishing primary four. Another move could be a disaster. She said Ginny, now in her second year at high school, was making friends far and wide and doing really well.

Josie suggested taking things one step at a time, putting a bit more thought behind a move and keeping in mind that the house might take a while to sell. She suggested I continue with the renovations rather than leaving jobs unfinished but I was fed up with renovating. I'd outgrown the idea. I was restless.

She didn't win the argument. The next day, without her knowing where I was going, I arranged for Laburnum Cottage to go on the market. The speed of my decision concerned her, but that was the only way to get moving. Don't hang around and miss good opportunities. Not only that, but I brought back listings of houses in the surrounding area. I had changed my mind about Falkirk being the only area we could go to. Now I argued that if we moved without going out of the Tayside area; Ginny could stay at school, and I would get my wish for another house. I would forego moving to my preferred area for the family. That's how flexible I was prepared to be.

The estate agent visited the cottage and told me to tidy up the outstanding jobs and get the garden looking better. He mentioned that the cottage was attractive, but the only drawback was the lack of parking, which would be reflected in the asking price. This was a disaster and I wondered why Josie hadn't warned me about such a pitfall when I spoke about buying the cottage in the first place. She had plenty to say about the other properties we looked at so it was her fault that I was going to lose money with this sale.

But it was a done deal. We were on the market and people would come out of the woodwork, desperate to buy the cottage. I went back to work on the rigs and called Josie more than normal over the following weeks. The disappointment that no-one had viewed the property was depressing me.

'All I want is to come home and hear that we have sold it.' That was what I said every time I called her.

My impatience grew and, at the end of each trip, I went out searching for houses. Months passed. One day, I came in with a listing and told Josie I'd driven to Arbroath, fifteen miles away, to see a property. It belonged to a retired widow who was finding the stairs too difficult.

'It's amazing. It's the oldest house in the street. It used to be a steading in a field, but the family sold the ground off to a builder and now it stands out because it's so different from the other houses. It's got an enormous garage and parking for three cars.' I was beaming. 'I told her we'd go back and see it tomorrow afternoon.'

Josie

The minute Josie saw the old, immaculate, stone-built house, she knew it was Dave's dream. He reminded her that because Iona lived nearby, Ginny and Jon would be close to their cousins. Dave had argued that the distance to Ginny's school would be no different and there was a primary school round the corner for Jon. The owner was lovely and made it clear she wanted a family to have the house. Her son and daughter were advising her and she said she'd consult them to ask if they agreed with Dave's request to reduce the asking price by £1,000.

There was nothing at fault; it was ideal. But Josie couldn't understand the feeling that swept through her body as she wandered about the house and the grounds. She started to shake and a wave of confusion washed over her. Not only was something physical happening to her but she also had a bewildering perception that she would never live there. She tried to fight off the negativity; it was as though she had a premonition that she might be swapping one prison for another. She couldn't find herself and quietly went along with everything. Inside her swirling head, she decided that she was going to follow her instincts and wasn't intending to forget that she had a voice. She would use it eventually.

Dave contacted a friend, a female solicitor, who lived and worked in Braeness. This was someone he had met on his many overnight stays away from the cottage. Chris dealt in family law. Josie had never met her, but Dave wanted to use her because he liked her; it didn't matter that conveyancing was not her speciality. She suggested Dave put in an offer with an entry date as far away as possible to give time for Laburnum Cottage to sell. He dealt with the bank and mortgage paperwork, but Josie certainly wouldn't ask for her name to be put on any legal documents after his last response.

No-one came to look at Laburnum Cottage. Dave put a fixed price on it, but still there were no takers. Between the bank manager, Chris and Dave, Josie was left out of the loop.

'So, I guess I need to know what dates we're looking at here,' Josie said one morning after he'd spoken to Chris on the phone for half an hour.

'In six weeks' time, we'll be moving. That's the agreement.'

Josie put her elbows on the table and steepled her forefingers at her lips.

'So, you're going away on Friday for three weeks, then three weeks after that we've got to move?'

'Yes, you can do the sums, can't you?'

He left for work, hopeful that someone would view and put in an offer immediately. In Josie's estimation, this was all going at rocket speed with too many loose ends. Dave had only been away a week when Chris called.

'I've heard from the other solicitor and there's been a change to the agreement. Seems the woman's family are not happy that she's promised to reduce the price so I'm afraid you'll have to decide immediately. It's going at the original price, and it's a case of *yes* or *no* so that I can either amend the offer or withdraw it. What do you think?'

'I've no idea. I don't know what to say and I can't contact Dave. He is head over heels for this house and can't wait for the cottage to be sold. He'll be so disappointed if he loses it over the sake of £1,000.' Josie crossed her fingers as she spoke.

Chris took the decision to go ahead and so the offer for the new place was amended and accepted. Dave called four days later. When Josie told him she hoped they hadn't made a mistake, she couldn't believe it when she heard him say she had been wrong. He would have told them to *shove it*! After all his bleating and wanting out of Laburnum Cottage, him singing the praises of the new house to others and his excitement at almost finishing the outstanding jobs; he made it her mistake.

Josie didn't know what to expect when he arrived home, but he wasn't as angry as she'd thought he might be. They weren't to worry because he'd just speak to the bank manager again.

'How is that supposed to work?' Josie enquired. 'It's not long until the entry date. Do you realise you need to hand over £33,000 a week on Friday?'

He looked at her in disbelief. It was as though he didn't realise they were dealing with actual houses and real money. If the cottage didn't sell, a highly likely scenario, he wouldn't have £33,000. Josie already knew that the bank manager was refusing a bridging loan because once Dave had taken over the housekeeping, he had faulted on more than a few loan payments.

The entry date came and went. No money exchanged hands and Chris hadn't put in a *get-out* clause that the sale would be subject to them selling Laburnum Cottage. Dave's dream house was put back on the market and sold for £2,000 less than he had initially offered. The woman's solicitors sued him for the difference. That had been the deal. Now he was stuck in a cottage that he had grown to hate. The people who surrounded him bored him and his bank balance was not only down but also very much overdrawn. Josie couldn't help him. He was in debt up to the hilt.

Dave and Josie would not make it. The sad thing was that they had both given up a lot and expected much more. They had struggled along the road to find success in their relationship, jobs and houses. They had dragged Ginny and Jon along with them. On one hand, it was a sad ending, but after a year and a half together in the cottage, Josie had to get out of her marriage. In fact, it wasn't even a year and a half because Dave had been away for almost a third of that time. Nothing had moved forward; everything had moved backwards. Dave thought his move from a Ford Granada to an Alpha Romeo or a BMW was progress. His irrational buying was digging a bigger hole for them all. The fundamental problem there was that whatever was bought was out of favour with him within a month. Nothing lasted. He was making all the wrong decisions and it was a steep learning curve for Josie. She had to be responsible for her children's future.

She decided this was no life for them. Josie would never deny Jon his father, but they couldn't be a family. Dave wasn't a family man. It was time to make plans to leave him and get on with life the way she wanted, because it was disrupting the children and making her ill. The uncertainty of what lay ahead for them was stressful.

Josie had been with Dave for ten years and there had been very few good times. His jealousy had spoiled a lot of opportunities for fun and socialising and because of his anger, Josie had ended up with ruined clothes, destroyed property, cracked bones and a broken spirit. He was impulsive, childish and erratic and felt entitled to everything, including her. He overcame his low self-confidence by demeaning her and her friends.

The control he needed to have over the family left them nervous and unable to fulfil their own needs. She had had to re-educate the children in manners every time he left on a trip. This wasn't the life she had dreamed of but, after a decade, she knew she had to stop thinking about the years she had wasted and leave before she gave him any more. The woman in the toilets all those years ago had been right. She had called Dave a bully. He had stopped her laughing with others that night and nothing had changed. That had been a signal, an alert that she let pass by.

Josie attended her weekly GP appointment. Sitting in front of the doctor, she thanked him for the medication he had prescribed a few weeks before but, against his advice, she had stopped taking the tablets and wouldn't need them anymore.

'So, what's brought this on?' Dr Boyd asked.

'I've been thinking about what my problem is. It's my husband and I'm going to get rid of my problem. I'm leaving him so I won't need the anti-depressants.'

After asking her a few more questions, Dr Boyd knew he was now dealing with a stronger woman, one who was going to fight for the success and survival of herself and her children.

'You know I'm here if you ever feel you need me. I've got a funny feeling I won't be seeing you again.' He said goodbye.

Josie worked slowly towards her goal.

In October, she finally got her dream and, despite Dave's negative comments, registered for college two mornings a week. It wasn't difficult to get back into studying after a break from evening classes; it was more the new-fangled equipment they expected her to use that baffled her. Instead of a typewriter, she faced a computer. It was alien that something behind a screen was creating carriage returns and that, with the tap of a button, the complete document would either be saved or disappear somewhere into the ether. The others in the class were fun, and it surprised Josie how much she laughed and cracked jokes again. She had been hesitant at first in class. Dave's influence on how inappropriate it had been for her to join in with any amusing company soon wore off. Josie never knew where she found her old independent, fun-loving self. Maybe Iona was right, it had only been lying dormant.

Her support network grew when she finally admitted to others she wasn't happy and was planning to go back to her old life. Moira hugged her, Iona promised to help in any way she could, Sheila said she'd be at the end of the phone if she wanted to talk and Erynn told her never to be without a bed for the night if things didn't go well and she found herself on the street with the children.

But it was Iona who turned out to be Josie's backbone. She explained where to apply for council housing and made sure Josie knew about the right forms. Josie didn't want to antagonise Dave by telling him too soon she was leaving. It was highly unlikely, but there was still something in her that knew if he became considerate, she might want to give him another chance.

Strangely, Josie felt very calm and unperturbed when, despite Dave still earning decent money while working onshore, he only parted with a couple of pounds now and again. Friends rallied round and gave her bread or milk, they knew Josie would pay them back once she got on her feet again. Dave had begun to leave with his overnight bag each weekend and head down south without saying goodbye. He filled up the car with pounds' worth of petrol to travel almost two hundred miles there and back and spend time with his mates or whoever at the bar while the children were eating out of someone else's fridge.

Dave

Late one Friday afternoon, I put my overnight bag at the back door. Heading down south to see friends would hopefully make me feel better. Josie went upstairs to be with the children for about five minutes and I was just about to pick up my set of car keys from the rack when I saw both hers and mine were gone. She was playing silly buggers again.

This was going to delay me; I didn't have time for all this rubbish. She came downstairs, went straight into the kitchen and sat down at the table. It looked like she was reading a magazine. I strolled in.

'Keys!' I clicked my fingers as I towered over her.

This wasn't an unusual pose for me. Whenever I wanted her attention, I would get her to sit down and stay there. Then I would stand over her, giving her a piece of my mind. Depending on what the problem was, I could go on for a while, but I didn't have time for that. My plan was to cover the two-hour journey in time for the pool competition at eight o'clock.

'What is it?' She was being cheeky: it was clear what I wanted.

'Keys, car keys. Give me them,' I demanded.

'I want to talk to you.' Josie stood up, then became uncharacteristically bold as she barked at me. 'Sit down!'

Surprisingly, I did. I think I was a bit shocked at her antics and wondered what was going on. She stood close to me and assumed the same pose as I normally did, one hand on her hip, the other leaning on the table. She looked wild as she stared down into my eyes. She was losing the plot.

'Why do you want the keys? Where are you going?'

'I'm going to see my family.' I retorted, although my scoff wasn't my usual forceful one.

'Listen, you walk away every weekend you're home. You never say goodbye to us. We don't know where you are, yet you expect us to stay here with nothing, no car, no money. And the minute you come back, you want to know what *I've* been doing. You can go wherever you like, but I'm telling you, you're teaching the children bad habits. All the smart remarks they hear and the way you talk down to me. One way or the other, this will stop.' Josie continued to stand over me.

'I've told you, I'm going to see my family,' I repeated.

'Dave, guess what? *We're* your family. If you go away and take the car, we're limited to what we can do. Not that it's a problem, but I got into this relationship because I thought you wanted to be part of a family. Seems I was mistaken. Now I'm going to get the keys for you.'

Josie made her way over to a kitchen cupboard where she picked my set of keys out of a pot. Very clever. She held them in her hand, but kept standing as she went on.

'Before I hand these over, here's something to think about. If you leave here tonight to go to your *family,* it's only fair you should know now. We're finished.'

She laid the keys on the table. I snatched them and bounced them in my hand twice before standing up. I left a minute later. There was no need for a goodbye because she didn't deserve it.

She was a weak, miserable woman who had nowhere to go. Her empty threats didn't bother me. I had told her often enough she would never manage without me.

Chapter 29

Josie

Once the door closed behind him, Josie called up to the children. They spent the evening telling funny stories and finding old clothes to dress up in. After imitating different people and playing games where the winner had to ask the others truth or dare, they watched Jaws for the fifth time. The children got ready for bed. It had been a long time since Josie asked them what they'd like to do the following day. This time, she knew she would follow through. She didn't have to wait for Dave. They wanted to go to Iona's house to see their cousins and then to the beach where they could buy enormous ice-cream cones. Josie had enough for the bus fare and knew that Iona would see them alright for the ice cream.

Josie lay awake that night. She thanked the gods that Dave hadn't disposed of their original mattress when he decided on a three-quarter bed. It didn't matter that it hung over the sides. It was easier to sleep on her own because she could get into the middle and reduce the risk of falling out. But she didn't sleep much that night.

She wondered what she had done in giving Dave an ultimatum. Now she had to be a woman of her word if nothing else and she was certain Dave knew that from the few times he had witnessed her saying to others that it would be the last time for this or the last time for that.

'You're only saying that!' He used to mock her.

'Watch me,' she had replied each time and stuck to her word.

She had never done it with Dave because he pulled the strings and instilled fear in her although now she realised she had let so many opportunities slip through her fingers.

As she stretched out, she gazed upwards and, in the glow from the streetlight, saw the circled designs on the ceiling imitating her swirling thoughts. She questioned herself about how she would manage and where she would live, but Iona and the application forms for the housing list came flooding back to her. She wondered how she would get to college until she recalled someone in class talking about a bus. Then she pondered over how she would survive financially but relaxed when she remembered the benefits system would entitle the children to government help. Josie wasn't too proud to ask for that. She turned over and snuggled in, content in the knowledge that she would manage without Dave.

Always alert for unusual noises and thinking it might be one of the children, Josie sat bolt upright and looked at the clock. It was five-thirty in the morning. She wrapped her housecoat tightly around her shivering body and tip-toed out of the bedroom. Standing on the landing, she looked down and through the French windows into the kitchen. Jon would have come in to wake her if there had been a problem so maybe it was Ginny who wasn't feeling great. She put her foot on the top step when she noticed a pair of legs through the glass doors, legs complete with men's trousers, walking towards the kitchen table. Dave was back.

She crawled into bed again and whispered to herself, *Too late, boy. You knew the deal.*

She surfaced an hour later but never mentioned their intentions of an outing. After all, he had said he would be away for the weekend and wasn't expected to be part of their plans. Later, when they packed a picnic bag and some spades, Dave asked the children what was going on.

'We're going to the beach!' they cried in chorus.

'In November?' Dave gave his usual snort.

'And I can't wait because I'm going upstairs on the bus!' Jon announced.

Dave hated the beach, so he certainly wouldn't be joining them and, if he had any thoughts of offering to take them, Jon's excitement about the bus had drawn a line under that.

It was an unusually bright winter's afternoon when Ginny and Jon helped their much younger cousins up to the café table full of ice-cream and juice. Iona and Josie sat nearby and chatted about life. Josie looked out at the whirling waves and shivered.

'Iona, I've got something to tell you. I'm going to apply to go on the housing list as you suggested. I just don't know if I'll get a place quick enough. It's November now and I'd like to be out of the cottage at the start of the year if I can.'

Iona slid along the café bench and hugged her.

'Look, there's no worry. Get the form in and tell them you and the kids are staying with me. And you can do that. I know it'll be a squeeze, but here's the thing. There'll be far too many of us living in a two-bedroomed house, so they must get you into suitable accommodation as quickly as possible.'

This was reassuring. Josie didn't dare believe things might all go in her favour. Iona said she would accompany her to the housing department and, sure enough, it was straightforward. There wasn't a house available but, the minute one came up, they would offer it to her because she was practically at the top of the list.

Dave

I didn't have to go away for another two weeks and so life continued. One morning, once the children had left for school, Josie was getting ready for college. I hadn't been able to stop her from going despite reminding her studying was a waste of time. She really wasn't as clever as she thought she was. I must admit, she seemed to enjoy it and made sure she never missed a class.

She packed a bag with her notebook and pencils and left it on the kitchen table.

'I don't know why you persist with this college caper. You're nowhere near smart enough to pass exams. I doubt you'll ever have the self-discipline. But, if you insist on going today, how are you getting through?' I asked.

'I'll catch the bus at the top of the road. No problem.' She smiled.

'I can take you.'

Josie shrugged but agreed, and we made our way out to the car. Halfway into the twenty-minute journey, I kept glancing at her. She had said very little, but it must have been clear by my sideways glances I had something on my mind. Finally, I spoke.

'I've got something I need to ask you.'

Josie didn't say a word but she turned to look at me. I could see her out of the corner of my eye.

'I've got a problem with money, and I wonder if you could help me?' I eventually got it out.

It didn't take any length of time for her to answer me so there's no doubt she had a reply ready, just waiting for me to talk about money.

'Of course I can help. I'm going to leave you and I'm taking the children. You won't have to pay for us. That should help you with your money problems. I'll wait until the children have had their Christmas and then we'll be off.'

There wasn't a hint of anger or disappointment in her voice. Nothing more was said while I digested her words. I felt a bit lost and knew then that Josie wasn't the woman for me. She wasn't a supportive wife and I was wasting my time and energy with her. I could tell she was slipping away from me and didn't want to let me be in charge. This was no position for a man of my standing to be in.

Reflecting on her words, I was in limbo. She had said she would wait until after Christmas, so I had four weeks yet. She was right, though. If she and the children were out of the way, and the cottage finally sold, I could get something more manageable. Even better, if she found a place and, if I wanted, I'd be able to slip back into her life once she'd cooled off. Just like old times.

I decided to give her time to sort out schools for the children. That was her department and if she got a place that needed a few jobs done, even better. She'd never refuse an offer of help with the move or any improvements. It was all looking good. A new project for me. With any luck, I'd be back on my feet with the proceeds from the cottage in my pocket and win time back in Josie's bed.

Josie

It was the first time in a while since Josie had taken the time to stare at the man driving, the one she had given up ten years of her life for. This was the man who had been caring and kind in the beginning, often generous and loving, but then had turned into a brutal and demeaning man who found it was second nature to be manipulative and accusing. These traits had reared themselves on and off over the years and not only with her. Other people and family had pushed away from Dave and ultimately she had been forced out too because she was his wife. She had interpreted times when he had given her attention and gifts as him being remorseful after the violence or when his insulting remarks had reduced her to a crumbling wreck. Really it was part of his manipulation game.

But there came a moment in the car when she couldn't look at him any longer because of other things he had done to her, things that women didn't talk about then because they felt shameful, used and abused. These times would have to remain Josie's secret. She reckoned he wouldn't even bat an eyelid if she told him how degraded she'd felt about the despicable things he had expected of her. That didn't matter now anyway.

Josie had waited for this moment. She had known it would come. Her answer about helping him with his money hadn't made her happy or left her feeling she had got revenge. She felt she had failed in her marriage, but she was strong now. She had a plan B.

The following day, Josie spied a newspaper on the kitchen counter. Folded over at the properties section, Dave had circled two places for rent.

That'll be right! Josie thought.

There was no way he was getting involved in this move.

He was at her tail for a few days, unsure of how to bring up the conversation about her moving out.

It took him back to how she had found somewhere to live after the caravan incident and her forward thinking about keeping her flat as a safety net.

Josie's forms had been sitting with the council for three weeks. Just as before, she didn't need his input to find a place to stay.

One morning, the children set off for school half an hour before Iona called.

'Josie! I'm glad I got you in. Listen, any chance you could pop through at some point? I've got a Christmas present for you.'

'Not a problem. I need to buy some wrapping paper so I'll just come through soon.' She lowered her voice to a whisper. 'With any luck, I'll have the car, so I should be there in about half an hour.'

Josie pulled on her old togs. If she dared to wear a smart pair of trousers or a skirt, the questioning would begin. He'd likely want to tag along to see what she was up to. Walking towards the back door, she saw he was only halfway through the job of repairing the coal bunker.

'I'm going to Iona's. We've got some Christmas presents to exchange. If I go soon, I can stop off at Woolworth's and get some wrapping paper. Is there anything you want me to bring back?'

'What do you mean? I want to go to the garage so you're not getting the car.'

'I can take the bus, but that means I'll be a couple of hours. If I take the car, I'll be back by the time you've finished the bunker. Unless you want to come with me.'

He looked her up and down, satisfied that she wasn't dressed for a party at half-past nine in the morning. He said she could take the car providing she was back by midday. She left without any criticism and arrived at Iona's in record time.

Iona pointed to a letter, stamped with the council postmark, sitting on top of her TV.

'There you go, sis. Your Christmas present.'

So, there it was. Confirmation that there was a house for her, keys waiting at the office and she could view the property as soon as she was able. She hadn't even moved in with Iona yet.

They both squealed and jumped around the living room, holding hands like school children.

'I'll need to be quick!' Josie bit her bottom lip. 'Remember, in case he asks, the queue at Woolworth's was a mile long. Come on. Let's get down to the office and pick up the keys.'

They practically skipped up the garden path to the typical council-style door that creaked open. Unfamiliar smells hit them.

'The smell of the floorboards reminds me of when I was pregnant with Ginny. That and cardboard made me want to vomit!'

'Well, you're not vomiting now, are you?'

As quickly as they could, the flat got the once over. An L-shaped hall, a living room with a door to the kitchen, three bedrooms and a bathroom. With front and back gardens, it was a dream come true. Josie overlooked the old cooker, the broken grate in the coal fire and the badly stained toilet. These were minor issues in the entire scheme of things.

'That's not a garden, that's a field!' Iona looked around the concrete outhouse towards yards of uncut grass and took a step back.

'I need to get back. I'll call them this afternoon when Dave's at the garage.'

Iona took the keys to hand back in until the paperwork was signed.

Almost in tears of happiness, Josie agreed on an entry date over the phone with them. Exactly as she wanted, the third week in January. Perfect timing.

Christmas came. The children were excited, but Josie could hardly muster up the energy to put up the tree. She peppered each action with thoughts of, *This will be the last time*. Christmas went.

Looking around, she sorted out in her head what she would take to her new flat. Nothing that Dave had bought in the last year and a half since they moved into the cottage interested her. Anything left from her old house was all she wanted. As a little bonus for him, she intended to leave him Ginny's sawn-up wardrobe unit.

Dave left on a short ten-day trip to a job in the south of England. The company had sent him train tickets from Dundee to London so, if Josie could afford to put petrol in, she would have the car for almost two weeks. Finally, it was the week before Josie officially took ownership of the flat.

Every second day, she and Iona brushed and scrubbed the floors. Once festivities were over, Josie registered Jon in a new school and found out bus and train times for Ginny. Iona organised two men and a removal van. Josie's next task was to tell the children.

Once back from his trip, Josie saw Dave's old habits returning. His overnight bag sitting at the back door. That was her chance. Dave left around four o'clock one Friday but he hadn't even turned the engine of the car on when she shouted to Ginny and Jon.

'Guess what? We're going out for Chinese food. Let's get ready!' It was a big treat for everyone.

By five, they were tucking into spring rolls. Gently, she explained things weren't going well at the cottage for any of them. It didn't completely surprise her that they agreed. They couldn't avoid seeing and hearing what had been going on. It hadn't been so long since they'd had a more peaceful life in their old house. The only benefit they had living at the cottage was that they had a bedroom each and a wider range of food and drinks.

Finally, she revealed that there was another flat waiting for them near their cousins in Arbroath. They would still have a bedroom each, but it would take a while before the place was decorated with carpets in every room. Dave remaining at the cottage didn't appear to bother them. He was away most of the time anyway, working or spending time with his *family* or whoever was waiting for him down south.

'But what about school?'

Josie explained the schooling arrangements and how Jon would make new friends from the area. Ginny already knew some classmates who travelled by train to school, so Josie suggested she met in town to make a plan for travelling together.

'When can we see it? The new place.'

'We'll go tomorrow, then we'll take the furniture and move next Friday.'

By the time they left the restaurant, a sense of relief had swept over each of them.

The next day, they were ready early. The tension and apprehension about his reaction was something Josie still had to work through. Although Arbroath wasn't far away from Forfar, the bus took the hour-long route, weaving in and out of little villages. Once it dropped them at the bus station, there was either a half-hour walk or a ten-minute ride on another bus to the house. The sun was shining and the sense of distance from Dave gave Josie a calm and strong demeanour. The children picked up on her relaxed mood. They walked to save money and took a trip through the main street to see what awaited them.

Iona had a set of keys and met them at the front door of the flat. Jon darted up and down the hall with his cousins before the issue of which bedroom they would have came up; they both wanted the front room. They tossed a coin with the proviso that the winner could choose which room they wanted, but the other would have theirs decorated first. Jon won. Ginny's room would be wallpapered and Josie would sleep on the floor until she could afford a bed.

Chapter 30

Dave

Exhaustion had overtaken me. I'd told Josie I was going to see my family, she didn't protest. Thank goodness. I had a late Saturday night with the boys and didn't get back to my nephew's flat until almost four in the morning. By that time, I'd sunk a few beers. Then the drive home had zonked me.

The minute I walked through the door of the cottage, I chucked my bag in the corner and made straight to put the kettle on. Josie was stoking the kitchen fire but she put the poker down and turned towards me, hands on hips.

Here we go, I thought.

'Right, you might as well know. I've found a place for me and the kids. We'll be moving on Friday.'

After lowering the kettle, I stood still momentarily. I let my jacket slowly slide off but the sleeve caught the fruit bowl and knocked it onto the tiled floor. Staring first at her then at the pile of boxes in the corner, I shook my head.

'So, you've finally managed to do something on your own then.' I bent down and picked up two bananas.

It surprised me that she didn't say thanks for seeing to the fruit bowl or wasn't irritated by my comment. Maybe she missed the implication that she was incapable of doing much without my help. Remarks that I made to remind her I was the boss had started to go over her head so I was in a dilemma. A decision had to be made. Did I ramp up the pressure or calm it down? It was possible I might need her in the future so I opted to calm my jets. She went on.

'You'll notice there's no food. I didn't have any money, and there's no point in stocking up because we won't be here. You can get your own. You'll manage to do that, won't you?'

Once again, I could only stare at her. She was beginning to insult me and I wasn't thinking straight.

Josie lifted two empty boxes and made her way upstairs. I followed her.

'Can I help?' I stood over her as she emptied the shelves in Ginny's room.

She didn't answer.

'I'm going to the shops. Is there anything special you want?'

She shook her head.

Over the next few days, I hung around doing nothing much. I didn't go to the bar but I pottered around doing a couple of minor jobs in the house. I watched what Josie was doing. She was on a mission and her leaving didn't appear to be a joke.

This might work out perfectly. I smiled as my mind worked overtime.

My immediate thoughts were related to what she would leave me to dispose of. And this might be the end of the cottage, which was wonderful. I wanted a reason to get rid of it and everything in it anyway. I had asked where she was going but she was vague with her answer. Inwardly, I admired her ability to get things done straightforwardly. She accepted what was available rather than arguing about something that was out of reach. Those were the moments when things fell apart for me, I wanted, and deserved, the stars. I knew she looked at what others had, but it didn't bother her as much as me when things weren't handed to her on a plate. How could she spend all these weeks sitting in a classroom to gain a few paltry certificates? How could she wait for months to buy a pair of shoes? What stopped her from craving the holiday she couldn't afford?

I took Jon out for the day and suggested to the boy that we drive to the new house so that we could count the miles on the speedometer. Jon innocently agreed and was happy that he only made two wrong turns before we arrived. I stopped in a parking bay, smarting at how close it was to the front door Jon pointed to. Just what I had always wanted. Mentally, I dug out part of the garden to make a driveway.

'It's a shame we don't have keys with us, but let's look through the windows and you can tell me which room is yours.'

It wasn't difficult to imagine the layout. When I saw the simpleness of the empty rooms and the potential the flat had, in an instant I knew what I could offer to do to make it a pleasant home. From what I could see, the old fireplace looked as though it had seen better days. Although I couldn't see clearly, I thought I could incorporate the back hall with the dated kitchen to make it more spacious. If Jon was right that there was a cupboard next to the bathroom, that could be space for a shower. Plenty of scope for development.

'Nice place you've got there,' I announced as soon as we were back and Jon had run upstairs to pack his small toys.

Bet she's mad that I found out where they're going! The thought went through my mind as I waited for her to explode.

She just smiled. But it didn't really matter that I knew where her new place was because I'd be going to see Jon now and again and would have found out, eventually.

'I'll be around tomorrow to help,' I told her on Thursday afternoon.

'Don't worry. It's all in hand.'

With the boxes taped up and the bunk beds dismantled, I watched as Josie put the screws in her rucksack.

Josie

The removal van came while the children were at school and Dave was sulking in the bedroom. Josie had to let the men into the cottage so Iona arranged to be at the new flat for their arrival. Jon said goodbye to his school friends before Josie picked him up and took him through to Arbroath by bus with their few remaining bags. Ginny was coming from school by train for the first time on her own. None of them remembered leaving the cottage for the last time, except that Dave didn't come out to wave goodbye.

Jimmy waited with his toolbox at their new place and set about assembling the bunk beds as soon as the removal men unpacked them. Josie arrived.

'Keep the snacks for tomorrow,' Iona instructed them. 'I'm taking the children to buy fish and chips. We'll be back in about fifteen minutes. Make sure you've got that table set.'

Josie emptied what boxes she could, then stopped. Her laughter brought Jimmy through from the room.

'What the hell is wrong with you?'

Josie held her hands, prayer-like, while moving from side to side with laughter.

'It's just dawned on me. I can do what I like when I like.'

She hummed as she took a folding table, four chairs and three stools out to the back garden.

Epilogue

Josie

It didn't surprise Josie that, for the first few months, Dave made a production of coming to collect Jon for a day out. The boy was over the moon about spending time with his dad but Josie detected a deterioration in his attitude when he returned, especially towards her. For almost ten years she had re-educated him on acceptable behaviour, especially towards females. Now it was starting again.

It also annoyed Josie when he came home saying things like, 'I wish my dad wouldn't ask me to remind you of things. He tells me you've to stop asking him for money.'

Josie had never asked Dave for money. She didn't need or want his money. He was using the children yet again, blackening her name and saying she was badgering him, making out that she was someone she wasn't.

Ginny very rarely saw Dave but when she did, the story was the same.

'I wish he would stop asking me what you are doing, if you're working and who your boyfriends are.'

It wasn't fair to go through the children to try to find out how Josie's life was working out.

Six months passed and Josie held her ground firmly. The marriage was over.

Dave got an offer for Laburnum Cottage. But, before it could be sold, Josie had to take paperwork to a solicitor because her signature was needed to make the sale legal. Although she couldn't understand it fully, it seemed that even his refusal to put her name on the title deeds didn't exclude her from an entitlement to part of any profit. But there was none. On the advice of her solicitor, who asked why on earth she was still married to him, she filed for divorce. She had to give her solicitor examples of Dave's treatment towards her. One thing that stood out for her was the many names he used to call her.

'So, you'll have to give me an idea of the words he used.'

'Well, one thing that was hurting was he constantly called me Fatty.'

The solicitor looked Josie's size twelve figure up and down. His saucer eyes gave away his thoughts. He turned back to his notes with a shake of his head.

Later that day, when she walked into Iona's, she could hardly speak for laughing.

'To think some typist will have to create a document that states, "He used to call me Fatty". These office girls will have a scream and I'll bet they'll be having a right old look at me the next time I go in.'

The cottage sold at a loss and, because of his debts, there was no money to be shared. The divorce went through in record time. Josie became single and Jon told her his dad had met up with his ex, Evelyn, the one who had worn Pagan perfume that clearly didn't smell like cat's piss on her.

Because Jon would always be the connection, there were times when Josie heard news about what was going on with Dave and Evelyn.

Seems they bought a house together and Dave said he could renovate it. History was repeating itself, but this time, he was using Evelyn's money. There came a point where Josie met the woman and was astounded at what a lovely person she was.

He doesn't deserve her. She is far too nice. Josie kept her thoughts secret.

It wasn't long before the same old stories surfaced. He kept changing his car and losing money. He wanted to sell up their beautiful house and found himself jumping from job to job because the bosses didn't like him. Evelyn had to bear the brunt of life with the bully and his trail of destruction.

Josie never asked about his situation, even when he missed a few months of picking Jon up. He eventually arrived on the boy's twelfth birthday and stood in the doorway wearing designer sunglasses and a brown leather bomber jacket. She wondered if he had shrunk as she stifled a laugh. Something about his stature was different. One arm looked limp and one eyebrow was raised higher than the other.

He waited until Josie asked him in.

'Is everything OK? You seem distracted,' she quizzed him.

Josie wasn't really that interested, but given his ability to fly off the handle, she needed to know if his mood involved her. He handed her a plastic bag, and, without being invited, plonked himself on the couch.

'That's for Ginny. Yes, I'm just a bit distracted.'

His right hand was shaking and he smoothed the leg of his corduroy trousers to steady it.

There were a few moments of awkward silence.

'What's the letter?' Dave pointed to the A5 official looking brown envelope on the table.

'Oh that. It's just to tell me I've got a place with the Open University.'

She waited for a retort but none came. He looked down at his feet before straightening the collar on his jacket. Josie could smell his nervousness.

'So how is life?' Josie was only being polite, she didn't really want an answer.

'Remember Charlie? Well, you wouldn't ever have heard this but, along with John Clark, they were involved in a fight a few years ago. It all started with a broken pint glass in a bar. You won't know anything about it but it involved a baby. Seems it's caught up with them now. They're saying I was with them when it happened and the word on the street is I'm for the chop. To be honest, I was a bit worried that somebody might be looking for me here. It's a well-known fact that this is where I come for Jon.'

'What do you mean? That the police are looking for you here?'

'That's what I don't know.'

'And *were* you involved?'

Josie didn't know why she had asked. There was nothing she could have done if he'd said yes and she couldn't have thought any less of him. So his answer was immaterial.

Dave gave a quick shake of his head and turned away. He looked vulnerable, less threatening. A liar.

She read between the lines of his story when he recounted a recent confrontation. In his Braeness local, he had done his usual and asked a couple of the guys to buy him a pint. Full of alcohol and bravado he had left for the short walk home. He never noticed the three fit young men step out of a doorway behind him as he passed by the old miners' cottages. But he clocked another one who walked towards him.

'Got a light?' he had called out to Dave.

'Don't smoke. Don't use them.'

Before he knew what was happening, the four men pinned him to the ground. He said they battered him to within an inch of his life, then one of them whispered, 'This is from my son. He won't be able to use his eyes, ears, arms or legs now, never mind cigarettes. But he can use a feeding tube. Thanks to you and your mates.'

The final kick in his face had seen Dave carted off to hospital where he left two weeks later minus an eye. He looked pleadingly at Josie.

'I wish I lived in America. That way, I could use a gun to protect myself.'

That sounded vicious. But a flashback flooded her mind, the conversation with John, the story of the broken pint glass and revenge which ultimately involved a little baby. She had been sure Dave was part of the group that launched the attack.

So, they finally caught up with him.

Josie stood up and looked out the window. She didn't pay a great deal of attention when three cars drew up together, followed by two patrol cars. It was as though in synchronisation the car doors opened. Three men walked towards Dave's car while four uniformed officers made their way towards Josie's flat.

Dave reached over for her hand. She didn't pull away but looked down at him sitting there, oblivious to the activity in the street. He seemed smaller, shrivelled, broken.

'You could help me. Just in case the cops ever ask and think I was part of it. If I told you the date and time when all this happened, you might even remember that I was with you.'

The rattle of the letter box brought Jon running out of his bedroom. He dived forward to open the door holding a Super Mario instruction booklet.

'Yes, he's here. My dad's here for my birthday and guess what? I'm going away for the weekend with him.'

That plan would have to wait.

Josie went from strength to strength, never hearing from or seeing Dave. He disappeared into the ether for years during which time she enrolled for university.

Jon and Ginny flourished. After completing four years of study, she emerged with a Masters.

On the morning of her graduation, Josie beamed as her shoulder-length hair sprung back into soft waves with each brush stroke. She tied it into a loose ponytail, then put on some pink lipstick. Holding the mortarboard in one hand, she caught the reflection of her black gown and white graduation hood in the living room window. Humming along to a familiar tune on the radio, she slipped into her new shoes.

This is déjà vu. What makes me think I've done this before?

She shrugged and picked up the keys for her Volkswagen Golf.

THE END

www.ingramcontent.com/pod-product-compliance
Lightning Source LLC
Chambersburg PA
CBHW071148070526
44584CB00019B/2709